1881/10½"
Plate

1881/8½"
Plate

1881/4½"
Nappy

1881
Ice Tea

1881
Goblet

1881/1 Pt.
Jug

1881/
Jug

1881/5"
la dinière

1881
Pickle

1881
Puff Box/Jelly

Stars and Str

DESSERT SER

SPAR

COLLECTIBLE GLASSWARE

from the 40s 50s 60s...

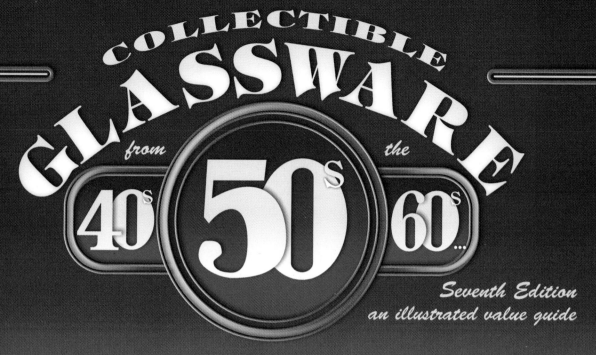

Seventh Edition
an illustrated value guide

Gene & Cathy Florence

COLLECTOR BOOKS
A Division of Schroeder Publishing Co., Inc.

ABOUT THE AUTHOR

Gene Florence, born in Lexington in 1944, graduated from the University of Kentucky where he held a double major in mathematics and English. He taught for nine years in Kentucky at the junior high and high school levels, one unforgettable year at a school for gifted students, before his glass collecting "hobby" became his full-time job.

Mr. Florence has been interested in collecting since childhood, beginning with baseball cards and progressing through comic books, coins, bottles, and finally, glassware. He first became interested in glass after buying a large set of pink Sharon Depression at a garage sale for $5.00… and studying to find out what it was.

By the time this is published, he will have written over eighty books, at least seventy of them on glassware. Titles include the following: *Collector's Encyclopedia of Depression Glass* now in its sixteenth edition; *Kitchen Glassware of the Depression Years*, sixth edition; *Collectible Glassware from the 40s, 50s, 60s*, seventh edition; *Elegant Glassware of the Depression Era*, tenth edition; *The Collector's Encyclopedia of Akro Agate; Stemware Identification; Glass Candlesticks of the Depression Era*; three volumes of *Pattern Identification*; two editions of *Anchor Hocking's Fire-King and More; Very Rare Glassware of the Depression Years, Six Series; Treasures of Very Rare Depression Glass; The Collector's Encyclopedia of Occupied Japan, Volumes I through V; Occupied Japan Collectibles; Pocket Guide to Depression Glass*, thirteen editions. He also wrote six editions of an innovative *Standard Baseball Card Price Guide* and two volumes about Degenhart collectibles.

If you know of any unlisted or unusual pieces of glassware from the examples shown in this book, you may write Mr. Florence at Box 22186, Lexington, KY 40522 or Box 64, Astatula, FL 34705. If you would like a reply, enclose a self-addressed, stamped envelope — and be patient. The volume of mail/e-mail from his web page (www.geneflorence.com) has begun to soar exponentially. He still answers it when time permits, but much of the year is spent writing, traveling, doing research, and sometimes, fishing.

On the Cover

Front: Fostoria Willow water tumbler, $18.00; Westmoreland Paneled Grape candy, $75.00; Fostoria Heirloom epergne, $225.00; Fostoria Lido blue ice bucket, $195.00; and Pyrex "Blue Willow" platter, $42.50. Back: Clover Blossom.

Cover Design: Beth Summers
Book Design: Beth Ray and Terri Hunter

COLLECTOR BOOKS
P.O. Box 3009
Paducah, Kentucky 42002-3009
www.collectorbooks.com

or

GENE AND CATHY FLORENCE

| P.O. Box 22186 | or | P.O. Box 64 |
| Lexington, KY 40522 | | Astatula, FL 34705 |

CONTENTS

ACKNOWLEDGMENTS

Thanks to all the friends, readers, collectors, and dealers who have contributed extensive data on patterns for this book. This *Collectible Glassware from the 40s, 50s, 60s...* has grown from 144 pages when started in 1992 to 256. Were it not for you sharing with me through writing, e-mailing, calling, and talking to me directly, it would not have grown the way it has.

Thanks, particularly to Cathy, my wife. Computers and the Internet are wonderful — when they work. Writing in Florida and Cathy correcting in Kentucky has been an adventure. We had attachments not downloading or AOL compressing and not being able to decompress. We had a wireless card give up, e-mails which are still out there some place, a computer tech son living too far away to help as often as we would have liked, all of which was "entertainment" we did not need. I hope the book enriches you in some way.

Specific thanks regarding this particular book need to go to Dick and Pat Spencer, Dan and Geri Tucker, Sonny and Maxine Larson, Bud and Dorothy Hines, Verlon Webb, and Denise S. Neri.

Various readers throughout the United States, Canada, Australia, New Zealand, England, and Puerto Rico have sent glass photos and information. Data given and not yet used is recorded for future works.

Richard Walker of New York and Charles R. Lynch of Kentucky took most of the photographs during one fourteen-day session. The usual photo session hassles of unwrapping, sorting, arranging, carting, and repacking glass was handled by Cathy Florence, Dick and Pat Spencer, Jane White, Zibby Walker, and the guys from the shipping department at Collector Books.

Thanks to Beth Ray and members of the editorial department at Collector Books who did design and layout for this book and who worked overtime to help me meet my deadline. If I've omitted the name of anyone who contributed, please forgive me; know that I, as well as all readers, thank you for your contributions.

PREFACE

Collecting has made impressive inroads into everyday life. Today, non-collectors are being exposed to collector finds through a variety of weekly television shows. Few of these feature glassware per se; but the national exposure is good for collectibles as a whole. Collecting has a great deal to do with nostalgia. People buy dishes because someone they loved, such as a grandmother, used them while they were growing up. Over thirty years ago when I started accumulating Depression glass, it was a part of my mother's generation of childhood memories and my grandmother's everyday dishes. Today, these memories have moved up a couple of generations and include the late 40s through 60s, and, lately, even early 70s. Furniture and glassware made in this era have been embraced by a generation of collectors who never sought collectibles before. Collecting glassware also has a tie to accessibility in the markets. Glassware from the 1950s upward, not surprisingly, is more available now than that made in the 1920s and 1930s.

This evolution of collecting interests is what led to the development of this book in 1992, a culmination of several years work finding the glassware to include. Both machine-produced and handmade glassware from the 50s era are incorporated herein given that both classifications are being collected. A few handmade glassware patterns included actually had their beginning near the end of 1930s, but their prevailing production was during the 1940s and 1950s, or even later. We've added over 40 patterns to the last two books to accommodate burgeoning interest in these wares, if that tells you anything. Some of these added patterns are very 50s, a little ultramodern, a little "out there" as befitted the space era. It is definitely more exhilarating to collect a pattern that you can have some hope of getting your hands on with time and determination.

Neophytes to collecting should know that some patterns were never nationally distributed, and that a number of nationally known companies closed in the 50s and 60s. Labor, environmental requirements, and material costs made American glassware more expensive and cheaper foreign-made glass took their markets. We must not forget the invasion of household plastic, either. All these factors conspired to ultimately enhance these wares for today's collectors because it shortened supply.

Not everyone looks for the pulse beat of the glass-collecting world as I do. Some have a collection they want to enhance the value of and feel they can do so by writing a book and sticking big prices on the items (hoped-for pricing). Some want the glamour of being a published author and have little clue about markets or the harm they can inflict pricing willy-nilly. My goal is a book that shows color photos, that will inform you about what is being collected and what is hard or easy to find, as well as one that will show you realistic pricing of what glass really sells for in our world of economic uncertainty. I sincerely hope I've accomplished that.

If you have glassware that you think should be included or would be willing to lend for photography purposes or copies of glass company advertisements listing pieces which you received with your sets, let me hear from you. Keep me apprised of your discoveries regarding the wares already listed. I will try to pass your information along to other collectors, something that is getting easier with laptop computers.

PRICING

All prices in this book are retail prices for mint condition glassware. This book is intended to be only a guide since there are some regional price differences that cannot reasonably be dealt with herein. You may expect dealers to pay from 50% to 60% less than the prices quoted. Glass that is in less than mint condition, i.e., chipped, cracked, scratched, or poorly molded, will bring only a small percentage of the price of glass that is in mint condition. Since this book covers glassware made from 1940 onward, you may expect that dealers and collectors will be less charitable of wear marks or imperfections than in glass made earlier.

Prices are now fairly standardized due to the Internet, national advertising of glassware, and dealers who market it at numerous glass shows held from coast to coast. I have attended shows in Florida, Houston, and Seattle in the last month to study price trends. Still, there are some regional differences in prices due partly to glass being more readily available in some areas than in others. West Coast prices are higher in most cases, but those prices are being resisted in our present economic status. Many companies charged more initially for wares shipped to the West Coast.

Prices tend to increase significantly on rare items if they are being sought by numerous collectors. In general, prices increase due to demand from additional collectors entering the field and from people becoming more aware of the worth of this 1950s glass.

MEASUREMENTS

All measurements are taken from company catalogs or by actually measuring each piece if no catalog lists are available. Capacities of tumblers, stemware, and pitchers are always measured to the top edge until nothing more can be added. Heights are measured perpendicular to the bottom of the piece, not up a slanted side. In company catalogs, plate measurements were usually rounded to the nearest inch or half inch (especially Fostoria plates), across the widest point.

ANNIVERSARY, JEANNETTE GLASS COMPANY, 1947 – 1949; LATE 1960s – MID 1970s

Colors: crystal, iridescent, pink, and Shell Pink

Anniversary pattern has recently had a piece re-introduced in the market. The crystal vase, shown as a pattern shot, was made in India according to a label on it. The vase may be purchased for $4.99 in some major discount stores. The satinized frosting on it is actually enhancing. I was rather astounded by the item; but with the demise of so many of the glassmaking companies in the last few years, we in the collecting world are going to have to get used to seeing items appearing in incongruous fashion from the dispersal of many of the glasshouse molds.

Pink Anniversary was considered to be Depression glass by collectors for years since earlier authors put it in their books as such. It was made well beyond the Depression era, though admittedly, it has echoes of the Deco linear look in its design. Crystal and iridescent could be purchased in boxed sets in "dish barn" outlets as late as 1975. Dinner plates are an older 9" size in pink, but are 10" in crystal and iridescent. Crystal is sometimes found trimmed with either silver (platinum) or gold; but, so far, these trims do not add to the price of the items.

Even though iridescent Anniversary can often be found in antique malls, it has sometimes been banned from being displayed at Depression era glass shows since it was made in the 1970s. Iridescent is collectible and prices are actually surpassing those of crystal. You will find it shown in carnival glass books now, though I doubt anyone ever pitched pennies in it at carnivals. However, that fact does create a second market for that particular color of Anniversary.

Snack plates with a cup indent have been seen in iridescent and crystal, but not in pink. There was a trend for collecting snack plates in all patterns for a time; and at least three people in the last few years have told me they are writing a book on these fifties, television tray necessities for serving quick sandwich meals before the wonder box; but, so far, I have not seen one. Have you?

Both square and round crystal cake plates have been found, usually with an aluminum lid sporting a variety of decals.

Taxing to find are the pink Anniversary butter dish, pin-up vase, wine glass, and sandwich plate. Both the wine and pin-up vase are reasonably priced considering how few of them are ever displayed for sale.

The 1947 Jeannette catalog lists the open, three-legged candy as a comport rather than compote. Terminology used for glassware varies from company to company and from time period to time period. For instance, older glassware catalogs often used "cream" to describe a creamer.

	Crystal	Pink	Iridescent
Bowl, 4⅞", berry	3.00	10.00	4.00
Bowl, 6¾", soup w/o rim	7.00		
Bowl, 7⅜", soup w/rim	7.00	20.00	7.00
Bowl, 9", fruit	12.00	32.00	12.00
Butter dish bottom	15.00	30.00	
Butter dish top	15.00	30.00	
Butter dish and cover	30.00	60.00	
Candy jar and cover	25.00	60.00	
*Cake plate, 12½"	12.00	20.00	
Cake plate, round, w/metal cover	17.50		
Cake plate, 12⅜", **square,** w/metal cover	25.00		
Candlestick, 4⅞", pr.	20.00		25.00
Comport, open, 3-legged	5.00	17.50	5.00
Comport, ruffled, 3-legged	6.00		
Creamer, footed	4.00	12.00	6.00

	Crystal	Pink	Iridescent
Cup	3.00	8.00	4.00
Pickle dish, 9"	6.00	18.00	7.00
Plate, 6¼", sherbet	2.00	4.00	2.00
Plate, 9", dinner		15.00	
Plate, 10", dinner	6.00		6.00
Plate, 12½", sandwich server	10.00	22.00	8.00
Relish dish, 8"	8.00	15.00	6.50
Relish, 4-part, on metal base	20.00		
Saucer	1.00	2.00	1.00
Sherbet, ftd.	4.00	11.00	
Sugar	3.00	9.00	5.00
Sugar cover	4.00	11.00	5.00
Tidbit, berry & fruit bowls w/metal hndl.	13.00		
**Vase, 6½"	16.00	30.00	
***Vase, wall pin-up	20.00	45.00	
Wine glass, 2½ oz.	10.00	17.00	

*Shell Pink $275.00   **Reproduced in crystal

***Shell Pink $295.00

ATTERBURY SCROLL, IMPERIAL GLASS COMPANY, C. LATE 1960s

Colors: amber, blue, carnival red, custard, crystal, Dynasty jade, some milk

Atterbury Scroll was first only a crystal production, and, though attractive, judging by the short run, apparently didn't attract much notice. Lately, however, with all the emphasis on collecting jadite colored items, Dynasty jade items began appearing rather regularly at my show table, having been brought in to be identified. Unfortunately, only five different pieces of jade were made in the "Scroll" as it is generally called by collectors. This color is illustrated by the goblet below. However, because of the production timing, pieces are turning up at markets right now in the various colors. So, if you like this, you need to buy it quickly, for unlike many of Imperial's patterns, you will have to work at finding pieces of Atterbury Scroll. The jade and other colors were made as a part of various color productions after 1963. Imperial also used these molds as a basis for their Antique Button line; so you will discover similar items sporting a "button" feature.

	Crystal	Jade		Crystal	Jade
Basket	22.00		Plate, dessert	8.00	
Bowl, 3-toed	25.00		Plate, lunch	10.00	18.00
Bowl, cereal	10.00		Plate, sq.	15.00	
Bowl, salad	20.00		Shaker	15.00	
Bowl, sq., w/ladle	30.00		Sherbet	10.00	15.00
Candle	22.00		Stem, water	15.00	20.00
Candy compote w/lid	28.00		Stem, wine	12.00	
Compote	18.00		Sugar, ftd.	25.00	
Compote, sm, crimped	15.00		Tumbler, juice	12.00	
Creamer, ftd.	25.00		Tumbler, tea	20.00	
Pitcher	45.00	90.00	Tumbler, water	15.00	22.00

BEADED EDGE, PATTERN #22 MILK GLASS, WESTMORELAND GLASS COMPANY, LATE 1930s – 1950s

Westmoreland did, in at least one catalog, refer to this pattern as Beaded Edge. The majority of glass companies issued line numbers for patterns and not names. The line number for Beaded Edge was 22. (Previous editions have shown an assortment of catalog pages if you wish to refer to them; new patterns causing space limitations prevented showing them this book.)

Decorated fruits, flowers, and birds were initially released in sets of eight designs. It took me almost 10 years and many miles of searching to find dinner plates with eight different fruit patterns and tumblers with eight floral decorations. That was before the Internet. The birds have been more elusive. You may also find an occasional Christmas decoration. Collectors seem to latch on to any Christmas-themed Beaded Edge as soon as I put it out for sale.

Fruit designs include strawberries, plums, raspberries, grapes, apples, cherries, peaches, and pears. Apples, pears, and peaches occupy most of the 15" torte plates I've encountered. However, a couple of years ago a lady e-mailed me that she had one with the strawberry design. Dinner plates, crimped bowls, and even sherbets can be hard to find; buy them when you see them. Be sure to check plates for use marks. The three-part relish, oval celery, and platter are more difficult to locate than I had previously thought. I have seen a few of these without decorations; decorated ones are rare. Basic luncheon sets (plates, cups, saucers, and tumblers) are found without difficulty. Pastel-bordered plates present an interesting contrast to those with white backgrounds. A Beaded Edge set can also be found with red trim.

A covered creamer and sugar appears with cherries on one side and a rendering of grapes on the opposite side. That sugar and creamer is Westmoreland's Pattern #108 and not Beaded Edge.

The reverse side of 15" plates shows the twelve zodiac symbols. Its opaque white color hides this revelation until the plate is turned over.

BEADED EDGE

	Plain	Red Edge	Decorated
Creamer, ftd.	11.00	13.00	20.00
Creamer, ftd., w/lid #108	20.00	25.00	38.00
Cup	5.00	7.00	12.00
Nappy, 5"	5.00	8.00	17.50
Nappy, 6", crimped, oval	10.00	15.00	30.00
Plate, 6", bread and butter	5.00	7.00	10.00
Plate, 7", salad	7.00	10.00	15.00
Plate, 8½", luncheon	7.00	10.00	14.00
Plate, 10½", dinner	15.00	28.00	45.00
Plate, 15", torte	25.00	40.00	70.00
Platter, 12", oval w/tab hndls.	35.00	50.00	100.00
Relish, 3-part	30.00	55.00	100.00
Salt and pepper, pr.	30.00	35.00	75.00
Saucer	2.00	3.00	4.00
Sherbet, ftd.	9.00	12.00	15.00
Sugar, ftd.	12.50	15.00	20.00
Sugar, ftd., w/lid #108	18.00	25.00	38.00
Tumbler, 8 oz., ftd.	10.00	12.00	16.00

"BIG TOP," GOTHIC, "PEANUT BUTTER GLASS," HAZEL ATLAS COMPANY, c. 1950s

Color: crystal, milk glass

A locally owned company (W.T. Young, Lexington, Kentucky) manufactured Big Top peanut butter and used this glassware to distribute its product. Growing up in Lexington, I saw thousands of these containers over the years and never gave much thought to them. I am one of the few people in America who didn't care for peanut butter; so that was a further reason for ignoring them.

Since the last book, a couple of things have been discovered about this ware. I told previously that the accountant I interviewed could only remember that it was a West Virginia glass company who shipped this glassware to the factory by the boxcar load two or three times weekly. I have now found that Hazel Atlas was that company. A lady in West Virginia found a set of 10 ounce tumblers in an original box, pictured here. Note the box indicates these were called Gothic; so we now have an original name for this pattern.

All known pieces are shown except the white milk glass tumbler. The seven ounce juice tumbler is the item most collectors are missing; evidently avid peanut butter fans didn't buy the smaller size. The price on these juices has almost doubled in a couple of years. I took a few to a show last year and one dealer grabbed them and asked if I had anymore. It seems her daughter had been searching for juice tumblers for over five years without success. Other collectors have informed me of struggles finding the luncheon plate, cup, and saucer. Obviously, these three pieces were marketed in some other manner than as peanut butter containers.

The tea goblet with the original peanut butter inside was a garage sale find about 20 years ago. I had no idea then I'd be using it in a book. It wasn't Depression glass — just interesting; it was a "comment piece" in my shop for a long time.

Thanks for all the help with new information on Gothic.

	Crystal
Cup	6.00
Saucer	3.00
Plate, 8", luncheon	7.50
Sherbet, 3⅝", 8 oz.	4.00
Tumbler, tea, 5¾", 10 oz.	7.00
Goblet, 5¼", 7 oz., juice	17.50

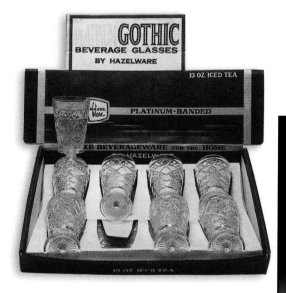

"BOUQUET," ETCHING #342, FOSTORIA GLASS COMPANY, 1950s

Colors: crystal

Bouquet is found on #2630 Century line and stems and tumblers are on line #6033. You may find additional pieces. Let me know if you do.

Basket, 10¼", reed hdld.	75.00	Plate, 9½", dinner	27.50
Bowl, 4½", 1-hdld.	14.00	Plate, 10¾", cracker	32.50
Bowl, 5", fruit	17.50	Plate, 14", torte	37.50
Bowl, 6", cereal	27.50	Platter, 12"	55.00
Bowl, 9", 2-hdld, oval, serving	37.50	Preserve w/cover	40.00
Bowl, 9", 2-hdld, serving	35.00	Relish, 7⅜", 2-part	20.00
Bowl, 9½", oval	35.00	Relish, 11⅛", 3-part	30.00
Bowl, 10½", salad	32.50	Salver, 12¼", 2⅛" high	60.00
Bowl, 10¾", ftd.	45.00	Saucer	4.00
Bowl, 11¼", lily pond	35.00	Shaker, pr.	30.00
Bowl, 11", ftd., rolled edge	45.00	Stem, 3¾", 4 oz., oyster cocktail	22.50
Bowl, 12", flared	42.50	Stem, 3⅝", 1 oz., cordial #6033	55.00
Butter w/cover, ¼ lb.	40.00	Stem, 4¼", 4 oz., cocktail #6033	23.00
Cake plate, 2-hdld.	27.50	Stem, 4", 6 oz., low sherbet #6033	20.00
Candlestick, 4½"	20.00	Stem, 4¾", 4 oz., claret-wine #6033	32.50
Candlestick, 7", duo	40.00	Stem, 4¾", 6 oz., saucer champagne #6033	22.50
Candlestick, 7¾", trindle	50.00	Stem, 5⅝", 6 oz., parfait #6033	20.00
Candy w/cover, 7"	45.00	Stem, 6¼", 10 oz., water #6033	25.00
Cheese comport, 2½" high	20.00	Sugar, ftd.	12.50
Comport, 4⅜"	25.00	Sugar, individual, ftd.	12.50
Creamer, ftd.	12.50	Tidbit, 8⅛", 3-toed	22.00
Creamer, individual, ftd.	12.50	Tray, 7⅛" for ind. cr/sug	17.50
Cup, ftd.	15.00	Tray, 9½", 2-hdld., muffin	35.00
Ice bucket	75.00	Tray, 9⅛", 2-hdld., utility	35.00
Mayonnaise, plate and spoon	40.00	Tumbler, 4½", 5 oz., juice #6033	25.00
Mustard, 4", w/cover and spoon	35.00	Tumbler, 5⅞", 13 oz., tea #6033	30.00
Oil bottle, 5 oz.	45.00	Vase, 5", #4121	
Pickle, 8¾"	20.00	Vase, 6", bud	22.50
Pitcher, 6⅛", 1 pint	75.00	Vase, 6", ftd. bud, #6021	85.00
Pitcher, 9½", 3 pint	135.00	Vase, 6", ftd., #4143	75.00
Plate, 6½", bread and butter	7.50	Vase, 7½", 2-hdld	75.00
Plate, 7½, crescent salad	45.00	Vase, 8¼", oval	85.00
Plate, 7½", salad	10.00	Vase, 8", flip, #2660	125.00
Plate, 8", party w/indent	20.00	Vase, 8", ftd. bud, #5092	85.00
Plate, 8½", luncheon	15.00	Vase, 10", ftd. #2470	125.00

"BUBBLE," "BULLSEYE," PROVINCIAL, ANCHOR HOCKING GLASS COMPANY, 1940 – 1965

Colors: pink, Sapphire blue, Forest Green, Royal Ruby, crystal, iridized, Vitrock, and any known Hocking color

"Bubble" has always been one of Anchor Hocking's most collected patterns. There is a plentiful supply of most pieces in all colors and even new collectors can readily recognize the simple, circular design sometimes called "Bullseye." Only a few items are hard to find. Blue creamers have always been scarce, and the 9" flanged bowl has for all intents and purposes left the collecting field, though it materialized in two styles. Both styles are shown in my *Anchor Hocking's Fire-King & More* book. You will search long and hard for blue grill plates and 4" berry bowls without inner rim damage. Grill plates are divided into three sections and were used in restaurants to keep the food separated and allowed smaller servings to fill the plate.

Original labels found on crystal "Bubble" read "Heat Proof." A 1942 ad (referring to Sapphire blue) guaranteed this Fire-King tableware to be "heat-proof," indeed a "tableware that can be used in the oven, on the table, in the refrigerator." This added feature is exclusive to Fire-King since earlier Depression glass patterns do not permit sudden changes in temperature without breaking. Forest Green or Royal Ruby "Bubble" stickers do not illustrate these corresponding heat-proof capabilities. Be forewarned!

If you find original factory labels on "Bubble" pieces, it will be for the color and not the name which collectors have assigned to it. Forest Green (dark) and Royal Ruby (red) "Bubble" dinner plates have both become challenging to find in mint condition (without scratches or knife marks on the surface). There are two styles of green and crystal dinner plates. The first plate measures ⅛" larger than the normally found dinner plate. The center of this plate is smaller and there are four rows of bubbles outside the center. A collector recently told me that she remembered the larger diameter, smaller centered crystal plates were given as a flour premium and offered as a cake plate. The typically found dinner plate has three rows of bubbles. The plates with four rows (cake?) are in shorter supply than those with three rows.

Many collectors use red and green "Bubble" for Christmas tables. Green and red water goblets are frequently found with advertising, suggesting they were premium items. A few pieces of amber and iridescent "Bubble" are found. The iridized pieces I found a couple of years ago have now settled into several collections. The small set consisted of dinner plates, cups, saucers, soup, and salad bowls. These iridized items have to be rare since so few are seen; but few collectors seem to know they exist.

Pink "Bubble" is hard to find except for the 8⅜" bowl that sells in the $10.00 to $12.00 range. That 8⅜" berry bowl can be found in almost any color that Anchor Hocking made (including all the opaque and iridescent colors). The recent demand for the Jade-ite "Bubble" bowl has it selling $20.00+ range. Milk White bowls were listed only in the 1959 – 60 catalog, but many of them still exist today. The inside depths of these bowls vary. Price all other colors of "Bubble" as you would crystal. I have found no new information on the plastic "Bubble" bowls made by S & K pictured in a previous edition.

"Bubble" stemware was originally called "Early American" line. The other stemware line sold along with "Bubble," sometimes called "Boopie," was actually named Berwick. Both of these stemware lines were manufactured after production of blue "Bubble" had ceased; thus, there are no blue "Bubble" stems to be found.

Royal Ruby Berwick is priced in the same range as Royal Ruby "Bubble" stemware; but the Forest Green Berwick is selling for less than the Forest Green "Bubble" stemware. The catalog lists an iced tea in Berwick with a capacity of 15 ounce. All I can find measure 14 ounces. Measurements for capacity are done by filling to the top rim (spilling-out-point) of the object to be measured.

"BUBBLE"

	Crystal	Forest Green	Light Blue	Royal Ruby
Bowl, 4", berry	4.00		17.50	
Bowl, 4½", fruit	4.50	11.00	15.00	9.00
Bowl, 5¼", cereal	8.00	18.00	15.00	
Bowl, 7¾", flat soup	10.00		15.00	
Bowl, 8⅜", large berry (Pink – $8.00)	6.00	16.00	19.00	22.00
Bowl, 9", flanged			450.00	
Candlesticks, pr.	25.00	150.00		
Creamer	7.00	12.00	35.00	
*Cup	3.50	8.00	4.00	8.00
Lamp, 3 styles	50.00			
Pitcher, 64 oz., ice lip	125.00			60.00
Plate, 6¾", bread and butter	3.00	18.00	4.00	
Plate, 9⅜", grill			22.50	
Plate, 9⅜", dinner	7.00	25.00	6.00	24.00
Platter, 12", oval	12.00		13.00	
**Saucer	1.00	4.00	1.00	4.00
***Stem, 3½ oz., cocktail	4.00	14.00		10.00
***Stem, 4 oz., juice	4.50	15.00		10.00
Stem, 4½ oz., cocktail	4.00	12.50		12.50
Stem, 5½ oz., juice	5.00	12.50		12.50
***Stem, 6 oz., sherbet	3.00	9.00		7.00
Stem, 6 oz., sherbet	3.50	9.00		9.00
***Stem, 9 oz., goblet	7.00	15.00		12.50
Stem, 10¾ oz., goblet	7.00	13.00		13.00
***Stem, 14 oz., iced tea	10.00	16.00		
Sugar	6.00	12.00	25.00	
Tidbit, 2-tier				75.00
Tumbler, 5 oz., 4", juice	3.50			8.00
Tumbler, 8 oz., 3¼", old fashioned	10.00			16.00
Tumbler, 9 oz., water	5.00			9.00
Tumbler, 12 oz., 4½", iced tea	12.00			12.50
Tumbler, 16 oz., 5⅞", lemonade	15.00			16.00

*Pink – $125.00   **Pink – $40.00   ***Berwick

BUTTERCUP, ETCHING #340, FOSTORIA GLASS COMPANY, 1941 – 1960

Color: crystal

Many brides who chose Buttercup as their crystal pattern in the 1940s are now passing on their precious crystal due to retirement or even death. Often, as families reduce or disburse their estate, glassware is either sold into the collectible market or split up within the family and either situation may create new collectors. Buttercup was a term of endearment made famous in Hollywood movies. Consequently, it was a natural choice as a name for Fostoria's bridal crystal, which was produced for 20 years, a testament to its popularity. Buttercup is certainly a more enchanting term of endearment than "dog breath," which is used in a current commercial.

More collectors are noticing this pattern that is not as plentiful as others from this time period. Prices are slowly beginning to rise. Slowly is the operative word; but it's the rising which is more important in an economic time when many pattern prices are not. Vases are difficult pieces to find in almost all Fostoria crystal patterns, and Buttercup is no exception. Stemware is more plentiful than other Buttercup items. Many brides bought only stems to go with their china and did not purchase glass serving dishes.

The small pieces shown in front are an individual ashtray and a cigarette holder. That cigarette holder might make a better toothpick holder, today, when we've been made so well aware that smoking is not as fashionable as it was depicted during this era. Stemware and salad and luncheon plates were in catalog listings as late as 1960 and that is why those items are easier to find today than many of the other Buttercup listings. Buttercup also had a corresponding Gorham silver pattern that could be purchased to use with this Fostoria crystal.

Item	Price	Item	Price
Ashtray, #2364, 2⅝", individual	27.50	Plate, #2337, 8½"	17.50
Bottle, #2083, salad dressing	295.00	Plate, #2337, 9½"	42.50
Bowl, #2364, 6", baked apple	20.00	Plate, #2364, 6¾", mayonnaise	7.50
Bowl, #2364, 9", salad	50.00	Plate, #2364, 7¼" x 4½", crescent salad	55.00
Bowl, #2364, 10½", salad	55.00	Plate, #2364, 11¼", cracker	32.50
Bowl, #2364, 11", salad	55.00	Plate, #2364, 11", sandwich	35.00
Bowl, #2364, 12", flared	60.00	Plate, #2364, 14", torte	60.00
Bowl, #2364, 12", lily pond	55.00	Plate, #2364, 16", torte	110.00
Bowl, #2364, 13", fruit	65.00	Relish, #2364, 6½" x 5", 2-part	25.00
Bowl, #2594, 10", 2 hndl.	65.00	Relish, #2364, 10" x 7¼", 3-part	35.00
Candlestick, #2324, 4"	17.50	Saucer, #2350	5.00
Candlestick, #2324, 6"	32.50	Shaker, #2364, 2⅝"	35.00
Candlestick, #2594, 5½"	30.00	Stem, #6030, 3¾", 4 oz., oyster cocktail	20.00
Candlestick, #2594, 8", trindle	60.00	Stem, #6030, 3⅞", 1 oz., cordial	42.50
Candlestick, #6023, 5½", duo	60.00	Stem, #6030, 4⅜", 6 oz., low sherbet	16.00
Candy w/cover, #2364, 3¾" diameter	155.00	Stem, #6030, 5¼", 3½ oz., cocktail	20.00
Celery, #2350, 11"	27.50	Stem, #6030, 5⅝", 6 oz., high sherbet	18.00
Cheese stand, #2364, 5¾" x 2⅞"	25.00	Stem, #6030, 6", 3½ oz., claret-wine	32.50
Cigarette holder, #2364, 2" high	35.00	Stem, #6030, 6⅜", 10 oz., low goblet	22.50
Coaster	22.00	Stem, #6030, 7⅞", 10 oz., water goblet	27.50
Comport, #2364, 8"	45.00	Sugar, #2350½, 3⅛", ftd.	15.00
Comport, #6030, 5"	40.00	Syrup, #2586, sani-cut	325.00
Creamer, #2350½, 3¼", ftd.	16.00	Tray, #2364, 11¼", center handled	35.00
Cup, #2350½, ftd.	15.00	Tumbler, #6030, 4⅝", 5 oz., ftd. juice	25.00
Mayonnaise, #2364, 5"	25.00	Tumbler, #6030, 6", 12 oz., ftd. iced tea	30.00
Pickle, #2350, 8"	25.00	Vase, 6", ftd., #4143	100.00
Pitcher, #6011, 8⅞", 53 oz.	295.00	Vase, 6", ftd., #6021	100.00
Plate, #2337, 6"	7.00	Vase, 7½", ftd., #4143	155.00
Plate, #2337, 7½"	12.00	Vase, 10", #2614	155.00

CABOCHON, A.H. HEISEY & COMPANY, 1950 – 1957

Colors: amber, crystal, and Dawn

Cabochon: the name itself means a gem cut in a convex curve with no facets. Obviously, the original designers of the Cabochon pattern intended the design to stand alone… as a "gem" of glassware. Cabochon is mostly found in crystal. This minimalistic pattern holds tremendous appeal for some Heisey collectors; but others disregard it as too plain.

Cabochon in amber or Dawn is rarely seen outside a major Heisey glass show. The amber plate illustrated is rarely witnessed. Dawn can be found, but you will pay a dear price for the privilege of owning it. Prices overall remain moderate for this pattern manufactured in those last years before the closing of the Heisey plant in 1957. This listing is copied from a 1953 catalog. Most patterns made in the declining years of the factory are more difficult to find than those manufactured during the prime years of the 30s and 40s.

The 6¼" candy dish is rare in Dawn. You will find a few pieces of Cabochon that are cut or etched, but finding Orchid and Rose etchings on Cabochon fascinate a majority of Heisey collectors. The cordial pictured below has Heisey's Debutante cut which, for me, adds to this pattern.

	Crystal
Bonbon, 6¼", hndl.	
(sides sloped w/squared hndl.), #1951	24.00
Bottle, oil, w/#101 stopper #1951	60.00
Bowl, 4½", dessert, #1951	4.00
Bowl, 5", dessert, #1951	5.00
Bowl, 7", cereal, #1951	6.00
Bowl, 13", floral or salad, #1951	18.00
Bowl, 13", gardenia	
(low w/edge cupped irregularly), #1951	18.00
Butter dish, ¼ lb., #1951	30.00
Cake salver, ftd., #1951	75.00
Candle holder, 2 lite, ground bottom, pr., #1951	165.00
Candlette, 1 lite (like bowl), pr., #1951	38.00
Candy, 6¼", w/lid (bowl w/lid), #1951	38.00
Cheese, 5¾", ftd., compote for cracker plate	17.50
Cream, #1951	13.00
Creamer, cereal, 12 oz., #1951	30.00
Cup, #1951	6.00
Jelly, 6", hndl. (sides and hndl. rounded), #1951	24.00
Mayonnaise, 3-pc. (plate, bowl, ladle), #1951	35.00
Mint, 5¾", ftd. (sides slanted), #1951	22.50
Pickle tray, 8½", #1951	20.00
Plate, 8", salad, #1951	6.00
Plate, 13", center hndl., #1951	42.00
Plate, 14", cracker w/center ring, #1951	18.00
Plate, 14", party (edge cupped irregularly), #1951	18.00
Plate, 14", sandwich, #1951	18.00
Relish, 9", three-part, oblong, #1951	22.00
Relish, 9", three-part, square, #1951	20.00
Salt and pepper, square, w/#60 silver-	
plated tops, pr., #1951	13.00
Saucer, #1951	1.50
Sherbet, 6 oz., #1951 (pressed)	4.00

	Crystal
Sherbet, 6 oz., #6092 (blown)	4.00
Stemware, 1 oz., cordial, #6091	22.50
Stemware, 3 oz., oyster cocktail, #6091	4.00
Stemware, 3 oz., wine, #6091	8.00
Stemware, 4 oz., cocktail, #6091	4.00
Stemware, 5½ oz., sherbet, #6091	4.00
Stemware, 10 oz., goblet, #6091	8.00
Sugar, w/cover, #1951	18.00
Tidbit, 7½" (bowl w/sloped outsides), #1951	12.50
Tray, 9", for cream and sugar, #1951	45.00
Tumbler, 5 oz., #1951 (pressed)	7.00
Tumbler, 5 oz., juice, flat bottomed, #6092 (blown)	7.00
Tumbler, 5 oz., juice, ftd., #6091	7.00
Tumbler, 10 oz., beverage, #6092 (blown)	8.00
Tumbler, 10 oz., tumbler, #6092 (blown)	8.00
Tumbler, 12 oz., #1951 (pressed)	12.50
Tumbler, 12 oz., iced tea, #6092 (blown)	12.50
Tumbler, 12 oz., iced tea, ftd., #6091	8.00
Tumbler, 14 oz., soda, #6092 (blown)	11.00
Vase, 3½", flared, #1951	24.00

CAMELLIA, PLATE ETCHING #344, FOSTORIA GLASS COMPANY, 1952 – 1976

Color: crystal

This pattern is often called "Camellia Rose" rather than just Camellia. This was Fostoria's answer to Heisey's Rose, Cambridge's Rose Point, and Tiffin's Cherokee Rose; and even though Fostoria's Camellia production outlasted all the other companies' rose patterns, it never reached the collecting status of the Heisey or Cambridge patterns. Camellia is often confused by beginning collectors with the more desirable Heisey Rose pattern. Experience has shown me that unknowledgeable people nearly always believe that they have found the more expensive (desirable) patterns instead of lesser known ones.

With the advent of the Internet, I receive several e-mails per week asking me to vet auction sites to see if the pattern represented is the right one. It may help you to purchase my three *Pattern Identification* guides which will show you over 1,600 different patterns with a close-up photo of each. That way, you will have a quick reference on hand when you need it. Unfortunately, it is not unusual to have pieces misrepresented as more expensive wares. Whether that was done mistakenly or on purpose, the collector is always upset and may have paid too much. Sometimes the items were found mislabeled at an antique mall where you assume dealers are knowledgeable. Have you noticed that almost all antique malls have signs posted — "No Refunds or Returns?" You need to know what you are buying. If you buy it, and it is not what it was supposed to be, it still belongs to you.

All pieces in the listing below that have no line numbers were made on Fostoria's #2630 blank, better known as Century. Some collectors are finding Camellia looks better to them than the undecorated Century; and they are switching to this etched pattern which is only a little more expensive. You probably will find additional pieces in this pattern that are not listed.

Item	Price		Item	Price
Basket, 10¼" x 6½", wicker hndl.	100.00		Plate, 9½", small dinner	30.00
Bowl, 4½", hndl.	15.00		Plate, 10", hndl., cake	30.00
Bowl, 5", fruit	16.00		Plate, 10¼", dinner	47.50
Bowl, 6", cereal	30.00		Plate, 10½", snack, small center	30.00
Bowl, 6¼", snack, ftd.	22.50		Plate, 14", torte	60.00
Bowl, 7¼", bonbon, 3-ftd.	25.00		Plate, 16", torte	100.00
Bowl, 7⅛", 3-ftd., triangular	20.00		Platter, 12"	47.50
Bowl, 8", flared	35.00		Preserve, w/cover, 6"	65.00
Bowl, 8½", salad	40.00		Relish, 7⅜", 2-part	18.00
Bowl, 9", lily pond	40.00		Relish, 11⅛", 3-part	45.00
Bowl, 9½", hndl., serving bowl	45.00		Salt and pepper, 3⅛", pr.	55.00
Bowl, 9½", oval, serving bowl	50.00		Salver, 12¼", ftd. (like cake stand)	75.00
Bowl, 10", oval, hndl.	45.00		Saucer	4.00
Bowl, 10½", salad	50.00		Stem, #6036, 3¼", 1 oz., cordial	42.50
Bowl, 10¾", ftd., flared	50.00		Stem, #6036, 3¾", 4 oz., oyster cocktail	18.00
Bowl, 11, ftd., rolled edge	55.00		Stem, #6036, 4⅛", 3½ oz., cocktail	20.00
Bowl, 11¼", lily pond	47.50		Stem, #6036, 4⅛", 6 oz., low sherbet	10.00
Bowl, 12", flared	55.00		Stem, #6036, 4¾", 3¼ oz., claret-wine	30.00
Butter, w/cover, ¼ lb.	50.00		Stem, #6036, 4¾", 6 oz., high sherbet	14.00
Candlestick, 4½"	25.00		Stem, #6036, 5⅞", 5½ oz., parfait	27.50
Candlestick, 7", double	45.00		Stem, #6036, 6⅞", 9½ oz., water	25.00
Candlestick, 7¾", triple	60.00		Sugar, 4", ftd.	14.00
Candy, w/cover, 7"	60.00		Sugar, individual	10.00
Comport, 2¾", cheese	22.50		Tidbit, 8⅛", 3 ftd., upturned edge	30.00
Comport, 4⅜"	25.00		Tidbit, 10¼", 2 tier, metal hndl.	45.00
Cracker plate, 10¾"	30.00		Tray, 4¼", for ind. salt/pepper	17.50
Creamer, 4¼"	15.00		Tray, 7⅛", for ind. sugar/creamer	20.00
Creamer, individual	12.00		Tray, 9½", hndl., muffin	32.50
Cup, 6 oz., ftd.	17.00		Tray, 9⅛", hndl., utility	30.00
Ice bucket	75.00		Tray, 11½", center hndl.	40.00
Mayonnaise, 3-pc.	37.50		Tumbler, #6036, 4⅝", 5 oz., ftd. juice	22.00
Mayonnaise, 4-pc., div. w/2 ladles	45.00		Tumbler, #6306, 6⅛", 12 oz., ftd. iced tea	28.00
Mustard, w/spoon, cover	35.00		Vase, 5", #4121	65.00
Oil, w/stopper, 5 oz.	60.00		Vase, 6", bud	35.00
Pickle, 8¾"	25.00		Vase, 6", ftd., #4143	85.00
Pitcher, 6⅛", 16 oz.	95.00		Vase, 6", ftd., #6021	65.00
Pitcher, 7⅛", 48 oz.	195.00		Vase, 7½", hndl.	85.00
Plate, 6½", bread/butter	7.00		Vase, 8", flip, #2660	90.00
Plate, 7½", crescent salad	60.00		Vase, 8", ftd., #5092	80.00
Plate, 7½", salad	10.00		Vase, 8½", oval	85.00
Plate, 8", party, w/indent for cup	25.00		Vase, 10", ftd., #2470	115.00
Plate, 8½", luncheon	15.00		Vase, 10½", ftd., #2657	115.00

CAMELLIA, JEANNETTE GLASS COMPANY, 1950s

Colors: crystal, crystal with gold trim, iridized, flashed red and blue

Camellia is a small Jeannette pattern that looks good alone or when used as accessory pieces for other patterns. More and more collectors are using it to gain additional serving pieces for other patterns because it lends itself to "blending" and pieces are readily available.

The punch set features a 9⅜" bowl which is 4¼" deep. It is found seated on a rack with extended metal hooks from which hang the eight cups. You may find this on a gold stand as well as self standing with no stand. I have seen the punch bowl iridized and it should sell at about double the crystal bowl. This bowl also comes with gold lettering advertising it as an eggnog set. All Camellia pieces seem to come with or without the gold trim that could wear with use. Don't put these trimmed pieces in the dishwasher if you want the trim to remain, especially if you have lemon in your dishwasher soap. However, that will remove it rather well should you not like the gold trim.

Notice the sprayed red Camellia relish tray with the original label still attached. We've also seen this piece sprayed with an electric blue color. The two-handled tray and the relish have been the hardest items for us to find.

Most often the creamer and sugar are found without the flower. However, I've finally found one with the flower. Price those with the embossed flower about 50% more than the price listed for the plain ones.

	Crystal		Crystal
Bowl, 5"	6.00	Plate, 8", luncheon	7.00
Bowl, 1-hndl., nappy	9.00	Plate, 12", sandwich	12.00
Bowl, 8⅞", vegetable	12.50	Relish, 6¾" x 11¾"	14.00
Bowl, 9⅜", 4¼" deep, punch	18.00	Saucer	.50
Bowl, 10⅛", 3½" deep, salad	15.00	Sugar, ftd.	7.50
Candleholder	12.50	Sugar, ftd. (with design)	15.00
Creamer, ftd.	7.50	Tidbit, 2-tier	20.00
Creamer, ftd. (with design)	15.00	Tray, two-handled	15.00
Cup	1.00		

CAPRI, "SEASHELL," "SWIRL COLONIAL," "COLONIAL," "ALPINE,"
HAZEL WARE, DIVISION OF CONTINENTAL CAN, 1960s

Color: Azure blue

  Capri refers to the blue color of this ware. This electric blue coloring was popular in the 1960s and can be seen in wares from other companies as well. You will note some slight price reduction in many of the basic pieces. This has resulted from the multitude of pieces being made available outweighing the number of new collectors. More new collectors turned to Anchor Hockings' Fire-King wares than to Hazel Atlas's Capri. Lack of demand will always lessen price to some extent. Now might be a good time to stock up on this sea blue color if it is to your liking.

  I have tried to organize the various Capri designs into some form of reference. On the bottom of page 25 in the foreground are Colony pieces with a distinct twist to them which I called "Colony Swirl." The "Swirl" is my added name for this pattern. Notice that the bases of both patterns are square or rectangular. That sounds great except I do have a crystal Colony shaped bowl sent me by a reader that has a "Simplicity" label. The "Dots" patterned glasses on the right are Skol Swedish-style glasses according to a boxed set I have. The three sizes of tumblers in this boxed set were priced 12¢, 15¢, and 18¢. Maybe the whole design is Skol, but I can only say the glasses were named that for sure. Skol is a toasting phrase meaning "to your health," and perhaps that's what this name implied. That box was shown in the 4th edition. The "Hobnails" design is shown on the left. The cup, creamer, and sugar have the hobs on the base of those respective pieces.

  The bottom of page 26 shows "Pentagonal" Capri, flat-bottomed tumblers and an assortment of other colors and pieces that you can collect within the Capri umbrella. They are definitely Hazel Atlas wares made in other colors; you can blend these or ignore them completely. The choice is yours.

  Pictured on the top of page 27 are Colony "Square," "Hexagonal," and "Octagonal." The Colony name comes from actual labels on the square based items; square, hexagonal, and octagonal are descriptions coming from the shapes. Shape names seemed the only easy way to describe these. The square-based tumbler is the only item that will fit the square indentation plate. There may be a square-based cup, but I haven't seen one.

  The bottom of page 27 shows the designs known as "Seashell" and "Tulip." The "Seashell" (swirled) pattern is the most commonly found design in Capri and "Tulip" (petal edged with circular dotted center) the most sparsely distributed. The ashtrays are all the same moulds as Moroccan Amethyst. That intaglio floral ashtray seems to be unusual in both Capri and Moroccan. The round ashtray and the coaster are Capri, but not of any particular design. That tumbler has five rounded "petal" protrusions that remind you of the bases on Duncan's Canterbury flat tumblers. Even though these designs are different, they could be used together if you were so inclined.

  Pentagonal flat tumblers, hexagonal stems, and octagonal dinnerware items make for some interesting geometric settings. Only Capri labels have been found on these pieces so far.

CAPRI

Ashtray, 3¼", triangular	6.00	Cup, octagonal	4.00	Sugar, round	8.00
Ashtray, 3¼", round	6.00	Cup, round, "Hobnails" or "Dots"	4.00	Sugar lid	12.00
Ashtray, 3½", square, embossed		Cup, round, swirled	4.00	Tidbit, 3-tier (round 9⅞" plate,	
flower	17.50	Cup, round, "Tulip"	7.00	7⅛" plate, 6" saucer)	22.50
Ashtray, 5", round	8.00	Plate, 5¾", bread and butter,		Tumbler, 2¾", 4 oz., "Colony Swirl"	7.00
Ashtray, 6⅝", triangular	12.00	octagonal	4.00	Tumbler, 3", 4 oz., fruit, "Dots"	4.00
Bowl, 4¾", octagonal	7.00	Plate, 7", salad, round, "Colony Swirl"	7.00	Tumbler, 3", 5 oz., pentagonal bottom	7.00
Bowl, 4¾", swirled	6.00	Plate, 7⅛", round, salad, "Colony		Tumbler, 3¹⁄₁₆", Colony or	
Bowl, 4⅞", round, "Dots"	5.00	Swirl"	7.00	"Colony Swirl"	8.00
Bowl, 5⅜", salad, round, "Hobnails"	7.00	Plate, 7¼", salad, "Hobnails"	6.00	Tumbler, 3⅛", 5 oz., pentagonal	7.00
Bowl, 5⅝", "Colony Swirl"	8.00	Plate, 7¼", salad, octagonal	6.00	Tumbler, 3¼", 8 oz., old fashioned,	
Bowl, 5¾", square, deep, Colony	10.00	Plate, 8", square	8.00	"Dots"	8.00
Bowl, 6", round, "Tulip"	10.00	Plate, 8", square, w/square cup rest	8.00	Tumbler, 3⅝", 6 oz., "Dots"	5.00
Bowl, 6", round, "Dots"	7.00	Plate, 8⅞", square	10.00	Tumbler, 4", "Dots"	4.00
Bowl, 6", round, sq. bottom, Colony	7.00	Plate, 8⅞", square, w/round cup rest	9.00	Tumbler, 4¼", 9 oz., "Colony Swirl"	7.50
Bowl, 6¹⁄₁₆", round, "Colony Swirl"	7.00	Plate, 9½", round, snack w/cup rest,		Tumbler, 4¼", 9 oz., water, pentagonal	
Bowl, 7¾", oval, Colony	15.00	"Tulip"	9.50	bottom	7.50
Bowl, 7¾", rectangular, Colony	14.00	Plate, 9¾", dinner, octagonal	9.00	Tumbler, 5", 12 oz., "Colony Swirl"	10.00
Bowl, 8¾", swirled	12.00	Plate, 9⅞", dinner, round, "Hobnails"	8.00	Tumbler, 5", 12 oz., tea, pentagonal	
Bowl, 9⅛" x 3" high	25.00	Plate, 10", snack, fan shaped w/cup rest	7.00	bottom	10.00
Bowl, 9½" x 2⅞" high	22.00	Saucer, 5½", square	1.00	Tumbler, 5¼", "Dots"	5.00
Bowl, 9½" oval 1½" high	9.00	Saucer, 6", round, "Hobnails" or "Dots"	1.00	Tumbler, 5½", 12 oz., tea, swirl	10.00
Bowl, 10¾", salad, Colony	24.00	Saucer, octagonal	1.00	Tumbler, 6", 10 oz., "Dots"	7.00
Candy jar, w/cover, ftd.	32.00	Sherbet, 2¾" high, round footed,		Vase, 8", "Dots"	20.00
Chip and dip, 2 swirled bowls		"Dots"	5.00	Vase, 8½", ruffled	35.00
(8¾" and 4¾" on metal rack)	25.00	Stem, 4½", sherbet	7.50		
Creamer, round	12.50	Stem, 5½", water	9.00		

CASCADE, 4000 LINE, CAMBRIDGE GLASS COMPANY, 1950s

Colors: crystal; some Emerald Green, Mandarin Gold, and Milk White — infrequently Tahoe Blue, Crown Tuscan, and Carmen

This attention-grabbing Cambridge pattern has fewer collectors pursuing it than it should. The heavy, bold design is interesting and it has presence and texture. A number of pieces were made in color, a few of which were shown in previous editions.

No one has ever been able to explain to me why there are two styles of stems on the water goblets — something to notice if you are just beginning to buy this pattern. One design is turned upside-down from the other. It actually is not so noticeable until you get each style sitting side by side and then it becomes rather apparent.

Several Cascade pieces such as the 8" ashtray had numerous functions. Besides a lamp base and its conventional use, it also served as the punch bowl base when turned upside-down. Then, too, it held up the 21" plate to make a buffet set. That 21" plate also became the punch bowl liner in the punch set. It was an astute use of costly moulds at a time when Cambridge was headed toward insolvency.

Items frequently observed at the markets are bowls of assorted sizes and shapes. If you run across flatware, tumblers, or colored items, you may want to buy those even if you are not a collector of this pattern. Cascade collectors will be glad to take them off your hands. You can see examples of Crown Tuscan and Carmen in my rare books, but finding a Tahoe Blue piece will be even more difficult.

	Crystal	Green	Yellow
Ashtray, 4½"	6.00		
Ashtray, 6"	10.00		
Ashtray, 8"	20.00		
Bowl, 4½", fruit	7.50		
Bowl, 6½", relish	13.00		
Bowl, 6½", relish, 2-pt.	13.00		
Bowl, 6", 4-ftd., bonbon	12.00		
Bowl, 7", 2 hndl., ftd., bonbon	13.00		
Bowl, 10", 3-pt., celery	20.00		
Bowl, 10", 4-ftd., flared	32.00		
Bowl, 10½", 4-ftd., shallow	32.00		
Bowl, 12", 4-ftd., oval	33.00		
Bowl, 12½", 4-ftd., flared	35.00		
Bowl, 13", 4-ftd., shallow	35.00		
Buffet set (21" plate w/8" ashtray)	85.00		
Candlestick, 5"	17.50	35.00	35.00
Candlestick, 6", 2-lite	27.50		
Candy box, w/cover	35.00	75.00	80.00
Cigarette box w/cover	22.50		
Comport, 5½"	17.50		
Creamer	8.50	20.00	20.00
Cup	8.00		
Ice tub, tab hndl.	32.50		
Mayonnaise spoon	7.50		
Mayonnaise, w/liner	17.50	65.00	65.00

	Crystal	Green	Yellow
Plate, 6½", bread & butter	5.50		
Plate, 8½", salad	9.00		
Plate, 8", 2 hndl., ftd., bonbon	14.00		
Plate, 11½", 4-ftd.	30.00		
Plate, 14", 4-ftd., torte	32.50		
Plate, 21"	65.00		
Punch base (same as 8" ashtray)	20.00		
Punch bowl liner, 21"	60.00		
Punch bowl, 15"	130.00		
Punch cup	7.50		
Saucer	2.50		
Shaker, pr.	20.00		
Stem, cocktail	11.00		
Stem, sherbet	10.00		
Stem, water goblet	15.00		
Sugar	8.00	20.00	20.00
Tumbler, 5 oz., flat	10.00		
Tumbler, 5 oz., ftd.	10.00		
Tumbler, 12 oz., ftd.	13.00		
Tumbler, 12 oz., flat	12.00		
*Vase 9½"	35.00	75.00	80.00
Vase, 9½", oval	40.00		

*Milk White $45.00

Color: crystal, rare in pink

Century enjoyed a long life at Fostoria. They may have expected it to endure even longer should one judge by its name. This Fostoria blank was used for several of their etched patterns made after 1950, just as the Fairfax blank was used for etching patterns before then. Heather and Camellia are two of the most collected patterns found on this #2630 shape. See the pictures of those patterns for additional pieces in this line.

High end prices for Century have stabilized. Wines, water goblets, and footed iced teas have leveled off as more collectors have turned to etched Century wares instead of the blank itself. Nationally, prices are fairly consistent. I just came back from a show in Seattle and Century prices there were consistent with what I find in Florida.

Sizes in Fostoria catalog listings for Century plates differ from the actual measurements by up to ½". I have tried to use actual measurements for Fostoria patterns in this book. I recognize that this has been an endless problem for people ordering through the mail or via the Internet. Glassware is certainly alive and well on the Internet. You may want to check out my glass listings and other books at www.geneflorence.com.

The ice bucket has button tabs for attaching a metal handle. One is pictured. The 8½" oval vase is shaped like the ice bucket, but without those tabs. A few damaged ice buckets (sans handles) have changed hands as vases. Pay attention to the glass you buy. You can see where the tabs used to be upon careful inspection. Buying mint condition glassware initially should pay you additional benefits in the future. Damaged glassware will always be damaged (or repaired) and nothing changes that.

	Crystal		Crystal
Ashtray, 2¾"	10.00	Pitcher, 7⅛", 48 oz.	110.00
Basket, 10¼" x 6½", wicker hndl.	70.00	Plate, 6½", bread/butter	6.00
Bowl, 4½", hndl.	12.00	Plate, 7½", salad	8.00
Bowl, 5", fruit	15.00	Plate, 7½", crescent salad	45.00
Bowl, 6", cereal	25.00	Plate, 8", party, w/indent for cup	15.00
Bowl, 6¼", snack, ftd.	14.00	Plate, 8½", luncheon	12.50
Bowl, 7⅛", 3-ftd., triangular	15.00	Plate, 9½", small dinner	25.00
Bowl, 7¼", bonbon, 3-ftd.	20.00	Plate, 10", hndl., cake	22.00
Bowl, 8", flared	25.00	Plate, 10½", dinner	33.00
Bowl, 8½", salad	25.00	Plate, 14", torte	35.00
Bowl, 9", lily pond	30.00	Platter, 12"	47.50
Bowl, 9½", hndl., serving bowl	35.00	Preserve, w/cover, 6"	35.00
Bowl, 9½", oval, serving bowl	32.50	Relish, 7⅜", 2-part	15.00
Bowl, 10", oval, hndl.	33.00	Relish, 11⅛", 3-part	25.00
Bowl, 10½", salad	30.00	Salt and pepper, 2⅜" (individual), pr.	15.00
Bowl, 10¾", ftd., flared	40.00	Salt and pepper, 3⅛", pr.	20.00
Bowl, 11, ftd., rolled edge	40.00	Salver, 12¼", ftd. (like cake stand)	55.00
Bowl, 11¼", lily pond	32.50	Saucer	3.50
Bowl, 12", flared	37.50	Stem, 3½ oz., cocktail, 4⅛"	18.00
Butter, w/cover, ¼ lb.	35.00	Stem, 3½ oz., wine, 4½"	30.00
Candy, w/cover, 7"	37.50	Stem, 4½ oz., oyster cocktail, 3¾"	20.00
Candlestick, 4½"	17.50	Stem, 5½" oz., sherbet, 4½"	12.00
Candlestick, 7", double	35.00	Stem, 10 oz., goblet, 5¾"	20.00
Candlestick, 7¾", triple	45.00	Sugar, 4", ftd.	9.00
Comport, 2¾", cheese	15.00	Sugar, individual	9.00
Comport, 4⅜"	20.00	Tidbit, 8⅛", 3-ftd., upturned edge	18.00
Cracker plate, 10¾"	30.00	Tidbit, 10¼", 2 tier, metal hndl.	27.50
Creamer, 4¼"	9.00	Tray, 4¼", for ind. salt/pepper	14.00
Creamer, individual	9.00	Tray, 7⅛", for ind. sugar/creamer	14.00
Cup, 6 oz., ftd.	13.00	Tray, 9⅛", hndl., utility	25.00
Ice bucket	65.00	Tray, 9½", hndl., muffin	30.00
Mayonnaise, 3-pc.	30.00	Tray, 11½", center hndl.	30.00
Mayonnaise, 4-pc., div. w/2 ladles	35.00	Tumbler, 5 oz., ftd., juice, 4¾"	22.50
Mustard, w/spoon, cover	27.50	Tumbler, 12 oz., ftd., tea, 5⅞"	27.50
Oil, w/stopper, 5 oz.	45.00	Vase, 6", bud	18.00
Pickle, 8¾"	15.00	Vase, 7½", hndl.	70.00
Pitcher, 6⅛", 16 oz.	60.00	Vase, 8½", oval	67.50

CHINTZ, PLATE ETCHING #338, FOSTORIA GLASS COMPANY, 1940 – 1977

Color: crystal

Fostoria's Chintz pattern is considered an Elegant glassware pattern, but it was shifted to this 50s book because it was made during the era included herein rather than the time frame encompassed by *Elegant Glassware of the Depression Era*. Chintz, as well as Fostoria's Century pattern, have both been transferred from the Elegant book where they were first shown before a 50s era book was ever conceived.

Hard-to-get pieces of Chintz include the syrup pitcher (Sani-cut metal top) and the footed 9½" bowl. Other items not easily uncovered include the cream soup, finger bowl, oval vegetable, and any vase. All these pieces are considered to be in short supply, although a few more oval bowls are being stumbled upon than in past history. Fostoria called the 8" oval bowl a sauce dish. These came divided or not. Many collectors refer to them as gravy boats. The oval sauce dish liner came with both, but a pamphlet listed it as a tray instead of liner. These seem to be in shorter supply than once thought.

The 11" celery on the #2496 (Baroque) blank does not exist according to several collectors who have written; so I have removed that from my listing. However, if you should spot one, let me know. Advanced collectors who concentrate on only one or two patterns always know more about those patterns than I do. Bearing in mind that my books cover hundreds of patterns, it's difficult to keep up with all peculiarities of each pattern; but I surely do try. For novice collectors, a fleur-de-lis in relief is the design for the Baroque (#2496) blank.

Chintz stemware is abundant, a common occurrence for most Elegant patterns from this time. It appears that people in the 1950s acquired stemware and did without serving pieces — as did their 30s counterparts. Indeed, glass company advertisements show they were at pains to "sell" the use of glassware as entire table settings. Almost any serving piece is hard to acquire. Stemware was bought to use with china sets; thus, glass serving pieces were redundant and didn't sell well. That fact was underscored by an elderly lady whose Fostoria I was negotiating to buy. Condescendingly she stated that no one back then wanted to eat from glass dishes, so why purchase those pieces? It appears to have been a long-lasting prejudice.

Chintz has only one size dinner plate, which is different from other Fostoria patterns. There was no service plate (usually an inch larger which was used as a dinner plate). You have to settle for a 9½" plate. Scratched and worn plates are a problem and regrettably, the rule rather than the exception. Prices below are for mint condition plates.

Item	Price		Item	Price
Bell, dinner	125.00		Plate, #2496, 9½", dinner	55.00
Bowl, #869, 4½", finger	70.00		Plate, #2496, 10½", hndl., cake	45.00
Bowl, #2496, 4⅝", tri-cornered	22.50		Plate, #2496, 11", cracker	40.00
Bowl, #2496, cream soup	95.00		Plate, #2496, 14", upturned edge	65.00
Bowl, #2496, 5", fruit	33.00		Plate, #2496, 16", torte, plain edge	135.00
Bowl, #2496, 5", hndl.	25.00		Plate, 17½", upturned edge	165.00
Bowl, #2496, 7⅝", bonbon	32.50		Platter, #2496, 12"	110.00
Bowl, #2496, 8½", hndl.	65.00		Relish, #2496, 6", 2 part, square	30.00
Bowl, #2496, 9¼", ftd.	310.00		Relish, #2496, 10" x 7½", 3 part	40.00
Bowl, #2496, 9½", oval vegetable	150.00		Relish, #2419, 5 part	40.00
Bowl, #2496, 9½", vegetable	75.00		Salad dressing bottle, #2083, 6½"	425.00
Bowl, #2484, 10", hndl.	65.00		Salt and pepper, #2496, 2¾", flat, pr.	100.00
Bowl, #2496, 10½", hndl.	70.00		Sauce boat, #2496, oval	65.00
Bowl, #2496, 11½", flared	65.00		Sauce boat, #2496, oval, divided	65.00
Bowl, #6023, ftd.	50.00		Sauce boat liner, #2496, oblong, 8"	30.00
Candlestick, #2496, 3½", double	32.00		Saucer, #2496	5.00
Candlestick, #2496, 4"	20.00		Stem, #6026, 1 oz., cordial, 3⅞"	50.00
Candlestick, #2496, 5½"	35.00		Stem, #6026, 4 oz., cocktail, 5"	22.00
Candlestick, #2496, 6", triple	60.00		Stem, #6026, 4 oz., oyster cocktail, 3⅜"	25.00
Candlestick, #6023, double	50.00		Stem, #6026, 4½ oz., claret-wine, 5⅜"	40.00
Candy, w/cover, #2496, 3-part	150.00		Stem, #6026, 6 oz., low sherbet, 4⅜"	18.00
Comport, #2496, 3¼", cheese	30.00		Stem, #6026, 6 oz., saucer champagne, 5½"	20.00
Comport, #2496, 4¾"	32.50		Stem, #6026, 9 oz., water goblet, 7⅝"	30.00
Comport, #2496, 5½"	40.00		Sugar, #2496, 3½", ftd.	16.00
Creamer, #2496, 3¾", ftd.	17.50		Sugar, #2496½, individual	21.00
Creamer, #2496½, individual	22.50		Syrup, #2586, Sani-cut	450.00
Cup, #2496, ftd.	21.00		Tidbit, #2496, 8¼", 3 ftd., upturned edge	26.00
Ice bucket, #2496	135.00		Tray, #2496½, 6½", for ind. sugar/creamer	22.00
Jelly, w/cover, #2496, 7½"	85.00		Tray, #2375, 11", center hndl.	40.00
Mayonnaise, #2496½, 3-piece	55.00		Tumbler, #6026, 5 oz., juice, ftd.	25.00
Oil, w/stopper, #2496, 3½ oz.	115.00		Tumbler, #6026, 9 oz., water or low goblet	25.00
Pickle, #2496, 8"	32.00		Tumbler, #6026, 13 oz., tea, ftd.	30.00
Pitcher, #5000, 48 oz., ftd.	375.00		Vase, #4108, 5"	100.00
Plate, #2496, 6", bread/butter	8.00		Vase, #4128, 5"	100.00
Plate, #2496, 7½", salad	14.00		Vase, #4143, 6", ftd.	135.00
Plate, #2496, 8½", luncheon	19.00		Vase, #4143, 7½", ftd.	210.00

Left to right: water goblet, water tumbler, claret-wine, cocktail, low sherbet, cordial, tea, juice, oyster cocktail.

CHRISTMAS CANDY," NO. 624, INDIANA GLASS COMPANY, 1937 – EARLY 1950S

Colors: Terrace Green (teal) and crystal

Indiana's #624 line has been dubbed "Christmas Candy" by collectors. Indiana called this teal color Terrace Green. The soup and vegetable bowl prices have continued an upward trend, while the rest have slowed or declined a few dollars. This happens to patterns that make big price jumps. New collectors tend to avoid patterns that are rapidly rising and tend to seek those that are steady. That leaves a dearth of collectors buying common items (cups, saucers, plates, creamers, and sugars). The collectors who have those pieces are still searching for and buying the harder to find items which cause them to continue escalating in price.

The supply of teal ran out before everyone found what they were lacking; but that short supply is what drove the price up in the first place. Of course, pricing is relative. Years from now, we may think these were very reasonable prices for uncommon items. Frequently, teal "Christmas Candy" is found in large groupings rather than a piece here and there. Glassware made in the 1950s or later is often found as sets — having been stored unused in someone's attic, garage, or basement. Sets may even be discovered in unopened boxes. It used to be in bad taste to return gifts, even duplicate ones, unlike our national pastime of returning everything, today. A few years ago I received a copy of a letter from a lady who had written Indiana Glass Company about this pattern. They told her it was made in the late 1930s and the 1950s, which confirmed information found on the only known boxed set, i.e. "15 pc. Luncheon set (Terrace Green) To F W Newburger & Co. New Albany Ind Dept M 1346; From Pitman Dretzer Dunkirk Ind 4-3-52." This was valuable dating information because this color had only been attributed to the earlier production in other published material.

A majority of teal colored pieces encountered come from trips through Indiana. I used to see groupings in Florida when I first moved here twelve years ago, but that hasn't been true lately. One of the problems with teal in Florida comes from well water usage which clouds the glass. No, there is no miracle cure for this cloudiness. I wish there were. The cloudiness is in the top layer of glass and only polishing it out will remove it. This is an expensive process, but it can be done.

One good thing about buying glassware in Florida, besides shopping outside in winter, is that "snow birds" (northerners in the local native tongue) yearly bring glass to sell from all over the country. You never know what will show up. Retirees bring glassware south with them, and as they downsize or leave this world, much of that glass becomes available to collectors. That is often glassware from the 1950s and 1960s rather than older wares.

Crystal "Christmas Candy" prices have changed very little even though only a smattering is being found. That bowl on top of the crystal tidbit measures 5¾". That bowl without a hole is challenging to find and has never been found in Terrace Green.

	Crystal	Teal
Bowl, 5¾"	4.50	
Bowl, 7⅜", soup	7.00	57.50
Bowl, 9½", vegetable		625.00
Creamer	8.00	30.00
Cup	4.00	30.00
Mayonnaise, w/ladle, liner	22.00	
Plate, 6", bread and butter	3.50	11.00
Plate, 8¼", luncheon	6.00	28.00
Plate, 9⅝", dinner	11.00	50.00
Plate, 11¼", sandwich	15.00	65.00
Saucer	2.00	12.00
Sugar	8.00	30.00
Tidbit, 2-tier	17.50	

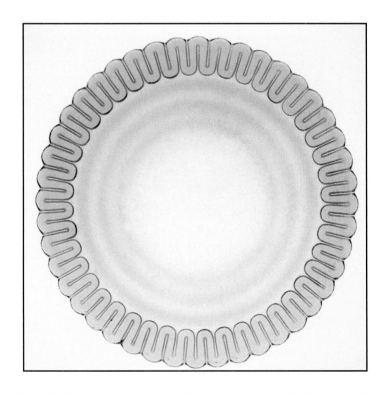

CHROMA, No. 123, IMPERIAL GLASS COMPANY, c. 1957

Colors: crystal, Burgundy, Evergreen, Indigo, and Madeira; some canary, custard, slag, and iridized

    Chroma was originally introduced in 1938 as Coronet; by 1942, it was known as Victorian and both were made in crystal and ruby and discontinued by end of WWII. The first goblets had one rough and one smooth ball on the stem; this was later made into just the rough patterned stem. The water goblet has two such balls; the tea goblet only one.

    I have not found Chroma at prices I was willing to pay for pieces to photograph. I kept running into groupings that were priced as a lot instead of pieces priced individually. There are a lot more customers looking for a piece or two rather than lots of six to 20 assorted pieces. In fact, I sell one shaker or one candle from a pair if that is what it takes to make the sale.

	*All colors
Cake stand	60.00
Compote, open	20.00
Compote w/lid ("Banquet")	65.00
Goblet, 8 oz. water	22.00
Goblet, 12 oz. tea	25.00
Plate, 8"	15.00
Sherbet, 6 oz.	18.00
Tumbler, 5½ oz. juice	18.00
Tumbler, 12 oz. tea	25.00

* deduct 25% for crystal

CLOVER BLOSSOM, DECORATION NO. 105, FEDERAL GLASS COMPANY, c. 1960

Color: milk glass white/pink and gray decoration

There has been little attention devoted to Federal's smaller patterns from the 1950s. Clover Blossom is one of them. In the catalog, this was advertised as "heat-proof and durable," "practically chip-proof" with "detergent resistant decoration." Regarding that last claim, there seems to be a variety of this pattern available not having full color decoration. The catalog also touted a "full size, 10" dinner plate." The set was packaged four ways: a five-piece place setting; a 16-piece starter set; a 35-piece dinnerware set; and a 53-piece dinnerware set. This was a contemporary of Golden Glory and the ever-present Rosecrest Snack set often encountered at markets.

If you have additional information, please let me know. You can always write or e-mail me through my web page, www.geneflorence.com.

Bowl, 4⅞" dessert	3.50
Bowl, 8" rim soup	10.00
Bowl, 8½"	15.00
Creamer	5.00
Cup	3.00
Plate, 7⅝" coupe	5.00
Plate, 10" coupe	8.00
Plate, 11¼" coupe chop	12.00
Saucer	.50
Sugar w/cover	10.00

COIN GLASS, LINE #1372, FOSTORIA GLASS COMPANY, 1958 – 1982

Colors: amber, blue, crystal, green, Olive, and red

Fostoria's Coin has seen price adjustments, both higher and lower in the last two years. Rare pieces and non-reproduced items are selling well in Fostoria's Coin Glass pattern. The reproductions that Lancaster Colony (who now own these Fostoria moulds) put out have resulted in a noticeable dip in sales of other items. I realize it is considered by some to be a continuance of the pattern since the original moulds are being used, but the pieces have different quality and, in some cases, a different color hue.

Coins in glassware design go all the way back to the late 1880s. In fact, Congress made it unlawful to reproduce actual currency images at some point and companies had to redesign their moulds for this popular type ware.

Those long-time collectors, who continue to acquire Coin, look for rarely seen items, bargains, and mistakes in pricing by uniformed sellers. Lack of collectors starting the pattern holds down sales of commonly found items. I originally included Coin in this book because it was becoming a desirable collectible — so desirable, in fact, that it became profitable enough to remake. I do not mean merely moulding a few pieces, but that they produced a whole line in many of the original colors. These colors deviate slightly from the cherished collectibles in amber, blue, and green; but there is virtually no way for new collectors to determine the red or crystal made yesterday from that made in the 1950s and 1960s; so, many won't even consider buying it. I used to tell collectors to look for frosted coins to identify older Coin; but, today, anyone can buy an acid for satinizing glassware at a crafters' store. Thus, frosted coins cannot be considered a true indication of older Coin glassware.

I have put an asterisk in the listing (*) by all pieces that have been manufactured in last ten years. Recognize that even that could change by the time this book becomes available. Obviously, this has caused chaos in pricing. Because the newly made pieces are priced so expensively initially, dealers are raising the prices on the older pieces. Who can blame them? Why sell an older piece for $50.00 when the newer item sells for $40.00? The older piece is going to be raised to $60.00 or even $75.00. This has happened in other collectibles, oak furniture for an example. The quandary I now have is how to handle it. If you collect Fostoria Coin, never has the following been truer. Know your dealer. Ask him if he can date the piece and keep the dated information with the piece. Remember, if the price sounds too good to be true, it probably is. Buying in an antique mall or over the Internet may not be so great an idea unless the dealer guarantees the piece. Then, too, phone calls, postage, and aggravation can all be costly.

Olive green is sometimes referred to as avocado, but Olive was the official name. Collectors often call the green most desired "emerald." This color is represented by the pieces in the bottom photo on page 41.

If you enjoy this pattern, collect it. People should collect what they like. Just be aware that future selling may be somewhat endangered by the remaking of older colors. Buy accordingly. This used to be an absolute law in collecting; the piece had to be authentically old. That, too, is changing. Today, it just has to be physically present in some cases. Remember the Beanie Baby, miniature racing cars, Lladro, and Department 56 wares? You don't have to be very old to recall these and they all fall under the "collectible" parameters of our present day society.

	Amber	Blue	Crystal	Green	Olive	Ruby
Ashtray, 5", #1372/123	17.50	25.00	18.00	30.00	17.50	22.50
Ashtray, 7½", center coin, #1372/119	20.00		25.00	35.00		25.00
Ashtray, 7½", round, #1372/114	25.00	40.00	25.00	45.00	30.00	20.00
Ashtray, 10", #1372/124	30.00	50.00	25.00	65.00	30.00	
Ashtray, oblong, #1372/115	15.00	20.00	10.00	25.00	25.00	
Ashtray/cover, 3", #1372/110	20.00	25.00	25.00	30.00		
Bowl, 8", round, #1372/179	30.00	50.00	25.00	70.00	25.00	45.00
Bowl, 8½", ftd., #1372/199	60.00	90.00	50.00	125.00	55.00	75.00
Bowl, 8½", ftd. w/cover, #1372/212	100.00	175.00	85.00	225.00		
*Bowl, 9", oval, #1372/189	30.00	55.00	30.00	70.00	33.00	50.00
*Bowl, wedding w/cover, #1372/162	70.00	90.00	55.00	150.00	55.00	85.00
Candle holder, 4½", pr., #1372/316	30.00	55.00	40.00	50.00	30.00	50.00
Candle holder, 8", pr., #1372/326	60.00		50.00		50.00	125.00
Candy box w/cover, 4⅛", #1372/354	30.00	60.00	30.00	100.00	33.00	60.00
*Candy jar w/cover, 6⁵⁄₁₆", #1372/347	40.00	50.00	25.00	125.00	25.00	50.00
*Cigarette box w/cover, 5¾" x 4½", #1372/374	50.00	80.00	40.00	115.00		
Cigarette holder w/ashtray cover, #1372/372	50.00	75.00	45.00	90.00		
Cigarette urn, 3⅜", ftd., #1372/381	25.00	45.00	20.00	50.00	22.00	40.00
Condiment set, 4 pc. (tray, 2 shakers and cruet), #1372/737	225.00	335.00	135.00	250.00		
Condiment tray, 9⅝", #1372/738	60.00	75.00	40.00		75.00	
*Creamer, #1372/680	11.00	16.00	10.00	30.00	15.00	16.00
Cruet, 7 oz. w/stopper, #1372/531	65.00	165.00	55.00	210.00	80.00	
*Decanter w/stopper, pint, 10³⁄₁₆", #1372/400	125.00	265.00	100.00	350.00	175.00	
*Jelly, #1372/448	17.50	25.00	15.00	35.00	15.00	25.00
Lamp chimney, coach or patio, #1372/461	50.00	60.00	40.00			
Lamp chimney, hndl., courting, #1372/292	45.00	65.00				

	Amber	Blue	Crystal	Green	Olive	Ruby
Lamp, 9¾", hndl., courting, oil, #1372/310	110.00	190.00				
Lamp, 10⅛", hndl., courting, electric, #1372/311	110.00	210.00				
Lamp, 13½", coach, electric, #1372/321	145.00	250.00	100.00			
Lamp, 13½", coach, oil, #1372/320	145.00	250.00	100.00			
Lamp, 16⅝", patio, electric, #1372/466	175.00	295.00	145.00			
Lamp, 16⅝", patio, oil, #1372/459	175.00	295.00	145.00			
Nappy, 4½", #1372/495			22.00			
*Nappy, 5⅜", w/hndl., #1372/499	20.00	30.00	15.00	40.00	18.00	30.00
Pitcher, 32 oz., 6³⁄₁₆", #1372/453	55.00	145.00	55.00	195.00	55.00	150.00
Plate, 8", #1372/550			20.00		20.00	40.00
Punch bowl base, #1372/602			165.00			
Punch bowl, 14", 1½ gal., #1372/600			165.00			
Punch cup, #1372/615			35.00			
*Salver, ftd., 6½" tall, #1372/630	110.00	225.00	125.00	295.00	125.00	
Shaker, 3¼", pr. w/chrome top, #1372/652	30.00	65.00	25.00	90.00	30.00	65.00
Stem, 4", 5 oz., wine, #1372/26			33.00		55.00	100.00
Stem, 5¼", 9 oz., sherbet, #1372/7			24.00		45.00	70.00
Stem, 10½ oz., goblet, #1372/2			35.00		55.00	95.00
*Sugar w/cover, #1372/673	35.00	45.00	25.00	65.00	35.00	45.00
Tumbler, 3⅝", 9 oz., juice/old fashioned, #1372/81			28.00			
Tumbler, 4¼", 9 oz., water, scotch & soda, #1372/73			28.00			
Tumbler, 5⅛", 12 oz., iced tea/highball, #1372/64			35.00			
Tumbler, 5⅜", 10 oz., double old fashioned, #1372/23			28.00			
Tumbler, 5³⁄₁₆", 14 oz., iced tea, #1372/58			35.00		40.00	75.00
*Urn, 12¾", ftd., w/cover, #1372/829	80.00	125.00	75.00	200.00	80.00	100.00
Vase, 8", bud, #1372/799	22.00	40.00	20.00	60.00	27.00	45.00
Vase, 10", ftd., #1372/818			45.00			

"COLONIAL COUPLE," HAZEL ATLAS GLASS, C. 1940

Colors: Platonite w/trims

Since adding "Colonial Couple" to this book two years ago I have had several letters and e-mails wanting to know where to buy some of it. I had a chance to buy a larger set, but chose only to buy one of each piece for photography. It gets rather expensive buying a whole set for photography when you only need one representative piece. In hindsight, I could've sold all the other pieces twelve times over. I have still not located a cup for the saucer shown.

There are likely other pieces to be found in this charming ware made by Hazel Atlas Glass Company around 1940. I suspect that most of the pieces found with Windmills or the black leaf and floral decoration (page 174) will turn up in this pattern. I am only listing pieces verified, however. If you should find additional pieces with this decoration, I'd appreciate hearing from you.

Though Hazel Atlas had first come out with a line of Platonite in the early 1930s, much of their early ware had translucent edges and was presented as white ware. Toward the late thirties and early forties when color trims were taking the glass world by storm (see Rainbow pattern by Anchor Hocking), they started affixing various designs to their white Platonite which by now had wonderful, full white coloring and was a perfect background on which to display images of nursery rhymes, Dutch children, windmills, Hopalong Cassidy, Tom and Jerry, red birds, forget-me-nots, black and red stripes — or a "Colonial Couple" as we see here.

The refrigerator bowl with lid was part of a four-piece stacking set that could be used individually if needed. Lids are therefore a premium today. The milk pitcher can also be found with an egg beater attachment. Those mechanical items are becoming highly collectible in their own right.

Bowl w/lid, round, refrigerator	35.00
Bowl, 5"	15.00
Cup	15.00
Egg cup	22.00
Pitcher, 16 oz., milk	38.00
Plate, dessert	10.00
Saucer	5.00
Shaker, kitchen, pr.	65.00
Tumbler, 8 oz., flat	20.00

CONSTELLATION, PATTERN #300, INDIANA GLASS COMPANY, C. 1940;
YELLOW MIST AND SUNSET CONSTELLATION, TIARA HOME PRODUCTS, 1980s

Colors: crystal; amber; amberina, yellow mist, red, green

After including Constellation in last book, I haven't noticed as many $150 price tags on the cake stands or tags claiming them to be early 1900s ware. We saw those in several states in the past. Indiana made some pieces with intaglio fruit centers and these appear less frequently than the plain ones. They should be priced at 10% to 20% more.

Again, in a bit of irony that everyone thinks, "only happens to them," we started accumulating Constellation to put in a book several years ago. It was hard going, a piece or two at a time. Slowly the box filled with what we deemed was an adequate amount of pieces to include in a book photo. Just as we got ready to do so, it appeared to rain Constellation pattern in the markets — and in dazzling colored wares. Yes, Indiana had foiled collectors again by deciding to resurrect this line for their Tiara Home Products division. We decided to include it anyway, since Tiara has closed down.

No doubt moulds are still in storage; but even so, these wares won't ever be again under these patronages; and Constellation pattern did begin in the early 40s, the era this book covers. Too, if someone wants to do a colored rainbow effect with his or her crystal collection, now would definitely be the time to do that. All colored pieces priced below are most likely Tiara products; and who knows? Fifty years from now these colored items may be eagerly sought by those future collectors.

	Crystal	Colors		Crystal	Colors
Basket, 11", lg. centerpiece	30.00	27.50	Mug	12.00	
Basket, sm. centerpiece	22.50		Pickle, oval, 2-hndl.	15.00	
Bowl, 6", nut, cupped	10.00		Pitcher, 7½", ½ gal.	40.00	60.00
Bowl, jumbo salad	25.00		Plate, dessert	5.00	
Bowl, 11", 2-hndl., oval	20.00		Plate, lunch	7.50	
Bowl, 11½", flat rim, ftd. console, belled	25.00	20.00	Plate, mayonnaise liner	5.00	
Bowl, nappy, 3-toe	12.50		Plate, salad	10.00	
Bowl, punch, flat	35.00		Plate, 13½", serving/cake	22.00	25.00
Cake stand, round	50.00		Plate, 18", buffet	32.00	
Cake, sq. pedestal. ft.	50.00		Platter, oval	22.50	
Candle, triangle. pr.	18.00	25.00	Relish, 6", 3 pt.	15.00	
Candy w/lid, 5½", 3-toe	22.50	18.00	Stem, 6¼", 8 oz., water	12.50	15.00
Celery, oval, compote, low centerpiece	25.00		Sugar	10.00	
Cookie jar & lid, 9"	25.00	30.00	Tumbler, flat, 8 oz.	12.50	
Creamer	10.00		Vase, 3 ftd.	15.00	
Mayonnaise bowl, flat, w/ladle	25.00				

Color: crystal

Corsage pattern has gained collectors of late and, therefore, has seen some slight price increases of recent years. This etched motif echoes many of those seen in the 1920s. There is enough available to collect a significant set. If you like this, now would be a good time to stock up on it.

Corsage is one Fostoria dinnerware line found on several blanks. Some may find the different shapes objectionable, but few patterns allow such a variety of profiles; and variety is supposedly the spice of life. One new collector told me she chose the pattern *because* of the variety of styles. There are three lines portrayed in the picture on the right. The creamer and sugar on row three are #2440, or Lafayette blank with its fancy curlicue handles. The ice bucket (pictured) and individual creamer and sugar are found on #2496 that is known as Baroque, which has a stylized fleur de lis design. I can't think of any other Fostoria pattern that has different lines for two sizes of sugar and creamers. Oddly enough, the basic plates are from the #2337 line that has plain, round plates like those found in Buttercup.

All these different lines were intriguing as I scrutinized this pattern for the book. Was Fostoria etching superfluous inventory, a practice at factories which often resulted in highly collectible, short supplied wares? Perhaps you'll spot another ware line that I missed. If so, let me know.

Bowl, #869, finger	32.00	Plate, 10", hndl., cake, #2496	40.00
Bowl, 4", #4119, ftd.	25.00	Plate, 11", cracker, #2496	35.00
Bowl, 4⅝", 3-corner, #2496	22.00	Plate, 13", torte, #2440	60.00
Bowl, 7⅜", 3-ftd., bonbon, #2496	25.00	Plate, 16", #2364	110.00
Bowl, 9", hndl., #2536	65.00	Relish, 2-part, #2440	27.50
Bowl, 9½", ftd., #2537	165.00	Relish, 2-part, #2496	22.50
Bowl, 10", hndl., #2484	60.00	Relish, 3-part, #2440	35.00
Bowl, 12", flared, #2496	60.00	Relish, 3-part, #2496	32.50
Bowl, 12½", oval, #2545, "Flame"	60.00	Relish, 4-part, #2419	40.00
Candelabra, 2 light w/prisms, #2527	110.00	Relish, 4-part, #2496	40.00
Candlestick, 5½", #2496	30.00	Relish, 5-part, #2419	60.00
Candlestick, 5½", #2535	35.00	Sauce bowl, 6½", oval, #2440	75.00
Candlestick, 6¾", duo, #2545, "Flame"	65.00	Sauce tray, 8½", oval, #2440	30.00
Candlestick, duo, #2496	50.00	Saucer, #2440	5.00
Candlestick, trindle, #2496	60.00	Stem, #6014, 3¾", 1 oz., cordial	45.00
Candy, w/lid, 3-part, #2496	115.00	Stem, #6014, 3¾", 4 oz., oyster cocktail	16.00
Celery, #2440	32.00	Stem, #6014, 4½", 5½ oz., low sherbet	15.00
Comport, 3¼", cheese	25.00	Stem, #6014, 5¼", 3 oz., wine	30.00
Comport, 5½", #2496	30.00	Stem, #6014, 5⅜", 5½ oz., high sherbet	20.00
Creamer, #2440	17.50	Stem, #6014, 5", 3½ oz., cocktail	20.00
Creamer, ind., #2496	12.50	Stem, #6014, 7⅜", 9 oz., water	28.00
Cup, #2440	18.00	Stem, #6014, 7⅞", 4 oz., claret	35.00
Ice bucket, #2496	85.00	Sugar, #2440	17.50
Mayonnaise, 2-part, #2440	30.00	Sugar, ind., #2496	12.50
Mayonnaise, 3-pc., #2496½	50.00	Tidbit, 3-footed, #2496	18.00
Pickle, #2440	25.00	Tray, 6½", ind. sug/cr., #2496½	15.00
Pitcher	295.00	Tumbler, #6014, 4¾", 5 oz., ftd. juice	20.00
Plate, 6½", #2337	8.00	Tumbler, #6014, 5½", 9 oz., ftd. water	22.00
Plate, 7½", #2337	10.00	Tumbler, #6014, 6", 12 oz., ftd. iced tea	28.00
Plate, 8½"	12.50	Vase, 8", bud, #5092	65.00
Plate, 9½", #2337	37.50	Vase, 10", ftd., #2470	155.00
Plate, 10½", cake, hndl., #2440	40.00		

CROCHETED CRYSTAL, IMPERIAL GLASS COMPANY, 1943 – EARLY 1950s

Color: crystal

I first started noticing Crocheted Crystal because the shapes and styles reminded me of Laced Edge, also made by Imperial. You will encounter a number of "go-with" pieces for this pattern as other companies made similar wares.

The punch bowl also came with closed handle cups, although the catalog ad shows open-handled ones. Open handled cups are more desired. There is no punch liner listed, but the 14" or 17" plate could serve as such. The most abundant piece of Crocheted Crystal is the double candle which is everywhere but in my picture.

Buying pieces of Crochet is sometimes an adventure in prices. The unknowing often have lofty prices because it is "pretty good glass" or "elegant looking glass." One individual I encountered before I first introduced this to the book swore that her epergne set was Heisey and was pictured in the Heisey book as rare. By the way, Heisey and Cambridge did not make every elegant looking piece of glass in the country.

I have always been told by knowledgeable Imperial buffs that Crocheted Crystal was made by Imperial exclusively for Sears, Roebuck, and Company. However, I found pieces from an auction in Florida, where a large set of floral cut mixed wares was sold with labels proclaiming it to be "CRYSTALWARE, Genuine Hand Cut Open Stock Pattern by R. G. Sherriff, Toronto." The major portion of the ware was Viking's Princess pattern; but the other was Imperial's Crocheted Crystal. Obviously, this company came by these wares some way, either from Imperial or Sears. It was listed in Sears's catalogs for years. The listing below is mainly from the fall 1943 Sears catalog with some additional pieces that were not in that particular inventory.

I have shown the elusive stemware (page 47). No one seems to recognize these as Crocheted Crystal. Be sure to study them since collectors of this pattern really pay the prices listed below. We sold some at a show recently and the people buying them asked my wife if she had any idea what a trial they'd had trying to find a set for twelve. Twice I have bought these stems and had them shipped to me from California. Both times, most of the stems were battered and broken by the post office. We've had really good luck shipping by wrapping the items themselves three times, once with paper, second with bubble wrap and third with paper again. This gives the items padding enough to separate them from bouncing into each other in the box when they're dropped from heights to conveyor belts at the distribution centers.

The cake stand, 12" basket, *flat* creamer and sugar, and narcissus bowl are not abundant. The normally found creamer and sugar have the open lace work of the other pieces. The single goblet pictured is a wine, although size of photo makes it look like a water.

You may find that many of the pieces in this pattern will turn light amethyst from exposure to the sun. This is known as SCA (sun colored amethyst) and is becoming somewhat collectible for that reason alone.

Basket, 6"	30.00	Mayonnaise plate, 7½"	7.50
Basket, 9"	50.00	Plate, 8", salad	7.50
Basket, 12"	85.00	Plate, 9½"	12.50
Bowl, 7", narcissus	40.00	Plate, 13", salad bowl liner	25.00
Bowl, 10½", salad	30.00	Plate, 14"	25.00
Bowl, 11", console	30.00	Plate, 17"	40.00
Bowl, 12", console	35.00	Punch bowl, 14"	65.00
Buffet set, 14" plate, ftd. sauce bowl, ladle	50.00	Punch cup, closed hndl.	3.00
Cake stand, 12", ftd.	40.00	Punch cup, open hndl.	7.50
Candleholder, 4½" high, double	15.00	Relish, 11½", 3 pt.	25.00
Candleholder, 6" wide, single	20.00	Stem, 4½", 3½ oz., cocktail	30.00
Candleholder (narcissus bowl shape)	40.00	Stem, 5½", 4½ oz., wine	35.00
Celery, 10", oval	25.00	Stem, 5", 6 oz., sherbet	22.00
Cheese & cracker, 12" plate, ftd. dish	40.00	Stem, 7⅛", 9 oz., water goblet	30.00
Creamer, flat	35.00	Sugar, flat	35.00
Creamer, ftd.	22.00	Sugar, ftd.	22.00
Epergne, 11", ftd. bowl, center vase	130.00	Tumbler, 6", 6 oz., ftd. fruit juice	25.00
Hors d'oeuvre dish, 10½", 4-pt., round	30.00	Tumbler, 7⅛", 12 oz., ftd. iced tea	30.00
Lamp, 11", hurricane	75.00	Vase, 5", 4-ftd.	35.00
Mayonnaise bowl, 5¼"	12.50	Vase, 8"	35.00
Mayonnaise ladle	5.00		

CROWN COLLECTION, FOSTORIA GLASS COMPANY c. 1961 – 1965; INDIANA GLASS CO.
FOR TIARA HOME PRODUCTS, late 1980s

Colors: crystal, Royal blue, gold, Ruby in Fostoria; red, yellow mist, green in Indiana Glass

Most of the Crown Collection activity has been limited to the Windsor line and the Luxenberg tri-candle. The bottle with stopper is being sought by collectors of colognes and perfumes and without stopper by candle collectors. The bottles without stoppers were difficult to sell before it was discovered that many were sold that way as candles. This type of crossover collecting can make for some interesting price advances in a very short time.

According to Fostoria's advertising, the very elegant Fostoria Crown Collection was inspired by existing crowns for heads of state. These four crown lines came with as few as one item in the Luxemburg line to six in the Windsor Crown line; and nearly all items in each line were produced in every color. Should you be able, at this point, to gather them all, you'd have not quite 60 items. If you decide to add the Hapsburg chalice and lid, candy, or the basket made from this same piece that Indiana produced after Fostoria's passing in 1986, you'd have more than 60. Excepting the Indiana pieces, probably none can be had for under $50.00, today. I'm telling you this because collectors are overlooking these in the markets as too few (four or five pieces available) items for collections. Even if you just managed to obtain one of each piece made, your collection would be 15 plus items, depending upon if you wanted the Indiana wares or not.

The Luxemburg Crown is represented by the footed, three-candle bowl; the Hapsburg Crown by the green Indiana made basket; the Navarre Crown by the blue compote with the fleur de lis knobbed lid and the Windsor Crown line by the square knobbed lid small candy bowls with pointed edging. Notice that all covered pieces were also sold without covers.

Prices below are for Fostoria's Crown and not the later Tiara.

#2749 Windsor	Crystal	Blue/Ruby	Gold
Bottle w/stopper	110.00	175.00	135.00
Candleholder, 3½"	45.00	67.50	55.00
Candy, 3¾"	40.00	55.00	45.00
Candy & lid, 5½"	60.00	80.00	70.00
Chalice, 6¾", ftd.	50.00	70.00	60.00
Chalice & lid, 8½", ftd.	70.00	100.00	90.00

#2766 Luxemburg	Crystal	Blue/Ruby	Gold
Bowl, 7¼", tri-candle	85.00	195.00	135.00

#2752 Navarre	Crystal	Blue/Ruby	Gold
Bowl, 9"	50.00	70.00	65.00
Bowl & lid, 10½"	70.00	90.00	85.00
Bowl, 9" ftd.	90.00	120.00	110.00
Bowl & lid, 12", ftd.	110.00	145.00	135.00

#2750 Hapsburg	Crystal	Blue/Ruby	Gold
Candy, 5¾"	40.00	55.00	45.00
Candy & lid, 7¼"	55.00	75.00	65.00
Chalice, 7¼", ftd.	65.00	90.00	80.00
Chalice & lid, 9¼", ftd.	80.00	120.00	110.00

Colors: crystal w/cut

This smaller Fostoria pattern has the official name of Rose, but most collectors refer to it as "Cut Rose." This name probably came about from collectors trying to distinguish it from so many other companies' rose patterns. In fact, I had trouble finding the pattern when I bought some years ago and started searching for "Cut Rose" pattern.

Most Rose cuttings are on Blank #2666 (Contour) and the stems are found on Blank #6036 (Rutledge). Maybe a bouquet of these roses would be a better gift for a loved one as they will last longer.

Bowl, finger	25.00	Relish, 7⅜", 2-part	28.00
Bowl, 2¼" high, small salad	22.00	Relish, 10¾", 3-part	38.00
Bowl, 11", salad	42.50	Shaker, pr.	50.00
Celery, 9"	30.00	Stem, 3¼", 1 oz., cordial	35.00
Creamer	20.00	Stem, 3¾", 4 oz., oyster cocktail	15.00
Creamer, individual	20.00	Stem, 4⅛", 3½ oz., cocktail	12.00
Cup	20.00	Stem, 4⅛", 6 oz., sherbet	10.00
Saucer	6.00	Stem, 4¾", 3¼ oz., claret-wine	20.00
Mayonnaise	35.00	Stem, 5⅛", 6 oz., saucer champagne	12.00
Mayonnaise plate	12.00	Stem, 5⅞", 5½ oz., parfait	18.00
Pickle, 7¼"	24.00	Stem, 6⅞", 9½ oz., water	18.00
Pitcher, 32 oz., flat	125.00	Sugar	20.00
Pitcher, 53 oz., ftd.	250.00	Sugar, individual	20.00
Plate, 7"	12.00	Tray, 7", sugar/creamer	17.50
Plate, 8"	15.00	Tumbler, 4⅝", ftd., 5 oz., juice	15.00
Plate, 14"	50.00	Tumbler, 6⅛", ftd., 12 oz., tea	22.50

Colors: crystal, 1933 – 1940; fired-on red, late 30s; amber, 1940s; dark green and milk glass, 1960s, 1970s, 1980s

"Daisy" is one of several patterns that straddles the fence between *Collector's Encyclopedia of Depression Glass* and *Collectible Glassware of the 40s, 50s, 60s....* Seeing as there are more collectors in quest of amber or green "Daisy," I decided that it best met the requirements for this book. Realize that crystal was made in 1930s, but there are only a few collectors buying it today, though it may be harder to assemble a set than either of the other colors.

Avocado colored "Daisy" was sold by Indiana as Heritage in the 1960s through 1980s and not under the name "Daisy" or No. 620, as it was called when the pattern was first produced in the late 1930s. This generates confusion because Federal Glass Company's Heritage pattern is rare in green (see page 103). Federal's green is the brighter, normally found Depression glass color and not the avocado colored green shown here. (Anytime you see avocado colored glassware, consider it to be late 1960s or early 1970s, when all the decorators went into the kitchen color schemes of Harvest Gold and Avocado Green.)

Amber "Daisy" has its admirers and prices have advanced. The indented grill plate (pictured here in green) is rare. By the way, this grill with an indent is for the cream soup and not a cup as is usual. Note how large that ring is. It is much larger than the base of a cup, but fits the base of the cream soup exactly. I never have found out why the grill plate/cream soup combination came into being. Perhaps it was touted as a soup and salad set.

The 12-ounce footed tea, relish dish, 9⅜" berry, and cereal bowls are all hard to find, but not scarce. Perfect (without inner rim roughness) cereal bowls have become the most troublesome pieces to find, taking that honor away from the iced tea. It's amazing how many teas appeared from hiding when the price reached $40.00. Unfortunately, so many have materialized that the price has dropped under that for now.

Few pieces of fired-on red "Daisy" are being encountered. A reader's letter a few years back said that her family had a red set that was acquired in 1935. That helps date this production. There is a pitcher in a fired-on red being found with the No. 618 (Pineapple and Floral) tumblers. This pitcher does not belong to either pattern per se, but was sold with both of these Indiana patterns. Thus, it's a legitimate go-with pitcher. It has a squared base, if you spot one. Most of the red pieces are cloudy in appearance from years of use.

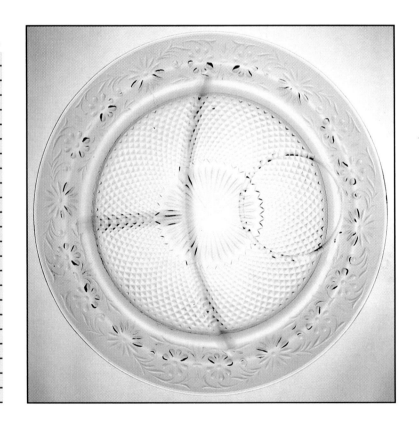

	Crystal	Green	Red, Amber
Bowl, 4½", berry	4.50	6.00	9.00
Bowl, 4½", cream soup	4.50	6.00	10.00
Bowl, 6", cereal	10.00	14.00	30.00
Bowl, 7⅜", deep berry	7.50	9.00	16.00
Bowl, 9⅜", deep berry	13.00	14.00	32.00
Bowl, 10", oval vegetable	10.00	10.00	15.00
Creamer, footed	6.00	5.00	8.00
Cup	4.00	4.00	4.50
Plate, 6", sherbet	2.00	2.00	3.00
Plate, 7⅜", salad	3.50	3.50	7.00
Plate, 8⅜", luncheon	3.00	4.50	6.00
Plate, 9⅜", dinner	5.00	6.00	8.00
Plate, 10⅜", grill	5.50	7.50	10.00
Plate, 10⅜", grill w/indent for cream soup		15.00	30.00
Plate, 11½", cake or sandwich	10.00	7.50	15.00
Platter, 10¾"	7.50	8.50	15.00
Relish dish, 8⅜", 3-part	12.50		25.00
Saucer	1.00	1.00	2.00
Sherbet, ftd.	5.00	5.00	8.00
Sugar, ftd.	6.00	5.00	8.00
Tumbler, 9 oz., ftd.	10.00	9.00	20.00
Tumbler, 12 oz., ftd.	20.00	20.00	38.00

Colors: crystal and iridized

Dewdrop tumblers remain elusive. For a pattern made for four years in the 50s, you would think that tumblers could easily be found. I have more requests for Dewdrop tumblers than for almost any other pattern in this book. The tumbler pictured below is the 6" tea and I haven't found any nine ounce water to picture beside it.

Dewdrop has struck the fancy of some new collectors and several items are beginning to be in short supply as sets are trying to be accumulated. Few dealers carry a supply of Dewdrop to shows, so it is a pattern you will have to ask for as you travel to shops, malls, and flea markets.

Dewdrop pitchers are causing a stir. There are two styles showing up and I may have pictured the wrong one previously. The footed one may be a go-with type while the flat, iridized one pictured may be the true Dewdrop pitcher. These are also found in crystal, but I was astonished to find one iridized. Notice how the top edge matches the edge of the creamer while the footed one has a non-scalloped edge. Since I have no catalog listing which shows a pitcher for this pattern, I will list both styles for now. The iridescent one is fetching $50.00 to $60.00.

In the past, many collectors bought the Lazy Susan in Dewdrop to obtain the missing ball bearings for their Shell Pink Lazy Susan or for a Candlewick tray, which the bearings also fit. I just came back from Seattle where I once paid for a complete Dewdrop Lazy Susan, picked up the ball bearings, stuck them in my pocket, and told the astonished lady to sell the other pieces for whatever she could get. I was flying; and besides, I needed the ball bearings for a Shell Pink set. The dealer remembered me and said she had a devil of a time selling the rest of that set. The boxed Lazy Susan pictured is an original. The Shell Pink Lazy Susan came in the same ornamented floral box, but with pink flowers instead of blue.

I have seen several boxed sets of snack trays in my travels. TV tray sets of various types were common in the mid-1950s and there are collectors beginning to accumulate them. Indeed, there is a cadre of collecting centered just on things from the 50s. Also, be forewarned; I watched a TV show hosted by a former Brady Bunch actress last night which was revisiting things from the 70s: avocado and green appliances; shag carpeting (with rakes to make it stand up again); and plastic, cardboard, and bean bag furnishings. This very well could be the next genre of collectibility — although I could do without garish daisy bedecked wallpapers and leisure suits again — not to mention sideburns.

Dewdrop will not break your bank account and makes a marvelous table setting with added color arrangements. Many crystal patterns are a delight in large groupings. Dewdrop is heavy and durable, but you'll have to eat off the snack sets, the leaf shaped relish, or the 11½" service plate for lack of other plates.

	Crystal
Bowl, 4¾"	5.00
Bowl, 8½"	17.50
Bowl, 10⅜"	20.00
Butter, w/cover	27.50
Candy dish, w/cover, 7", round	25.00
Creamer	8.00
Cup, punch or snack	3.00
Pitcher, ½ gallon, ftd.	22.00
Pitcher, flat	50.00
Plate, 11½"	17.50

	Crystal
Plate, snack, w/indent for cup	4.00
Punch bowl base	10.00
Punch bowl, 6 qt.	30.00
Relish, leaf shape w/hndl.	8.00
Sugar, w/cover	13.00
Tray, 13", Lazy Susan, complete, 2-pc. w/ball bearing ring	45.00
Tumbler, 9 oz., water	20.00
Tumbler, 12 oz., iced tea, 6"	30.00

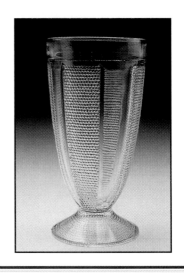

Colors: crystal, crystal w/ruby stain, crystal w/gold, blue satin, green satin, (Cameo)/black, yellow, teal, blue, amber, electric blue, carnival, milk

Diamond Point is one of the patterns I have received more requests to identify and to list than any other in recent years. Since the last edition of this book I have been able to sell a few extra books because of its being included. Cathy has researched most of the three *Pattern Identification Guides* and has found that Diamond point has its origins in some "mitered diamond" wares dating back to 1850, various versions of which have been produced by countless companies, including names we recognize today, such as Westmoreland, Kemple, Imperial and this production by Indiana. The names have differed — Diamond, Mitered Diamond, Sawtooth, Diamond Point — and stems, edge treatments, mould shapes, and clarity of glass have changed, but the four-sided cut diamond has not. That particular diamond shape has that seemingly timeless appeal for collectors.

It is very possible that I have missed some of the colors produced by Indiana. Frankly, I never expected to be putting this in a book when it was appearing all over the markets and I didn't pay the kind of attention I should have. People are now collecting this; and I've gotten some requests for it at shows, though its recent manufacture precludes it in the contracts of some shows. Too, my listings of items may not be complete. Therefore, if you have further knowledge regarding this Diamond Point pattern by Indiana, I'd very much appreciate your telling me so I can include it in the future. Prices are those I've encountered. Prices are only given for the crystal with ruby stain. It is the ruby stained crystal most collectors seek and the stories about the origin of this glass would make a book in itself.

	Crystal w/ruby		Crystal w/ruby
Ashtray, 5½"	5.00	Compote, 7¼"tall, crimp rim	12.50
Bowl, 3 toe, crimped	8.00	Creamer, ftd	4.00
Bowl, 6", flat rim	5.00	Duet server, stand w /6" bowls	14.00
Bowl, 6", scalloped rim	6.00	Stem, water	6.00
Bowl, 9¾", straight side	12.50	Ice tub, 11⅝", w/lid (looks like cookie jar)	18.00
Bowl, 11½", low foot, scalloped	15.00	Mug	8.00
Bowl, 13½", low foot, flared	18.00	Pitcher	20.00
Cake stand, 10"	22.00	Plate, 14½", serving	15.00
Candle, ftd.	7.50	Shaker	17.50
Candlelamp	10.00	Sherbet, ftd.	5.00
Candy, 4¾", w/lid	10.00	Sugar, ftd	4.00.
Candy, 12" high, 2½" deep, 6" dia., w/lid	15.00	Tumbler, 9 oz., water	4.00
Candy, 15½" tall, "Chalice" w/lid	25.00	Tumbler, 15 oz., tea	5.00
Compote, 7¼" tall, flat rim	12.50	Vase, ftd.	12.00

...rs: crystal, some amber, blue green, red, and black; some with painted designs

Early American Prescut (EAPC) is one pattern remembered by kids growing up in the 1960s and early 1970s just as the kids growing up in the late 1940s and 1950s remember Fire-King. I just did a seminar for an Altrusa club and displayed a variety of Depression, Elegant, and later glassware. The one piece recognized most readily was the piece of EAPC. No one knew what it was, but did know Mom or Grandma had some of it. It was recognized over Jade-ite, which was casually noticed because of the notorious television show, and not from its history.

All EAPC pieces are designated as the 700 line in Anchor Hocking's catalogs. There were other Prescut patterns made at Anchor Hocking, a dilemma I address on page 59. EAPC has to have the star in the design with two exceptions. The double candle has a knob in place of the star. That star was pictured in the catalog where the knob is attached; so probably the mould makers changed the design to better release the piece from the mould. That was an ongoing battle at glass factories — glass designers against mould makers. I met a family of four brothers who had all been mould makers in Lancaster, Ohio. They told me some interesting stories from "the good ole days." Also, the cup used with punch and snack sets does not have the star. It was borrowed from the "Oatmeal" line rather than having to make a new cup mould.

Four pieces of EAPC were introduced by Anchor Hocking in the 1960 – 1961 catalog. Most pieces were discontinued by 1978, but the creamer, sugar, cruet, and shakers with plastic tops were made as late as 1997. The only piece I can find listed in the latest catalog is the 8½" vase that is being sold to the florist industry.

The creamer, sugar, oil bottle, regular shakers, butter dish, gondola bowl, and 13½" plate are difficult to sell. Moreover, these pieces can sometimes still be found on the shelves of dish barns and closeout stores. The ever-present punch bowl can still be seen at prices ranging from $20.00 to $75.00. For me, they sell slowly at $25.00 and I have been able to move them more quickly at $22.00. Remember, these were sold for $2.89 a set with an oil and lube job in the middle and late 1960s. Lots of oil changes were purchased at Marathon gas stations and the punch set was reasonably priced; so one can assume there are multitudes of these around. A large number of Royal Ruby ashtrays have been discovered, but, so far, that is the only piece discovered in that color. You can also find pieces in laser blue, avocado green, and amber. Colored wares are uncommon and some are deceiving, having sprayed colors over crystal.

Some items were only made for a year or two. The most difficult, but desirable pieces to own are the oil lamp, 11", four-part relish plate with swirl dividers, and 11¾" paneled bowl. Additionally, the EAPC 40 ounce (square) pitcher, smooth rim 4¼" bowls, 6¾" plates with or without ring, individual shakers, and 13½" five-part relish are missing from many collections. There were several seemingly experimental pieces made including a bud vase, footed sherbet, and cocktail shaker. According to dealers, the following items are becoming hard to find: iced tea tumblers, Lazy Susans with a wire rack, and the frosted lampshade.

There are four and five inch round powder jars with a crinolated locking system that look like EAPC as well as a three-part small relish and heart-shaped dish. The asking price is in $15.00 – 20.00 range. These are not EAPC. If you look around the center of the pieces, the word "Italy" will be embossed. It is possible to find two unmarked halves of the covered powders that have been "married" that won't be marked.

For more detailed information on EAPC, check out my book, *Anchor Hocking's Fire-King & More.*

	Crystal
Ashtray, 4", #700/690	5.00
Ashtray, 5"	10.00
Ashtray, 7¾", #718-G	15.00
Bowl, 4¼", #726 (smooth rim)	22.00
Bowl, 5¼", #775 (scalloped rim)	7.00
Bowl, 6¾", three-toed, #768	4.50
Bowl, 7¼" (scalloped rim)	22.00
Bowl, 7¼", round, #767	5.00
Bowl, 8¾", #787	9.00
Bowl, 9", console, #797	14.00
Bowl, 9", oval, #776	6.00
Bowl, 9⅜", gondola dish, #752	4.00
Bowl, 10¾", salad, #788	12.00
Bowl, 11¾", paneled, #794	195.00
Bowl, dessert, 5⅜", #765	2.50
Butter, bottom w/metal handle and knife	15.00
Butter, w/cover, ¼ lb., #705	6.00
Cake plate, 13½", ftd., #706	32.00
Candlestick, 7" x 5⅝", double, #784	30.00
Candy, w/lid, 5¼", #744	10.00
Candy, w/cover, 7¼" x 5½", #792	12.00
Chip & dip, 10¾" bowl, 5¼", brass finish holder, #700/733	27.50
Coaster, #700/702	2.50
Cocktail shaker, 9", 30 oz.	795.00
Creamer, #754	3.00
Cruet, w/stopper, 7¾", #711	6.00
Cup, punch or snack, 6 oz. (no star)	2.00
Lazy Susan, 9-pc., #700/713	50.00
Oil lamp	295.00

	Crystal
Pitcher, 18 oz., #744	12.00
Pitcher, 40 oz., square	42.50
Pictcher, 60 oz., #791	17.00
Plate, 6¾", no ring, salad w/indent	55.00
Plate, 6¾", w/ring for 6 oz. cup	55.00
Plate, 10", snack, #780	10.00
Plate, 11", 4-part w/swirl dividers	175.00
Plate, 11"	12.00
Plate, 11¾", deviled egg/relish, #750	32.50
Plate, 13½", serving, #790	12.50
Punch set, 15-pc.	35.00
Relish, 8½", oval, 2-part, #778	5.00
Relish, 10", divided, tab hndl., #770	22.00
Relish, 13½", 5-part	30.00
Server, 12 oz. (syrup), #707	20.00
Shakers, pr., metal tops, #700/699	5.00
Shakers, pr., plastic tops, #725	5.00
Shakers, pr., 2¼", individual, #700/736	50.00
Sherbet, 3½", 6 oz., ftd.	395.00
Sugar, w/lid, #753	4.00
Tray, 6½" x 12", hostess, #750	10.00
Tray, cr/sug, #700/671	3.00
Tumbler, 5 oz., 4", juice, #730	3.00
Tumbler, 10 oz., 4½", #731	3.00
Tumbler, 15 oz., 6", iced tea, #732	20.00
Vase, 5", ftd., bud	595.00
Vase, 6 x 4½", basket/block, #704/205	16.00
Vase, 8½", #741	7.00
Vase, 10", #742	12.50

PRESCUT: "OATMEAL" & "PINEAPPLE," ANCHOR HOCKING GLASS CORPORATION, 1941 – 1970s

There has been uncertainty among collectors as to what comprises EAPC and what is not. Read page 56 on EAPC for that explanation. "Oatmeal" is presently defined as EAPC pieces without the "star" and is pictured in the top row. The "Oatmeal" name comes from the fact that seven of these pieces were premiums in boxes of Crystal Wedding Oats. The soap dish may not have been in the oatmeal boxes, but is the same pattern. You can tell by its price that it is not as common at the market as the others. Like the five pieces of Forest Green sandwich that were packed in oatmeal, these "Oatmeal" items are abundant today. "Oatmeal" and "Pineapple" discussed in the next paragraph were both listed in Anchor Hocking catalogs under the general term Prescut and collectors have given them these "oatmeal & pineapple" nomenclatures over the years, which I am now using so everyone can be on the same page.

The other pattern often mistakenly identified as EAPC has been called "Pineapple" by collectors. It is shown on the second and third rows above. It was first shown in the 1941 catalog, 20 years before the birth of EAPC. This can be found mostly in crystal with an occasional piece in white. You might even find white items decorated with painted flowers. The crystal cigarette box can be found with a Royal Ruby lid and is usually proffered that way.

"OATMEAL"

	Crystal
Bowl, 4¼", berry	2.00
Cup	2.00
Saucer, 4⅜"	1.50
Sherbet, 5 oz.	1.50
Soap dish, 5¼" x 3¾"	20.00
Tumbler, 4 oz., juice	2.00
Tumbler, 7 oz., old fashioned	2.50
Tumbler, 9 oz., water	2.00

"PINEAPPLE"

	Crystal	White
Box, 4¾", cigarette or dresser	15.00	12.50
Box, 4¾", w/Royal Ruby lid	25.00	
Butter, round	15.00	
Marmalade, w/Royal Ruby lid	20.00	
Pitcher, 12 oz., milk	8.00	10.00
Sugar w/lid, handled	12.00	
Sugar w/lid, no handles	10.00	
Syrup pitcher	12.00	
Tumbler, 10 oz., iced tea	6.00	8.00

EMERALD CREST, FENTON ART GLASS COMPANY, 1949 – 1955

Color: white with green edge

Emerald Crest was listed in Fenton catalogs from 1949 until January 1955. I had an interesting edict from a lady who was married in 1957 and received Emerald Crest as a wedding gift. She insisted that I correct my dates as I had to be wrong. Although manufacture almost certainly ended in 1956 since it was not in that year's catalog, that doesn't mean sales stock in stores had vanished, just that the stores could not reorder it from Fenton.

Emerald Crest had followed Aqua Crest (blue trimmed) which started in 1941, and Silver Crest (crystal trimmed) started in 1943. Since Aqua Crest is not in this book, you will find prices for Aqua Crest fall between those of Emerald Crest and Silver Crest (priced on pages 230 and 231).

A number of pieces of Emerald Crest have two dissimilar line numbers. Originally, this line was #680, and all pieces carried that designation. In July 1952, Fenton began issuing a ware number for each piece; that is why you see two diverse numbers listed for the different sized plates and vases.

Emerald Crest mayonnaise sets are commonly found with crystal spoons, but a green spoon was made. It is occasionally found in mayos and mustards, and the green spoons sell alone for $32.00 – 35.00. You can see green spoons in the mustards. The green stopper for the oil bottle is also difficult to locate. Most stoppers for those bottles were sold in crystal. Personally, I feel the green adds to the pattern appearance.

I do not buy or sell a lot of Fenton; as a result, I am grateful for the help from Fenton collectors and dealers as well as readers who have assisted with listings of Fenton patterns in this book. I appreciate their time and direction in attaining price listings for Emerald and Silver Crest.

Item	Price
Basket, 5", #7236	80.00
Basket, 7", #7237	110.00
Bowl, 5", finger or deep dessert, #7221	25.00
Bowl, 5½", soup, #680, #7230	37.50
Bowl, 8½", flared, #680	45.00
Bowl, 9½", #682	60.00
Bowl, 10", salad, #7220	72.50
Bowl, dessert, shallow, #7222	20.00
Bowl, ftd., tall, square, #7330	225.00
Cake plate, 13", high ftd., #680, #7213	130.00
Cake plate, low ftd., #5813	120.00
Candle holder, flat saucer base, pr., #680	75.00
Comport, 6", ftd., flared, #206	37.50
Comport, ftd., double crimped	37.50
Creamer, clear reeded hndls., #7231	35.00
Cup, #7208	35.00
Flower pot w/attached saucer, #7299	60.00
Mayonnaise bowl, #7203	33.00
Mayonnaise ladle, crystal, #7203	8.00
Mayonnaise ladle, green, #7203	35.00
Mayonnaise liner, #7203	18.00
Mayonnaise set, 3-pc., w/crys. ladle, #7203	65.00

Item	Price
Mayonnaise set, 3-pc., w/gr. ladle, #7203	95.00
Mustard, w/lid and spoon	85.00
Oil bottle, w/green stopper, #680, #7269	125.00
Pitcher, 6" hndl., beaded melon, #7116	70.00
Plate, 5½", #680, #7218	15.00
Plate, 6½", #680, #7219	16.00
Plate, 8½", #680, #7217	22.50
Plate, 10", #680, #7210	50.00
Plate, 12", #680, #7212	47.50
Plate, 12", #682	55.00
Plate, 16", torte, #7216	65.00
Saucer, #7208	10.00
Sherbet, ftd., #7226	22.50
Sugar, clear reeded hndls., #7231	35.00
Tidbit, 2-tier bowls, 5½" & 8½"	65.00
Tidbit, 2-tier bowls, 8½" & 10"	85.00
Tidbit, 2-tier plates, #7297	60.00
Tidbit, 3-tier plates, #7298	95.00
Vase, 4½", fan, #36, #7355	30.00
Vase, 6¼", fan, #36, #7357	35.00
Vase, 8", bulbous base, #186	65.00

EMERALD GLO, PADEN CITY AND FENTON ART GLASS COMPANY, 1940s – 1950s

Color: Emerald green

Emerald Glo was a big seller for us at a recent show in Texas. We set out over half a table full and packed four or five pieces when it was over. It was sold to collectors and to dealers who were buying it for resale. Emerald Go was made primarily by Paden City Glass Company for Rubel; however, the pattern was also made by Fenton Art Glass Company in the later years of its production. Labeled pieces have been found which specify "Cavalier Emerald-Glo Hand-Made." All "star cut" pieces were made by Paden City, but uncut pieces were made by both companies. Normally, the Fenton manufactured pieces are a slightly darker green color. Fenton pieces are most often found with cast-iron accoutrements as opposed to the gold-toned ones. Fenton also made pieces in white from these same moulds, but that is rarely seen. It is the green that is prized today, no matter who manufactured it.

Candleholders, pr., ball with metal cups	40.00
Casserole w/metal cover	45.00
Cheese dish w/metal top and handle	70.00
Cocktail shaker, 10", 26 oz.	65.00
Condiment set (2 jars, metal lids, spoons & tray)	65.00
Condiment set (3 jars, metal lids, spoons & tray)	80.00
Creamer	20.00
Creamer/sugar, individual (metal), w/metal lid, on metal tray	40.00
Creamer/sugar, individual, w/metal lid, on metal tray	40.00
Cruet	30.00
Ice bucket, metal holder & tongs	70.00
Marmalade w/metal lid & spoon	30.00
Mayonnaise, divided, w/metal underliner & spoons	40.00
Oil bottle	30.00
Relish, 9", divided, w/metal handle	35.00
Relish, 9", tab hndl., w/metal handle	40.00
Relish, heart shaped	35.00
Salad bowl w/metal base, fork, and spoon	55.00
Salad bowl, 10"	30.00
Server, 5-part, w/metal covered center	65.00
Sugar	20.00
Sugar w/metal lid & liner	25.00
Syrup w/metal lid & liner	45.00
Tidbit, 2-tier (bowls 6" & 8")	50.00
Tray, 8½", handled	35.00
Tumbler, 2⅝", 1 oz.	10.00

ENGLISH HOBNAIL, LINE NO. 555, WESTMORELAND GLASS COMPANY, 1920s – 1983

Colors: amber, crystal, and crystal with various color treatments and white

English Hobnail was one of the patterns originally listed in my first Depression glass book in 1972; but crystal and amber English Hobnail were being produced until Westmoreland closed in 1983. Consequently, I am now chronicling amber and crystal in this book. I acknowledge that crystal, crystal with amber or black bases or trims, and some shades of amber were made before 1940, but pricing is relatively the same for all crystal or amber no matter when it was made.

Milk glass English Hobnail was only made in this book's time frame. It sells for about the same price as crystal or even a little lower. You can double the price listed for any decorated milk glass English Hobnail. Ruby flashed English Hobnail seems difficult to sell at regular crystal prices. There is a fervent clientele for crystal English Hobnail, but collectors enthusiastically seeking amber seem uncommon.

The amber and crystal candy pictured on page 66 is actually Westmoreland's #300 line Waterford. It is often collected along with English Hobnail and appears to be better quality glass. The crystal punch set pictured has never been found in color, though one could always hope.

	Amber/Crystal		Amber/Crystal		Amber/Crystal
Ashtray, 3"	5.00	Bowl, 11", bell	35.00	Cup, demitasse	16.00
Ashtray, 4½"	7.00	Bowl, 11", rolled edge	32.00	Decanter, 20 oz.	55.00
Ashtray, 4½", sq.	7.50	Bowl, 12", celery	22.00	Egg cup	15.00
Basket, 5", hndl.	20.00	Bowl, 12", flange or console	30.00	Hat, high	20.00
Basket, 6", tall, hndl.	42.00	Bowl, 12", flared	35.00	Hat, low	18.00
Bonbon, 6½", hndl.	12.50	Bowl, 12", oval, crimped	45.00	Ice tub, 4"	22.00
Bottle, toilet, 5 oz.	22.00	Bowl, cream soup	16.00	Ice tub, 5½"	45.00
Bowl, 4", rose	18.00	Candelabra, 2-lite	25.00	Icer, sq. base,	
Bowl, 4½", finger	7.50	Candlestick, 3½", rnd. base	10.00	w/patterned insert	60.00
Bowl, 4½", round nappy	7.00	Candlestick, 5½", sq. base	15.00	Lamp, 6½", electric	45.00
Bowl, 4½", sq. ftd., finger	9.00	Candlestick, 9", rnd. base	26.00	Lamp, 9½", electric	65.00
Bowl, 4½", sq. nappy	7.00	Candy dish, 3-ftd.	30.00	Lamp, candlestick	
Bowl, 5", round nappy	9.50	Candy, ½ lb., and cover,		(several types)	32.00
Bowl, 5½", bell nappy	11.50	cone shaped	28.00	Lampshade, 17"	185.00
Bowl, 6", crimped dish	12.50	Chandelier, 17", shade		Marmalade w/cover	22.00
Bowl, 6", rose	18.00	w/200+ prisms	395.00	Mayonnaise, 6"	10.00
Bowl, 6", round nappy	10.00	Cheese w/cover, 6"	45.00	Mustard, sq. ftd., w/lid	25.00
Bowl, 6", sq. nappy	10.00	Cheese w/cover, 8¾"	65.00	Nut, individual, ftd.	6.00
Bowl, 6½", grapefruit	11.00	Cigarette box and cover,		Oil bottle, 2 oz., hndl.	20.00
Bowl, 6½", round nappy	12.00	4½"x2½"	20.00	Oil bottle, 6 oz., hndl.	30.00
Bowl, 6½", sq. nappy	12.50	Cigarette jar w/cover, rnd.	15.00	Oil-vinegar combination, 6 oz.	40.00
Bowl, 7", 6 pt.	30.00	Cigarette lighter		Parfait, rnd. ftd.	15.00
Bowl, 7", oblong spoon	18.00	(milk glass only)	15.00	Pitcher, 23 oz., rounded	55.00
Bowl, 7", preserve	15.00	Coaster, 3"	6.00	Pitcher, 32 oz., straight side	60.00
Bowl, 7", round nappy	15.00	Compote, 5", round, rnd. ftd.	12.00	Pitcher, 38 oz., rounded	70.00
Bowl, 7½", bell nappy	16.00	Compote, 5", sq. ftd., round	12.50	Pitcher, 60 oz., rounded	75.00
Bowl, 8", 6 pt.	30.00	Compote, 5½", ball stem,		Pitcher, 64 oz., straight side	85.00
Bowl, 8", cupped, nappy	25.00	sweetmeat	32.00	Plate, 5½", rnd.	4.00
Bowl, 8", ftd.	30.00	Compote, 5½", bell	16.00	Plate, 6", sq.	5.00
Bowl, 8", hexagonal ftd.,		Compote, 5½", sq. ftd., bell	18.00	Plate, 6", sq., finger bowl liner	5.00
2-hndl.	40.00	Compote, 6", honey, rnd. ftd.	20.00	Plate, 6½", depressed center, rnd.	6.00
Bowl, 8", pickle	16.00	Compote, 6", sq. ftd., honey	20.00	Plate, 6½", round	6.00
Bowl, 8", round nappy	27.50	Compote, 8", ball stem,		Plate, 6½, rnd., finger bowl liner	6.50
Bowl, 9", bell nappy	32.50	sweetmeat	38.00	Plate, 8", rnd.	6.00
Bowl, 9", celery	20.00	Creamer, hexagonal, ftd.	9.00	Plate, 8", rnd., 3-ftd.	15.00
Bowl, 9½", round, crimped	32.00	Creamer, low, flat	7.50	Plate, 8½", plain edge	8.00
Bowl, 10", flared	35.00	Creamer, sq. ftd.	8.50	Plate, 8½", rnd.	8.00
Bowl, 10", oval, crimped	40.00	Cup	8.00	Plate, 8¾", sq.	8.00

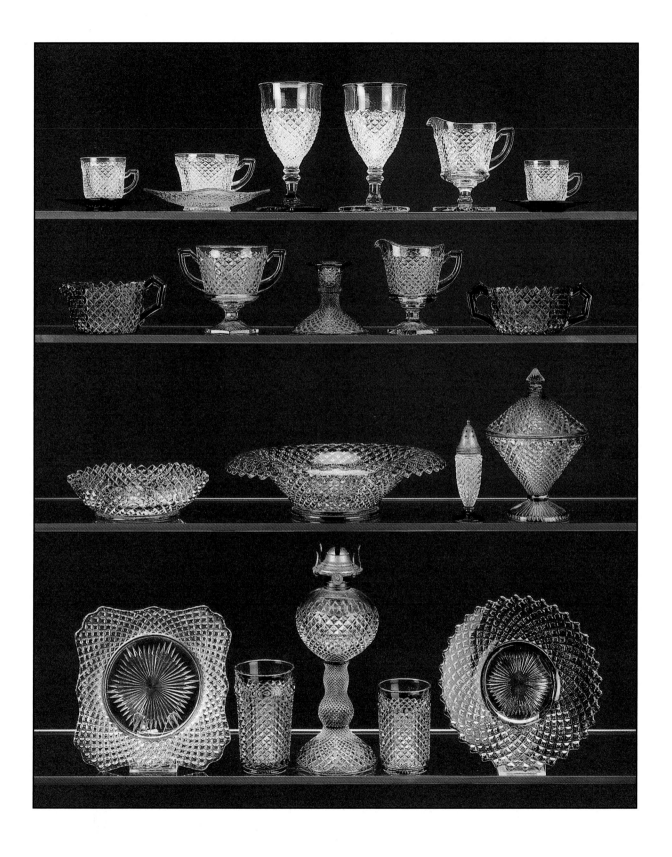

ENGLISH HOBNAIL

	Amber/Crystal		Amber/Crystal		Amber/Crystal
Plate, 10½", grill, rnd.	18.00	Stem, 5 oz., rnd. claret	12.50	Tumbler, 7 oz., sq. ftd., juice	9.00
Plate, 10", rnd.	18.00	Stem, 5 oz., sq. ftd., oyster cocktail	9.00	Tumbler, 8 oz., rnd., ball, water	10.00
Plate, 10", sq.	18.00	Stem, 8 oz., rnd. water goblet	10.00	Tumbler, 8 oz., water	10.00
Plate, 12", sq.	25.00	Stem, 8 oz., sq. ftd., water goblet	10.00	Tumbler, 9 oz., rnd., ball, water	10.00
Plate, 15", sq.	40.00	Stem, sherbet, low, one ball, rnd. ftd.	6.00	Tumbler, 9 oz., rnd. ftd., water	10.00
Plate, 14", rnd., torte	35.00	Stem, sherbet, rnd. low foot	7.00	Tumbler, 9 oz., sq. ftd., water	10.00
Plate, 20½", rnd., torte	75.00	Stem, sherbet, sq. ftd., low	7.00	Tumbler, 10 oz., iced tea	12.00
Plate, cream soup liner, rnd.	5.00	Stem, champagne, two ball, rnd. ftd.	8.00	Tumbler, 11 oz., rnd., ball, iced tea	10.00
Puff box, w/ cover, 6", rnd.	22.00	Stem, sherbet, high, two ball, rnd. ftd.	9.00	Tumbler, 11 oz., sq. ftd., iced tea	12.00
Punch bowl	200.00	Stem, sherbet, rnd. high foot	9.00	Tumbler, 12 oz., iced tea	12.50
Punch bowl stand	75.00	Stem, sherbet, sq. ftd., high	9.00	Tumbler, 12½ oz., rnd. ftd., iced tea	10.00
Punch cup	6.50	Sugar, hexagonal, ftd.	8.50	Urn, 11", w/cover	50.00
Punch set (bowl, stand, 12 cups, ladle)	395.00	Sugar, low, flat	7.50	Vase, 6½", ivy bowl, sq. ftd., crimp top	30.00
Relish, 8", 3-part	17.00	Sugar, sq. ftd.	8.50	Vase, 6½", sq. ftd., flower holder	28.00
Saucer, demitasse, rnd.	8.00	Tidbit, 2-tier	25.00	Vase, 7½", flip	32.00
Saucer, demitasse, sq.	8.00	Tumbler, 1½ oz., whiskey	12.00	Vase, 7½", flip jar w/cover	60.00
Saucer, rnd.	2.00	Tumbler, 3 oz., whiskey	12.00	Vase, 8", sq. ftd.	40.00
Saucer, sq.	2.00	Tumbler, 5 oz., ginger ale	8.00	Vase, 8½", flared top	45.00
Shaker, pr., rnd. ftd.	20.00	Tumbler, 5 oz., old fashioned cocktail	11.00	Vase, 10" (straw jar)	70.00
Shaker, pr., sq. ftd.	20.00	Tumbler, 5 oz., rnd. ftd., ginger ale	8.00		
Stem, 1 oz., rnd. ftd., cordial	12.00	Tumbler, 5 oz., sq. ftd., ginger ale	8.00		
Stem, 1 oz., rnd., ball, cordial	15.00	Tumbler, 7 oz., rnd. ftd., juice	9.00		
Stem, 1 oz., sq. ftd., cordial	14.00				
Stem, 2 oz., rnd. ftd., wine	10.00				
Stem, 2 oz., sq. ftd., wine	10.00				
Stem, 2¼ oz., rnd. ball, wine	9.00				
Stem, 3 oz., rnd., cocktail	8.00				
Stem, 3 oz., sq. ftd., cocktail	8.00				
Stem, 3½ oz., rnd. ball, cocktail	7.00				

WESTMORELAND GLASS COMPANY

Handmade Glassware of Quality

GRAPEVILLE, PENNSYLVANIA

Since 1889

FESTIVE, LINE #155, DUNCAN AND MILLER, C. 1950s

Colors: crystal, Aqua, Honey

Festive, perhaps better than any other glassware pattern from this era, reflects the space age interest of 1950s. This flame polished mold is attracting collectors more than any other Duncan and Miller pattern. From the swirling, circle optic in the glassware itself reminiscent of Saturn's rings, to the avant-garde shapes juxtaposed with wooden and metal parts, this glass was a wonderful departure from the norm. A vase was brought in for me to identify at a recent speaking engagement; so I am adding that to the listing. Notice that Duncan named their yellow color Honey.

	Honey	Aqua
Bowl, sauce dish w/ladle	45.00	55.00
Bowl, 14", flower w/stand, flare	50.00	65.00
Candlestick, 5½"	32.50	37.50
Candy box w/lid	45.00	55.00
Cheese tray, oval, w/wood bridge	65.00	75.00
Comport, 7½", high ft.	45.00	55.00
Comport, 9"	50.00	60.00
Creamer	20.00	25.00
Cruet, 8"	35.00	45.00
Plate, 16", buffet	75.00	90.00
Relish, 10", round, 3-pt. hndl.	70.00	80.00
Shaker, 4"	30.00	35.00
Sugar	20.00	25.00
Tray for sugar/creamer	20.00	25.00
Twin server, 9½", w/hndl	40.00	45.00
Vase, 10"	40.00	45.00

FIRE-KING "ALICE," ANCHOR HOCKING GLASS CORPORATION, EARLY 1940s

Colors: Jade-ite, Vitrock w/trims of blue or red

"Alice" is obtainable in plain, red or blue trimmed Vitrock, or Jade-ite. Some of the red-trimmed pieces fade to pink, and there are two shades of blue-trimmed pieces being found. You can see the red-trimmed "Alice" pictured in my *Anchor Hockings' Fire-King and More* book. Red-trimmed Alice turns out to be the hardest color to find and is missing from most collections. I remember seeing the red trimmed quite often in northern Texas about ten years ago while visiting shops on my way to the big Houston glass show. By the time I learned more about the true scarcity of red, those pieces I had thought were over priced and did not buy, had long since disappeared into collections.

I need to point out that white "Alice" is Vitrock. There are two well-defined hues of Vitrock "Alice," however, as shown in the photograph. These do not display very well together; so you need to decide whether you like the beige/gray shade or the white. Neither is plentiful in today's market.

Dinner plates are the pieces to embrace in this diminutive "Alice" pattern. It would seem few people would pay money for the plates to go with those cups and saucers that were free in oatmeal boxes. The quantity of dinner plates I see as I travel in the Missouri area between St. Louis and Joplin makes me believe plates may have been given away by someone in that area. Lucky you, if you live in that area because you should be able to find them a tad more easily than the rest of us.

	Jade-ite	Vitrock/Blue trim	Vitrock/Red trim	Vitrock
Cup	7.00	10.00	33.00	5.00
Plate, 9½"	26.00	28.00	65.00	16.00
Saucer	3.00	4.00	17.00	2.00

FIRE-KING BLUE MOSAIC, ANCHOR HOCKING GLASS CORPORATION, 1966 – LATE 1967

Blue Mosaic sugar, creamer, and cups have solid blue exteriors with a white indented band at the bottom. They have no little blue squares in concentric rings which make up the mosaic look on all other pieces. The sugar is a cup mould with no handles plus a white lid; the creamer is a cup mould with a spout. Note the sugar lid is a different style than found on most Fire-King patterns. The same cup was used for both the saucer and the snack tray, unlike the smaller sized snack cup in other Fire-King patterns. This briefly made (two years) Anchor Hocking pattern was illustrated only in a 1966 – 1967 catalog. The platter and round vegetable bowl are the most difficult pieces to find.

Blue Mosaic should be the first snack set that collectors of those items find for there is an abundance of these available; and surely Florida was a main allocation area for them. I see at least one Blue Mosaic snack set every time I go shopping here. The snack tray in this pattern is oval and not rectangular.

Bowl, 4⅝", dessert	6.00		Plate, 10", dinner	8.00
Bowl, 6⅝", soup plate	12.00		Platter, 9" x 12"	16.00
Bowl, 8¼", vegetable	16.00		Saucer, 5¾"	2.00
Creamer	6.00		Sugar	6.00
Cup, 7½ oz.	4.00		Sugar cover	5.00
Plate, 7⅜", salad	7.00		Tray, 10" x 7½", oval, snack	6.00

FIRE-KING CHARM, ANCHOR HOCKING GLASS CORPORATION, 1950 – 1954

Colors: Azur-ite, Forest Green, Ivory, Jade-ite, Milk White, pink, and Royal Ruby

Charm was the original designation for the square dishes made by Anchor Hocking from 1950 through 1954. Jade-ite and Azur-ite colors were advertised alongside their Forest Green and Royal Ruby counterparts; however, the color names of Forest Green and Royal Ruby prevailed on the red and green instead of the Charm appellation. I received repeated letters asking me to price Forest Green and Royal Ruby Charm under Charm and not under Forest Green and Royal Ruby which I had been doing. After I followed that appeal, I had at least a dozen complaints asking why I didn't price square pieces of Royal Ruby and Forest Green. When you say "Charm" to Fire-King collectors, red or green does not usually come to mind; Jade-ite and Azur-ite do.

There are only five different pieces of Royal Ruby Charm. You will note the large berry bowl is significantly higher priced now than it used to be. Mint condition large berry bowls have turned out to be terribly inadequate for the demand. Jade-ite Charm is the hardest jade ware to find. At present, the platter and dinner plates in Jade-ite are very elusive and Jade-ite Charm prices continue to soar on these. There appears to be an adequate supply of Azur-ite except for soups, platters, and dinner plates which have seen slight increases in price recently.

	Azur-ite	Forest Green	Jade-ite	Royal Ruby
Bowl, 4¾", dessert	6.00	6.00	15.00	8.00
Bowl, 6", soup	20.00	20.00	50.00	
Bowl, 7⅜", salad	25.00	17.00	60.00	70.00
Creamer	12.00	7.50	20.00	
Cup	4.00	5.00	10.00	6.00
Plate, 6⅝", salad	10.00	10.00	40.00	
Plate, 8⅜", luncheon	12.00	10.00	26.00	10.00
Plate, 9¼", dinner	25.00	30.00	50.00	
Platter, 11" x 8"	28.00	22.00	65.00	
Saucer, 5⅜"	1.50	1.50	4.00	2.50
Sugar	12.00	7.50	20.00	

FIRE-KING FLEURETTE, ANCHOR HOCKING GLASS CORPORATION, 1958 – 1960

Color: white w/decal

Fleurette first appeared in Anchor Hocking's 1959 – 1960 catalog printed in April 1958. Fleurette seems to have been replaced with Primrose by the 1960 – 1961 catalog. Some odd pieces with Fleurette decals have turned up recently in auctions of former Anchor Hocking employees' estates in Lancaster, Ohio. A Lace Edge candy and Napco vases with Fleurette decals both have been documented. Fleurette is in shorter supply than Primrose which replaced it, but it suffers from a lack of collectors or the price would increase dramatically with the short supply available. Be sure to watch for washed-out or missing designs on these decaled lines. Time has not been kind to many of them, but Fleurette seems to have suffered most.

I have seen only one size of tumbler in Fleurette and it is rarely found.

All Fire-King sugar lids are interchangeable though they all don't have the same knob design. They are plain white. Be sure to check these lids while shopping. More than once an American Sweetheart lid has been misplaced on a Fire-King sugar bowl.

Bowl, 4⅝", dessert	3.00		Plate, 9⅛", dinner	5.00
Bowl, 6⅝", soup plate	12.00		Platter, 9" x 12"	14.00
Bowl, 8¼", vegetable	12.00		Saucer, 5¾"	1.00
Creamer	5.00		Sugar	5.00
Cup, 5 oz., snack	3.00		Sugar cover	5.00
Cup, 8 oz.	4.00		Tumbler, 9 oz., water	100.00
Plate, 6¼", bread and butter	15.00		Tray, 11"x 6", snack	4.00
Plate, 7⅜", salad	10.00			

FIRE-KING "GAME BIRD," ANCHOR HOCKING GLASS CORPORATION, 1959 – 1962

Color: white w/decal

Anchor Hocking had advertisements calling this pattern both "Wild Bird" and "Game Bird." I preferred the "Game Bird" moniker when I first wrote *Collectible Glassware from the 40s, 50s, 60s....* The following game birds are depicted on this pattern: Canada goose, ringed-necked pheasant, ruffled grouse, and mallard duck. I have catalog sheets of mugs, cereals, and ashtrays listed for 1960 – 1961; but, as you can see below, there are many more pieces available than those.

I now have caged all these wild birds except for three juice glasses. I have a mallard juice. Note the listing of a water tumbler. So far, it has only been seen with a pheasant, but who knows?

That ringed-neck pheasant is the only feathered friend in town if you are looking for serving pieces. The sugar, creamer, 8½" vegetable, and platter have only been found with pheasant decals. It is possible to collect an entire set of pheasant decorated dinnerware, but no other bird can be collected in a full set as far as I can determine. I have chosen to show that pheasant set. The platter and vegetable bowl along with that water tumbler previously mentioned are the most difficult items to find; don't allow them fly by.

Great promotional sales or give-aways make Missouri and Oklahoma a haven for "Game Bird." I have encountered dozens of mugs and tumblers on my trips to that area although little else in the pattern was for sale.

Mugs are microwaveable and great for coffee, tea, or hot chocolate. In fact, mug collecting per se, is catching on, especially in Fire-King circles. It's amazing how many different types there are. You could decorate a whole wall and not use a duplicate mug — actually, maybe a whole room. Obviously they have been very useful and durable throughout all these years.

Ashtray, 5¼"	16.00	Plate, 9⅛", dinner	6.50
Bowl, 4⅝", dessert	5.00	Platter, 12" x 9"	65.00
Bowl, 5", soup or cereal	8.00	Sugar	20.00
Bowl, 8¼", vegetable	75.00	Sugar cover	5.00
Creamer	20.00	Tumbler, 5oz., juice	35.00
Mug, 8 oz.	8.00	Tumbler, 9 oz., water	100.00
Plate, 6¼", bread & butter	10.00	Tumbler, 11 oz., iced tea	12.00

FIRE-KING GRAY LAUREL, ANCHOR HOCKING GLASS CORPORATION, 1952 – 1963

A 1953 catalog is the only time that Gray Laurel is mentioned in Anchor Hocking records. I bought my first set of Gray Laurel on a trip through Phoenix years ago. It was all labeled and like new, so I purchased it. Actually, most of the items photographed here are from that original acquisition. Gray has turned out to be so scarce when compared to the quantity of Peach Lustre (laurel leaf design) found.

The 11" serving plate and 8¼" vegetable bowl are hard to locate, particularly with good color. That is the major detriment for Gray Laurel — the color wears through and shows white streaks. The color on Gray Laurel lingered on the surface of the glass much better than that of Peach Lustre, but it did wear with use. Dishwashers and abrasive detergents are deadly on this color as well as many other glassware patterns of this era. With the introduction of the dishwasher, glass companies had to learn to combat the abusive heat suddenly heaped upon their dishes. I'm told that there was much testing of color thereafter to get it to stay put on the glassware.

Three sizes of tumblers were made to go with Gray Laurel. These tumblers are "complementary decorated" with gray and maroon bands. There is a five ounce juice, a nine ounce water, and a 13 ounce iced tea. To date, I have not spotted any of these. Do you have any? I need one of each.

Crystal stemware, like the Early American Line shown under "Bubble," was also decorated with a laurel cutting to go with this pattern.

Bowl, 4⅞", dessert	6.00		Plate, 7⅜", salad	8.00
Bowl, 7⅝", soup plate	15.00		Plate, 9⅛", dinner	9.00
Bowl, 8¼", vegetable	28.00		Plate, 11", serving	18.00
Creamer, ftd.	5.00		Saucer, 5¾"	3.00
Cup, 8 oz.	4.00		Sugar, ftd.	5.00

FIRE-KING HONEYSUCKLE, ANCHOR HOCKING GLASS CORPORATION, 1959 – 1960

Color: white w/decal

Honeysuckle made its appearance in the spring 1959 Anchor Hocking catalog for 1960 – 1961. As with Fleurette, Honeysuckle seems to have been replaced by Primrose shortly after its introduction. Honeysuckle also is in shorter supply than Primrose and more collectors seek it than they do Fleurette. The seemingly non-existent 6¼" bread and butter plate has appeared in significant numbers of late effecting a cut of its former price. However, don't pass by any Honeysuckle mugs. They are selling in the $65 range if you can spot one. Be sure to watch for washed-out or missing designs on these decaled lines. There were three sizes of tumblers listed for Honeysuckle, but I have located only two sizes. These were shown in my *Anchor Hocking's Fire-King and More* book.

As with most of the decaled lines, the platter and round vegetable are difficult to locate. They were sold only with the largest sized sets; obviously, there were many smaller sized sets sold without those items.

Bowl, 4⅝", dessert	4.00		Plate, 9⅛", dinner	6.00
Bowl, 6⅝", soup plate	9.00		Platter, 9" x 12"	18.00
Bowl, 8¼", vegetable	16.00		Saucer, 5¾"	1.50
Creamer	5.00		Sugar	5.00
Cup, 8 oz.	4.00		Sugar cover	5.00
Mug	65.00		Tumbler, 5 oz., juice	20.00
Plate, 6¼", bread and butter	10.00		Tumbler, 9 oz., water	20.00
Plate, 7⅜", salad	5.00		Tumbler, 12 oz., iced tea	20.00

FIRE-KING "JANE RAY," ANCHOR HOCKING GLASS CORPORATION, 1945 – 1963

Colors: Ivory, Jade-ite, Peach Lustre, crystal, amber, white, and white trimmed in gold

"Jane Ray" is the most collected Anchor Hocking pattern from the 1950s. "Jane Ray" is the name collectors have called this ribbed Jade-ite pattern. "Jane Ray" was listed in catalogs for nearly 20 years, so there is an abundance of it around. A Jade-ite set is more economically priced today than it was two years ago when I last wrote about this pattern. Today, soups, cereal, and vegetable bowls are selling around 10% less and even the hard to find demitasse cup and saucers have declined a little more. What brought this about was the supply of jade color suddenly flooding the markets, old and newly manufactured at the behest of a certain famous TV personality, was more than collectors could handle; so price adjustments had to be made.

The large flanged soup is selling in the $250 range, yet I have seen them priced for three or four times that. They are rare, but dealers need to be aware that customers who know prices will see that exorbitant price on these wares and leave your booth thinking everything in there is priced "too high to buy." How do I know this? They come to my booth and tell me exactly that. "When I saw that, I knew I couldn't afford anything in *that* booth," they'll say.

A few years ago, boxes of "Jane Ray" went begging; today, some collectors are buying lowly saucers for $2.00 that couldn't be sold for 25¢ then. I once priced them five for $1.00 in a mall.

"Jane Ray" means Jade-ite to most collectors. I had it listed exclusively in Jade-ite in my first book. Notice that there were other colors manufactured.

There are demitasse cups and saucers in crystal, Peach Lustre, and amber. "Jane Ray" demitasse sets were the most difficult pieces to find until flat soups were unearthed.

A 1947 chain store catalog of glassware by Anchor Hocking lists this as "Jade-ite Heat Proof Tableware," which is the only bona fide name known. That record also lists the vegetable bowl as 8⅛" instead of 8¼", as indexed in later catalogs. I have never seen this smaller version, but there could be some. Probably, it's an incorrect measurement.

Availability, as with blue "Bubble" and green Block, puts "Jane Ray" in front of many new collectors. If you like this pattern, start collecting now and buy the harder-to-find pieces when you discover them.

	Ivory	Jade-ite	Vitrock
Bowl, 4⅞", dessert	25.00	11.00	10.00
Bowl, 5⅞", oatmeal		18.00	18.00
Bowl, 7⅝", soup plate		20.00	
Bowl, 8¼", vegetable		25.00	25.00
Bowl, 9", flat soup		250.00	
Cup	20.00	5.00	8.00
*Cup, demitasse		30.00	20.00
Creamer		10.00	

	Ivory	Jade-ite	Vitrock
Plate, 6¼"		85.00	
Plate, 7¾", salad		10.00	
Plate, 9⅛", dinner	40.00	10.00	20.00
Platter, 9" x 12"		24.00	
Saucer	10.00	2.00	2.00
**Saucer, demitasse		35.00	20.00
Sugar		8.00	
Sugar cover		18.00	

*Peach Lustre $10.00

**Peach Lustre $15.00

FIRE-KING MEADOW GREEN, ANCHOR HOCKING GLASS CORPORATION, 1967 – 1977

Color: white w/decal

Remember the avocado colored appliances in the late 1960s and 1970s? Meadow Green was a line of glassware and oven-ware introduced by Anchor Hocking at that time to complement that décor. As with Indiana's Daisy, this color was made specifically for matching kitchens of the day. Collectors today are beginning to notice it, and I keep hearing that green and gold may return as decorator colors. As with Blue Mosaic, cups, creamers, and sugars have solid colors; in this case, two different shades of green can be found on the exteriors without the floral decal. The lid for the sugar is white without a decal.

Meadow Green is still reasonable and, I'm told, can be used in both ovens and microwaves. (Be sure to test for hot spots before leaving it in the microwave for very long.) If hot and it cools too quickly after taking it from the microwave, it will crack or worse — explode. Casseroles came with non-decaled white lids as well as crystal. Crystal seems to be preferred by cooks since you can check on what's cooking without lifting the lid. However a premium of a couple of dollars is asked for white lids since they are more difficult to find. Add that to the price listed below since prices are for items with clear lids. If you want to collect a pattern without major competition right now, then this might a pattern for you.

Bowl, 4⅝", dessert	3.00		Creamer	3.00
Bowl, 5", cereal	3.50		Cup	2.50
Bowl, 6⅝", soup	6.00		Custard, 6 oz.	1.50
Bowl, 8¼", vegetable	12.00		Loaf pan, 5" x 9"	6.50
Cake dish, 8", square	6.00		Mug, 9 oz.	3.00
Cake dish, 9", round	6.50		Plate, 7⅜", salad	2.50
Casserole, 12 oz., hndl.	3.50		Plate, 10", dinner	4.00
Casserole, 1 qt., w/cover	7.00		Platter, 12" x 9"	8.00
Casserole, 1½ qt., w/cover	8.00		Saucer	.50
Casserole, 1½ qt., oval, w/cover	8.00		Sugar w/lid	7.00
Casserole, 2 qt., w/cover	9.00		Utility dish, 1½ qt.	6.00
Casserole, 3 qt., w/cover	12.00		Utility dish, 2 qt.	7.00

FIRE-KING PEACH LUSTRE, "LAUREL," ANCHOR HOCKING GLASS CORPORATION, 1952 – 1963

Anchor Hocking's 1952 catalog declared Peach Lustre as "The New Sensation." This laurel leaf design was also made in another color called Gray Laurel. The laurel design was integrated in the name of that pattern, but not so with Peach Lustre. The name Peach Lustre was also used to refer to the color used for other patterns, so don't be confused by that. For example, "Jane Ray" demitasse sets can be found in Peach Lustre. Twelve years of production of Peach Lustre should have made a rather large collecting base, and it would have, had the color held up.

Unfortunately, this color was not too resilient. Prices listed below are for pieces with excellent color and no wear and tear. The major detraction to collecting Peach Lustre is color deterioration. Dishwashers and abrasive detergents were deadly on the glaze. Wear creates white streaks on the surface. Recognize that worn or rubbed pieces will be hard to sell for even half the listed price. Because there is so much still around, collectors can afford to be picky about what they buy in Peach Lustre. The 11" serving plate was discontinued as of August 25, 1960. It is the most difficult piece to find, especially with good color. It's a great size serving dish, and was obviously well used. It is difficult to find in mint condition.

Crystal stemware like that shown under "Bubble" was also engraved with a laurel cutting to go with all laurel patterns.

Bowl, 4⅞", dessert	4.00	Plate, 7⅜", salad	8.00
Bowl, 7⅝", soup plate	10.00	Plate, 9⅛", dinner	5.00
Bowl, 8¼", vegetable	10.00	Plate, 11", serving	14.00
Creamer, ftd.	4.00	Saucer, 5¾"	1.00
Cup, 8 oz.	3.00	Sugar, ftd.	4.00

FIRE-KING PRIMROSE, ANCHOR HOCKING GLASS CORPORATION, 1960 – 1962

Color: white w/decal

Anchor Hocking's Primrose was the first pattern to try to bridge the gap between dinnerware and ovenware. Primrose was created with pieces intended for both functions. Many of Anchor Hocking's patterns made during this era were produced as dinnerware, even though they were embossed "ovenware" to allow customers to know that they were "heat-proof" and could be "pre-warmed" in the oven. No ovenware was intended for use on the stovetop, but most "ovenware" patterns can be used in the microwave with caution.

Primrose was only shown in the 1960 – 1962 catalogs. From its lack of availability today, it might be very limited or, as with the Sapphire Blue ovenware, Grandma may still be using it instead of parting with it to buy newer wares.

All tumblers, along with most of the lidded ovenware items, are difficult to find in this pattern. The 11 ounce white tumblers are the only Fire-King ones known besides those of the "Game Bird." Crystal Primrose tumblers were packed in boxed sets and came in at least two sizes. The crystal tumblers have become harder to find than the white ones. Many Primrose sets have been accumulated without finding tumblers of any kind.

There are some rarely seen pieces of Primrose being found. Check out my *Anchor Hocking's Fire-King and More* book for listings on these pieces including gravy boats, shakers, vases, and even an egg plate.

All Primrose casserole covers are clear crystal Fire-King. White covers were not made until later. All pieces of ovenware were guaranteed against oven breakage for two years. Dealers would exchange a new item for the broken pieces.

The deep loaf pan was sold as a baking pan by adding a crystal glass cover. All the crystal glass lids are harder to find than their respective pans.

Item	Price	Item	Price	Item	Price
Bowl, 4⅝", dessert	3.50	Casserole, 2 qt., knob cover	16.00	Plate, 9⅛", dinner	6.00
Bowl, 6⅝", soup plate	9.00	Creamer	5.00	Platter, 9" x 12"	14.00
Bowl, 8¼", vegetable	14.00	Cup, 5 oz., snack	3.00	Saucer, 5¾"	1.00
Cake pan, 8", round	12.00	Cup, 8 oz.	3.00	Sugar	5.00
Cake pan, 8", square	12.00	Custard, 6 oz., low or dessert	3.00	Sugar cover	5.00
Casserole, pt., knob cover	9.00	Pan, 5" x 9", baking, w/cover	18.00	Tray, 11" x 6", rectangular, snack	5.00
Casserole, ½ qt., oval,		Pan, 5" x 9", deep loaf	14.00	Tumbler, 5 oz., juice (crystal)	50.00
au gratin cover	12.00	Pan, 6½" x 10½", utility baking	12.00	Tumbler, 5 oz. (white)	28.00
Casserole, 1 qt., knob cover	12.00	Pan, 8" x 12½", utility baking	40.00	Tumbler, 10 oz. water (crystal)	50.00
Casserole, 1½ qt., knob cover	12.00	Plate, 7⅜", salad	5.00	Tumbler, 11 oz. (white)	22.00

FIRE-KING RESTAURANT WARE, ANCHOR HOCKING GLASS CORPORATION, 1948 – 1967

Colors: Jade-ite, Milk White

After "Jane Ray," Anchor Hocking's Restaurant Ware line is the most sought Jade-ite pattern. Unfortunately, there are now pieces being made in China that are similar in shape to this pattern that are in major department stores and Cracker Barrel restaurants. Most Restaurant Ware is marked and the newly made is not. Know your dealer and remember that if prices seem too reasonable to be true, there probably is a reason.

Restaurant Ware is usable for microwave ovens I'm told. Remember to put the dish in the microwave for just a little time to see if it gets hot, as you would test any other dish.

You can see a catalog sheet at the bottom of this page, which will show you the differences in the three sizes of Restaurant Ware cups and the mug. For more detailed information and to view some remarkably rare items in Jade-ite, pick up a copy of my *Anchor Hocking's Fire-King & More*.

White Restaurant Ware is being found in small quantities and is generating some new collector interest.

	Jade-ite		Jade-ite
Bowl, 4¾", fruit, G294	10.00	Plate, 5½", bread/butter, G315	10.00
Bowl, 9¼", flat soup	100.00	Plate, 6¾", pie or salad, G297	10.00
Bowl, 8 oz., flanged rim, cereal, G305	22.00	Plate, 8⅞", oval partitioned, G211	60.00
Bowl, 10 oz., deep, G309	26.00	Plate, 8", luncheon, G316	45.00
Bowl, 15 oz., deep, G300	28.00	Plate, 9⅝", 3-compartment, G292, 2 styles	25.00
Cup, demitasse	30.00	Plate, 9⅝", 5-compartment, G311	35.00
Cup, 6 oz., straight, G215	9.00	Plate, 9", dinner, G306	22.00
Cup, 7 oz., extra heavy, G299	10.00	Platter, 9½", oval, G307	48.00
Cup, 7 oz., narrow rim, G319	12.00	Platter, 11½", oval, G308	45.00
Mug, coffee, 7 oz., G212	10.00	Saucer, 6", G295	4.00
Mug, 8 oz.	10.00	Saucer, demitasse	30.00
Pitcher, ball jug, 3 styles	495.00		

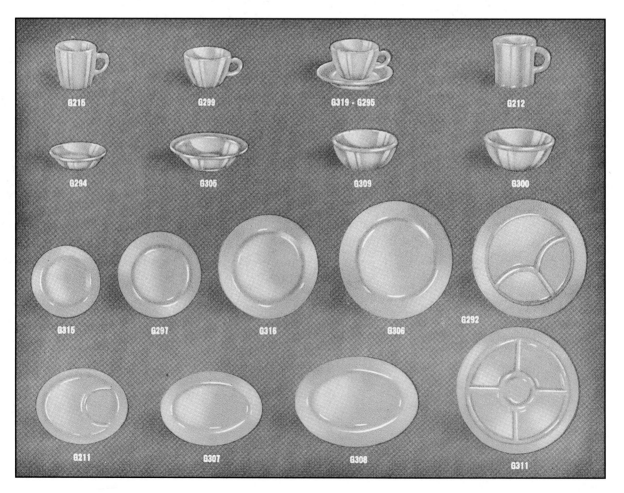

FIRE-KING SAPPHIRE BLUE OVEN GLASS, ANCHOR HOCKING GLASS CORPORATION, 1942 – 1950s

Colors: Sapphire blue, crystal; some Ivory and Jade-ite

Fire-King Sapphire blue was the choice ovenware for almost two generations. Both my mom and my grandmother baked in Fire-King. Many a tasty pie and bread pudding came from those dishes as I was growing up. Mom wouldn't consider using anything but half a large roaster for bread pudding made "from scratch biscuits." When my dad broke it years later, she went to my shop and commandeered one off the shelf. Sapphire was the ovenware that was recognized for its durability. Fire-King had a two-year guarantee. All you had to do was take the broken pieces to your local dealer and your piece was replaced at no charge if it failed while being used properly.

When Fire-King is mentioned today, it is automatically translated into Jade-ite. It used to be that when Fire-King was talked about, Sapphire blue oven glass was what instantaneously came to mind. Times are changing.

This blue remains usable for standard ovens, but it tends to develop heat cracks from sudden temperature changes if utilized in the microwave. We learned that the hard way. Don't use it in the microwave. A guy mentioned to me just last month that he'd learned that hard lesson also — and was at the show looking to replace for his wife the piece that he'd broken.

Collectors are inclined to favor the casseroles with pie plate covers before those with knobbed covers. Cooks prefer the knobbed lids because they are easier to lift when hot than the pie plate style — but there are fewer bottoms for these. Those knobbed lids survived better than their counterparts even though many were sold as bakers without lids.

That 8 ounce nurser (bottle) is not as available as the 4 ounce. Sporadically, nipple covers have surfaced. These blue covers are embossed "BINKY'S NIP CAP U.S.A." (and not Fire-King).

The dry cup measure looks like a mug with eight ounce measurements up the side and no spout for pouring. Beware of one spouted measuring cups with the spout removed. Without measurements on the side, you are speaking mug and not dry measure. Regular mugs come in two styles: thick and thin. The thin is uncommon.

The reason the juice saver pie plate is so highly priced comes from the fact that most were heavily used and are deeply scarred. To obtain the price below, this pie plate has to be mint. Jade-ite ones are very rarely seen, as that price indicates.

The prices with asterisks (under the Ivory listing) are for Jade-ite items with the Fire-King embossing. Those particular Jade-ite items (with asterisks) are not found in Ivory. Most Ivory is plain without an embossed design. You will find plain Ivory and Jade-ite mugs that hold eight ounces, not seven. The Jade-ite mug with the embossed Fire-King pattern is uncommon as the price illustrates.

	Ivory	Sapphire		Ivory	Sapphire
Baker, 1 pt., 4½" x 5"		8.00	Loaf pan, 9⅛" x 5⅛", deep	15.00	22.00
Baker, 1 pt., round	4.00	8.00	Mug, coffee, 7 oz., 2 styles	*110.00	28.00
Baker, 1 qt., round	6.00	12.00	Nipple cover		225.00
Baker, 1½ qt., round	6.00	16.00	Nurser, 4 oz.		20.00
Baker, 2 qt., round	8.50	16.00	Nurser, 8 oz.		33.00
Baker, 6 oz., individual	5.00	5.00	Percolator top, 2⅛"		5.00
Bowl, 4⅜", individual pie plate		22.00	Pie plate, 8⅜", 1½" deep		9.00
Bowl, 5⅜", cereal or deep dish pie plate	12.00	22.00	Pie plate, 9⅝", 1½" deep		10.00
Bowl, measuring, 16 oz.		27.50	Pie plate, 9", 1½" deep	10.00	10.00
Cake pan (deep), 8¾"		40.00	Pie plate, 10⅜", juice saver	*300.00	135.00
Cake pan, 9"	15.00		Refrigerator jar & cover, 4½" x 5"	**40.00	15.00
Casserole, 1 pt., knob handle cover	30.00	14.00	Refrigerator jar & cover, 5⅛" x 9⅛"	**75.00	32.50
Casserole, 1 qt., knob handle cover	25.00	18.00	Roaster, 8¾"		55.00
Casserole, 1 qt., pie plate cover		18.00	Roaster, 10⅜"		80.00
Casserole, 1½ qt., knob handle cover	20.00	22.00	Skillet, 7" x 4⅝", handle		6.00
Casserole, 1½ qt., pie plate cover		20.00	Table server, tab handles (hot plate)	18.00	22.00
Casserole, 2 qt., knob handle cover	25.00	22.00	Utility bowl, 6⅞", 1 qt.		20.00
Casserole, 2 qt., pie plate cover		25.00	Utility bowl, 8⅜", 1½ qt.		25.00
Casserole, individual, 10 oz.		13.00	Utility bowl, 10⅛"		28.00
Cup, 8 oz., measuring, 1 spout		30.00	Utility pan, 8⅛" x 12½", 2 qt.		125.00
Cup, 8 oz., dry measure, no spout		900.00	Utility pan, 10½" x 2" deep	18.00	25.00
Cup, 8 oz., measuring, 3 spout		30.00			
Custard cup or baker, 5 oz.	10.00	5.00	*Jade-ite w/embossed design (not Ivory)		
Custard cup or baker, 6 oz.	6.00	5.00	**Jade-ite (not Ivory)		

FIRE-KING "SHELL," ANCHOR HOCKING GLASS CORPORATION, 1965 – 1976

Colors: white, white trimmed in gold, Jade-ite, and Lustre Shell

The "Shell" pattern name was derived from the Golden "Shell" pattern which was milk white with a 22K gold trim and Lustre "Shell" which was a re-introduction of the old Peach Lustre. Jade-ite "Shell" was never really named that but was shown in Anchor Hocking catalog listings as having "English Regency" styling. Thus, some collectors, confusing things further, are now referring to it as "Regency Shell." Be aware that there are now two names for this pattern in Jade-ite, "Regency Shell" and "Jade-ite Shell."

The major concern for new collectors is distinguishing between "Shell" and "Swirl" patterns in Fire-King. "Shell" patterns (page 85) have scalloped edges on flat pieces while the "Swirl" patterns (pages 87 and 88) do not. Creamers and sugars in "Shell" are footed while "Swirl" creamer and sugars are flat except for the later made white ones. Those are footed but shaped differently, as can be seen on page 88.

Lustre "Shell" was introduced in 1966 and was in catalogs until 1976. This Lustre "Shell" was the same color used for Peach Lustre, introduced in 1952 and discontinued in 1963. Evidently, there was a great demand for Anchor Hocking to remake this color; however it suffered the same deterioration of its predecessor. Lustre "Shell" color is found only on the exterior of some pieces leaving me to believe that Hocking was aware of the problem.

A demitasse cup and saucer were introduced to the Lustre "Shell" line in 1972. As with other Fire-King patterns, demitasse saucers are harder to find than cups.

You may find pieces of Golden "Shell" adorned with some design. A popular decoration is of the 1964 New York World's Fair, though other artists' works are encountered. Some are well done and suitable for hanging in the den; others might add some color to the barn.

	Gold	Jade-ite	Lustre
Bowl, 4¾", dessert	3.50	12.00	4.00
Bowl, 6⅜", cereal	10.00	22.00	10.00
Bowl, 7⅝", soup plate	12.00	28.00	15.00
Bowl, 8½", vegetable	9.00	26.00	18.00
Creamer, ftd.	3.50	22.00	10.00
Cup, 8 oz.	3.25	10.00	5.00
Cup, 3¼ oz., demitasse	7.50		10.00
Saucer, 4¾", demitasse	10.00		10.00
Plate, 7¼", salad	4.00	22.00	3.50
Plate, 10", dinner	6.00	25.00	7.00
Platter, 9½" x 13"	9.00	85.00	
Saucer, 5¾"	1.00	4.00	2.00
Sugar, ftd.	4.00	22.00	10.00
Sugar cover	4.00	65.00	8.00

FIRE-KING "SWIRL," ANCHOR HOCKING GLASS CORPORATION, 1950s

Colors: Azur-ite, Ivory, Ivory trimmed in gold or red, white or white trimmed in gold, and Pink

"Swirl" was first introduced in 1950 in Azur-ite, which is the light blue; that was followed by Sunrise (red trimmed Ivory). In fact, if you find Sunrise pieces with original labels, they will say Ivory and not Sunrise. Color names seemed to take precedence over pattern names at Anchor Hocking. Ivory "Swirl" was introduced in 1953; later in the 1950s, Anchorwhite took over for the Ivory and Ivory was discontinued. Golden Anniversary was introduced in 1955 by adding 22K gold trim to Ivory "Swirl." In the latter 1950s, a gold border was added to Anchorwhite, but labels on this say "22K." The Ivory is a beige tint as opposed to the flatter white of Anchorwhite. They are sometimes confused when shopping by flashlight at early morning flea markets. Both patterns were heavily marketed and are available. Watch for worn gold edges, since most collectors avoid those pieces for collections. If you are buying these to use, pieces with worn gold edges may be a bargain.

Pink "Swirl" was introduced in 1956 as Pink. A pitcher and tumblers were made to complement the Pink "Swirl." The tumbler pictured is from an original boxed set. Actually, the catalog lists this pitcher and tumblers separately as "Wrought Iron."

	Anchorwhite Ivory	Azur-ite	Golden Anniversary	Jade-ite	Pink	Sunrise
Bowl, 4⅞", fruit or dessert	7.00	10.00	4.00		9.00	5.00
Bowl, 5⅞", cereal	24.00	20.00				24.00
Bowl, 7¼", vegetable					40.00	
Bowl, 7⅝", soup plate	10.00	16.00	10.00		18.00	16.00
Bowl, 8¼", vegetable	20.00	32.00	12.00		28.00	22.00
Bowl, 9¼", flanged soup	100.00	165.00				
Creamer, flat	10.00	10.00			8.50	10.00
Creamer, ftd.	2.75		3.25			
Cup, 8 oz.	8.00	6.00	4.00	40.00	6.00	6.50
Pitcher, 80 oz.					28.00	
Plate, 7⅜", salad	8.00	9.00	6.00		7.50	8.00
Plate, 9⅛", dinner	10.00	10.00	7.50	80.00	10.00	10.00
Plate, 11", serving					22.00	
Platter, 12" x 9"	20.00	20.00	12.00	350.00		18.00
Saucer, 5¾"	2.00	2.00	1.00	20.00	2.00	3.00
Sugar lid, for flat sugar	5.00	10.00			7.00	10.00
Sugar, flat, tab handles	10.00	8.00			8.00	10.00
Sugar, ftd., open handles	3.00		3.50			
Tumbler, 5 oz., juice					6.00	
Tumbler, 9 oz., water					8.00	
Tumbler, 12 oz., iced tea					14.00	

FIRE-KING TURQUOISE BLUE, ANCHOR HOCKING GLASS CORPORATION, 1957 – 1958

Color: Turquoise Blue

Turquoise Blue was cataloged by Anchor Hocking as dinnerware, but pieces are embossed ovenware on the reverse side except the egg plate, which is not marked at all. Evidently, the ribbed design on the bottom did not allow for a Fire-King logo. Most of Anchor Hocking's 1950s and 1960s dinnerware lines are marked ovenware. This enlightened the purchaser that the item could be pre-warmed in the oven before using. Turquoise Blue has become more collectible than any blue colored ware of this era. Availability of basic pieces started many collectors down a road that looked easy, but rarely found items slowed them from completing sets. Just when prices were slowing down in the States, along came Japanese collectors discovering it on the Internet. You really have to appreciate a pattern to pay as much for postage as you do in buying the piece itself.

Availability for cups, saucers, 9" dinner plates, creamers, and sugars is not a problem. Mugs and small berry bowls are the next easiest pieces to find. Although the 9" plate with cup indent is not as plentiful as the dinner plate, it does not command the price of the dinner since many collectors do not buy the snack sets...yet. Snack sets often have gold trim and a good dishwasher with lemon based soap will eliminate it. Be careful if you like the gold there.

We used Turquoise Blue as our dinnerware during the years my sons were reaching their teens. From that experience I can tell you that 10" serving plates are rarely found and the 6⅛" plate may even be harder to find. Many collectors are searching for one of either size. The traditional 9" dinner with its upturned edge does not make a satisfactory sized plate to feed teenage boys. We sold that set and replaced it with another set of dishes. Now that Turquoise Blue costs at least five times more than when we first bought it, our younger son has decided he'd like a set of his own. Nostalgia in action.

The batter bowl is rarely seen except in Illinois where it must have been a promotional item. They appear more frequently there.

There are two distinct mixing bowl sets that go with this Turquoise Blue. The three-piece set of round bowls was called Splash Proof and the four-piece set of oval spouted bowls was called Swedish Modern by Hocking. Collectors commonly call them "tear drop" bowls, today. The one quart round mixing bowl and the three quart tear-shaped mixing bowls are the most difficult sizes to find. However, the one quart tear-shaped bowl is usually the first to sell at shows. Many people want these to use as small serving dishes with their Turquoise Blue tableware.

Ashtray, 3½"	10.00
Ashtray, 4⅝"	12.00
Ashtray, 5¾"	14.00
Batter bowl, w/spout	375.00
Bowl, 4½", berry	10.00
Bowl, 5", cereal	17.00
Bowl, 6⅝", soup/salad	25.00
Bowl, 8", vegetable	25.00
Bowl, "tear drop," mixing, 1 pt.	33.00
Bowl, "tear drop," mixing, 1 qt.	38.00
Bowl, "tear drop," mixing, 2 qt.	38.00
Bowl, "tear drop," mixing, 3 qt.	63.00
Bowl, round, mixing, 1 qt.	23.00
Bowl, round, mixing, 2 qt.	28.00
Bowl, round, mixing, 3 qt.	30.00
Creamer	8.00
Cup	5.00
Egg plate, 9¾"	20.00
Mug, 8 oz.	10.00

Plate, 6⅛"	20.00
Plate, 7¼"	13.00
Plate, 9"	11.00
Plate, 9", w/cup indent	6.00
Plate, 10"	40.00
Relish, 3-part, 11⅛"	13.00
Saucer	1.50
Sugar	8.00

FIRE-KING WHEAT, ANCHOR HOCKING GLASS CORPORATION, 1962 – LATE 1960S

Anchor Hocking's Wheat production began in 1962, and it was one of their most prolific lines. Like the 1940s Sapphire blue Fire-King before it, everyone has seen the Wheat pattern of the 1960s. Several glass and pottery companies produced wheat patterns. It was a popular motif of that time. You will find crystal glasses with wheat cuttings that were made to go with all the wheat patterns being used. Not everyone is fond of Wheat, but there are enough that remember it to keep the collecting spark alive. Wheat will not break your checking account; so you can buy extra pieces if the occasion arises.

Ovenware lids create dilemmas today because casserole sizes of yesteryear do not accept most modern day lids. Replacement lids for the older casseroles will cost up to half of the price of the entire dish. Those lids are valuable possessions, so treat them gently. Both the oval and round 1½ quart casseroles and the 10½" baking pan were used with candle warmers. These candle warmers were brass finished with walnut handles plus the candle. Many were never used. They are being found with the original candles intact. Replacement candles can be found at most kitchenware stores should you need one. Several readers say that they still use these today for keeping food warm. Food never lasted that long with my boys. It never had a chance to get cold.

Bowl, 4⅝", dessert	3.50	Cup, 8 oz.	4.00
Bowl, 5", chili	30.00	Custard, 6 oz., low or dessert	3.00
Bowl, 6⅝", soup plate	8.00	Mug	65.00
Bowl, 8¼", vegetable	12.00	Pan, 5" x 9", baking, w/cover	16.00
Cake pan, 8", round	11.00	Pan, 5" x 9", deep loaf	12.00
Cake pan, 8", square	10.00	Pan, 6½" x 10½" x 1½", utility baking	12.00
Casserole, 1 pt., knob cover	8.00	Pan, 8" x 12½" x 2", utility baking	20.00
Casserole, 1 qt., knob cover	10.00	Plate, 7⅜", salad	8.00
Casserole, 1½ qt., knob cover	11.00	Plate, 10", dinner	6.00
Casserole, 1½ qt., oval, au gratin cover	14.00	Platter, 9" x 12"	15.00
Casserole, 2 qt., knob cover	15.00	Saucer, 5¾"	1.00
Casserole, 2 qt., round, au gratin cover	15.00	Sugar	4.50
Creamer	5.00	Sugar cover	5.00
Cup, 5 oz., snack	3.00	Tray, 11" x 6", rectangular, snack	4.00

FLORAGOLD, "LOUISA," JEANNETTE GLASS COMPANY, 1950s

Colors: Iridescent, some Shell Pink, ice blue, and crystal

Floragold was called "Louisa" by some when first collected because it looked like an older carnival glass pattern called "Louisa." Eventually the correct name Floragold was found and all but the earliest collectors label it properly now. Though formerly in the *Collector's Encyclopedia of Depression Glass*, Floragold was made long after the Depression era and rightly belongs in this book; so when the 50s books was conceived in 1990, I moved the pattern here. I mention this because I recently received a humbling call from an incredulous collector who checked my Depression book out of the library and was incensed that Floragold and Holiday were not in it. That reader was on a 13 year between books program. It would be interesting to know what other surprises she regarded as exclamatory.

People on the Internet, who do not sell much glassware, price this early 1950s glassware quite high believing it to be original carnival glass made in the early part of the twentieth century.

At last, some of the larger ruffled bowls have begun to sell, albeit sales are rather slow. They remain inexpensive. Mint condition shaker tops are difficult to get. They were made of white or brown plastic, and rotating those too tightly cracked scores of them. Tops are worth $15.00 to $16.00 each, which makes the tops more costly than the shakers themselves. Remember that when you find these priced cheaply — but topless.

Cups abound because they were also sold in sets of eight or twelve as part of eggnog sets. Either the pitcher or the large bowl accompanied these cups. That 5¼" saucer (no cup ring) is the same as the sherbet plate and there is no cup ringed saucer.

Ice blue, crystal, red-yellow, Shell Pink, and iridized large comports were made in the late 1950s and into the early 1970s. All colored comports are selling in the $12.00 to $15.00 range except the iridized one which will fetch $35.00 with excellent applied color. These have a tendency to be unevenly sprayed and have crystal showing.

For those who have never seen the 5" square butter dish, it was pictured in the *Very Rare Glassware of the Depression Years, Fourth Edition.* There are two different 5¼" comports in Floragold. Both of these were pictured in the first edition of *Very Rare Glassware of the Depression Years.*

	Iridescent
Ashtray/coaster, 4"	5.50
Bowl, 4½", square	5.00
Bowl, 5½", round cereal	40.00
Bowl, 5½", ruffled fruit	7.00
Bowl, 8½", square	14.00
Bowl, 9½", deep salad	50.00
Bowl, 9½", ruffled	8.00
Bowl, 12", ruffled large fruit	7.00
Butter dish and cover, ¼ lb., oblong	25.00
Butter dish and cover, round, 6¼", sq. base	45.00
Butter dish bottom	14.00
Butter dish top	28.50
Butter dish and cover, round, 5½", sq. base	1,000.00
Candlesticks, double branch, pr.	60.00
Candy dish, 1 handle	12.00
Candy or cheese dish and cover, 6¾"	55.00
*Candy, 5¼" long, 4 feet	7.50
Comport, 5¼", plain top	1,000.00
Comport, 5¼", ruffled top	1,100.00
Creamer	9.00
Cup	6.00
Pitcher, 64 oz.	40.00
Plate or tray, 13½"	25.00
Plate or tray, 13½", with indent	75.00
Plate, 5¼", sherbet	12.00
Plate, 8½", dinner	40.00
Plate, 11¾" (Iris shape)	495.00
Platter, 11¼"	25.00
*Salt and pepper, plastic tops	55.00
Saucer, 5¼" (no ring)	12.00
Sherbet, low, footed	16.00
Sugar	6.50
Sugar lid	12.00

	Iridescent
Tidbit, wooden post (usually white)	45.00
Tumbler, 10 oz., footed	20.00
Tumbler, 11 oz., footed	20.00
Tumbler, 15 oz., footed	120.00
Vase or celery	450.00

* Shell pink $20.00

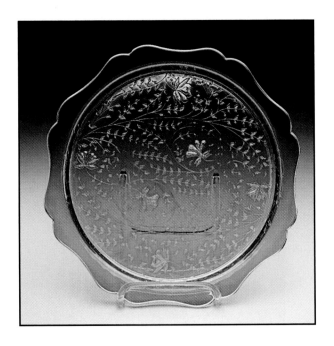

FOREST GREEN, ANCHOR HOCKING GLASS COMPANY CORPORATION, 1950 – 1967

Color: Forest Green

Forest Green was the color name of this Anchor Hocking glassware, but it has become synonymous as a pattern name, also. Forest Green was used for the square Charm blank, but that glassware became better known as Charm; so I have removed all the Forest Green and Royal Ruby Charm pieces from the listing below. You will now find them priced only under Charm on page 71 to eliminate duplications of listings.

Even Hocking's green "Bubble" was simply called Forest Green when it was first made. According to Anchor Hocking catalogs, "Bubble" stemware was primarily called Early American line. The other stemware line sold along with Early American was called "Boopie" by an earlier author; but records from Hocking show the name to be Berwick. On page 95, the Early American line is pictured on the left in row two and Berwick is pictured on the right in that row.

After you eradicate Charm from the listing below, Forest Green is diminished to being an accessory pattern, although a copious one. Forest Green can provide all sorts of beverage items, vases, and serving pieces. The Forest Green oval vegetable is scalloped along the edges and has a swirled effect on the sides. These were premium items for a flour company in the south; look for them there.

Not all dark green pieces on the market identified as Forest Green are Anchor Hocking wares. Forest Green has become synonymous with any dark green, but to be truly Forest Green, Anchor Hocking must have made it. They patented that name.

Decorated tumblers such as "A Bicycle for Two" will bring a dollar or two more than regular tumblers. However, undecorated tumblers sell faster to collectors.

Forest Green was widely distributed as premium items. Hocking must have furnished their products at an extremely attractive price since so many tumblers and vases are found today. In the Kentucky area, tumblers were used as containers for Sealtest brand dairy products. Honey and tea bags were other commodities often found in Anchor Hocking tumblers.

Massive quantities of 4" ball-shaped ivy vases testify to successful sales of Citronella candles packaged in those. I have previously pictured a boxed set of "Moskeeto-Lites." Those candles originally sold for $1.19. After using the candles, you had two free vases. There are many Forest Green and Royal Ruby vases in Florida where mosquitoes definitely increased sales.

Ashtray, 3½", square	5.00	
Ashtray, 4⅝", square	6.00	
Ashtray, 5¾", square	9.00	
Ashtray, 5¾", hexagonal	8.00	
Batter bowl w/spout	30.00	
Bowl, 4¾", dessert	4.50	
Bowl, 5¼" deep	10.00	
Bowl, 6", mixing	10.00	
Bowl, 8½", oval vegetable	25.00	
Cocktail shaker, w/lid	50.00	
Pitcher, 22 oz.	25.00	
Pitcher, 36 oz.	30.00	
Pitcher, 86 oz., round	38.00	
Plate, 6¾", salad	8.00	
Punch bowl	30.00	
Punch bowl stand	30.00	
Punch cup (round)	2.25	
Saucer, 5⅜"	1.00	
Sherbet, flat	8.00	
*Stem, 3½ oz., cocktail (1)	10.00	
*Stem, 4 oz., juice (3)	10.00	
Stem, 4½ oz., cocktail (8)	12.50	
Stem, 5½ oz., juice (7)	12.50	

Stem, 6 oz., sherbet (9)	9.00
*Stem, 6 oz., sherbet (2)	6.00
*Stem, 9 oz., goblet (4)	10.00
Stem, 10¾ oz., goblet (6)	13.00
*Stem, 14 oz., iced tea (5)	14.00
Tumbler, 5 oz., 3½"	4.00
Tumbler, 7 oz.	4.00
Tumbler, 9 oz., table	5.00
Tumbler, 9 oz., fancy	6.00
Tumbler, 9½ oz., tall	6.50

Tumbler, 10 oz., ftd., 4½"	6.50
Tumbler, 11 oz.	7.00
Tumbler, 13 oz., iced tea	8.00
Tumbler, 14 oz., 5"	7.50
Tumbler, 15 oz., long boy	11.00
Tumbler, 15 oz., tall iced tea	17.00
Tumbler, 32 oz., giant iced tea	25.00
Vase, 4", ivy ball	5.00
Vase, 6⅜"	7.00
Vase, 9"	12.50

*Berwick
Numbers in ( ) indicate items in row 2, page 95, from left to right.

Color: White with 22K gold decorations

Federal glass enthusiasts are seemingly the only collectors chasing down Golden Glory. It is a budding market at best. Be cautious since the 22K gold decorations deteriorate easily and detergents will lighten or remove them. You might run into some items that were rarely used or are still boxed. The boxed set pictured here was a wedding gift never used. Discovery of mint condition pieces always make collectors happy. A new find is the mug that has been selling in the $3.00 range. The operative word is selling — mainly to collectors of mugs.

I have received a couple of letters from readers asking about crystal tumblers with Golden Glory decorations. I received a picture of a stem with this decoration for documentation, but no measurements. Look for them.

Initially, only a dozen pieces of Golden Glory were offered. Federal reissued it in 1978 and three additional pieces were included in the line. These included the larger 10" dinner plate, the smaller 6⅜" soup, and the 11¼" round platter. Incidentally, this later release did not include the oval platter, larger soup, sugar, creamer, and tumblers. This ought to make those items harder to find; but, according to a dedicated collector, the hardest-to-find pieces are the 8½" vegetable bowl, tumblers, and the 7¾" salad plate. I have been unable to find the round platter, so they could be in short supply. I did see one, but you could barely make out an outline of the pattern on the plate. Dishwashers are a detriment to gold decorations.

Bowl, 4⅞", dessert	4.50	Plate, 9⅛", dinner	5.00
Bowl, 6⅜", soup	9.00	Plate, 10", dinner	7.00
Bowl, 8½", vegetable	12.00	Platter, 11¼", round	15.00
Bowl, 8", rimmed soup	12.00	Platter, 12", oval	12.00
Creamer	5.00	Saucer	.50
Cup	3.50	Sugar	4.00
Mug	15.00	Sugar lid	5.00
Plate, 7¾", salad	3.00	Tumbler, 9 oz., ftd.	12.00
		Tumbler, 10 oz., 5"	10.00

HARP, JEANNETTE GLASS COMPANY, 1954 – 1957

Colors: crystal, crystal with gold trim, and cake stands in Shell Pink, pink, iridescent white, red, and ice blue

    With so many new collectors starting smaller sized patterns such as Harp, the prices are rising. There is really not enough of it to provide everyone a set who wishes one. Harp has been used for bridge parties and smaller groups for years; and with a cake stand, cups, saucers, and 7" plates, it's an ideal pattern for entertaining. Cake plates are withstanding today's demand, but the supply of cups, saucers, and 7" plates is dwindling. If you run into the cup and saucers, do not hesitate — buy.

    If gold trim bothers you, an art gum eraser and a little elbow grease will take care of that. That trim is 22K gold which is a softer material and predisposed to erode with much use.

    The normally found vase is 7½", but there is a different style being found that has a little indentation at the foot. One of those was listed on an Internet auction with a high reserve and did not sell. Though rare, it is not an item in high demand. Demand for an item is what drives up price.

    That Harp cake stand is reminiscent of late 1800s and early 1900s glassware. Most patterns after that time had cake plates instead of a stand. The following thirteen types of Harp stands have been documented. Shell Pink, red, transparent pink, and iridescent ones are the most coveted.

1. 2. Crystal with smooth or ruffled rims
3. 4. Either of above with gold trim
5. Iridescent with smooth rim
6. 7. White or Shell Pink (opaque) with beads on rim and foot
8. 9. Ice blue with beads on foot and smooth or ruffled rim
10. Pink transparent
11. Platinum decorated with smooth rim
12. Red
13. Fired-on red

	Crystal
* Ashtray/coaster	5.00
Coaster	4.50
Cup	35.00
** Cake stand, 9"	28.00

	Crystal
Plate, 7"	14.00
Saucer	12.50
*** Tray, 2-handled, rectangular	40.00
Vase, 7½"	27.50

  * Platinum decoration $8.00
 ** Ice blue, white, pink, or Shell Pink $45.00
*** Shell Pink $60.00

HARVEST OR "GOLDEN HARVEST," COLONY GLASSWARE

Colors: Iridescent, milk

The ad for this ware in milk glass cautions to never pour hot or cold liquid directly onto cold dishes, which is good advice for most glassware unless it says it's heat-proof. This was sold in various package sets: punch bowl, three-piece console, luncheon, snack, and beverage. Therefore, many people may have some items; but you would've had to work at owning the entire pattern. The milk glass is most collected, but there are some starting to look at iridescent colored ware.

According to my sources, Harvest was obtained most often through the redemption of S&H green stamps in the midwestern states. You received a stamp for each $1.00 you spent and when a book of 300 or so was filled, you could redeem it for merchandise. Other companies had stamps. In my area it was Top Value, and our first dining table and two chairs (commonly called a card table by most folks) came from there in 1964 when we were married. When my aunt heard we only had two chairs, she gave us enough stamps to get two more. Kids of today probably wouldn't understand that.

	White
Bowl, 8 qt. punch	20.00
Bowl, 10" ftd. console	18.00
Butter, ¼ lb. w/cover	15.00
Candy box w/cover (or ftd. wedding bowl)	25.00
Cake stand, 12"	18.00
Candle, ftd. (sherbet design)	10.00
Creamer, ftd.	5.00
Cup	3.00
Cup, ftd. punch/snack	2.50
Goblet, ftd. water	6.00
Pitcher, 40 oz.	20.00
Pitcher, 65 oz.	25.00
Plate, 6" sherbet	1.00

	White
Plate, 8" salad	3.00
Plate, 10" luncheon	6.00
Platter, 14½"	14.00
Tumbler, 5 oz. juice	4.00
Tumbler, 10 oz. water	6.00
Tumbler, 14 oz. cooler	8.00
Tray, tea & toast (snack) oval	5.00
Tray, 2 hdld. oval sug/cream liner	4.00
Salt & pepper, ftd.	12.50
Saucer	.50
Sherbet, ftd.	5.00
Sugar, ftd. no handle	5.00

HEATHER, ETCHING #343, FOSTORIA GLASS COMPANY, 1949 – 1976

Colors: crystal

Heather is a fashionable girl's name, today; and I know of at least one collector who chose this pattern because that's her name. Heather was initially introduced in the *Elegant Glassware of the Depression Era* book due to requests from collectors who loved it. Although Heather certainly is elegant ware, its production dates best fit the era of this book. Heather is being encountered more often at markets, a definite plus for people now interested in it, trying to fill in partial sets that have been passed down.

All listings in Heather without a line number below are etched on Century blank #2630. The pattern shown below is a #2470, 10" footed vase. I have tried to give as accurate a listing for this pattern as possible from old catalogs, but I am sure there are additional pieces. Any help from Heather devotees will be included in future editions.

Heather, like all patterns etched on #2630 blank, has problems with abrasions and scrapes on the surfaces of flat pieces. All plates are subject to that abuse sometimes just from stacking them due to the ground bottoms scraping the top of the plate underneath. Protect them by what you serve on them and by how you store them between use. Many collectors use paper plates to separate stacked plates. These dishes were meant to be used and most were. No one knew that someday they would become valuable, particularly if they were pristine. There are a few people in the country who polish out scratches now; but it's expensive, sometimes costing more than the plate is worth.

Item	Price		Item	Price		Item	Price
Basket, 10¼" x 6½", wicker hndl.	95.00		Plate, 8½", luncheon	15.00		Tumbler, #6037, 4⅞", 5 oz., ftd.,	
Bowl, 4½", hndl.	15.00		Plate, 8", party, w/indent for cup	30.00		juice	20.00
Bowl, 5", fruit	18.00		Plate, 9½", small dinner	35.00		Tumbler, #6037, 6⅛", 12 oz.,	
Bowl, 6", cereal	28.00		Plate, 10", hndl., cake	30.00		ftd., tea	25.00
Bowl, 6¼", snack, ftd.	20.00		Plate, 10½", dinner,			Vase, 5", #4121	60.00
Bowl, 7⅛", 3 ftd., triangular	20.00		large center	45.00		Vase, 6", bud	40.00
Bowl, 7¼", bonbon, 3 ftd.	25.00		Plate, 10½", snack tray,			Vase, 6", ftd., bud, #6021	55.00
Bowl, 8", flared	32.50		small center	30.00		Vase, 6", ftd., #4143	55.00
Bowl, 9", lily pond	37.50		Plate, 14", torte	65.00		Vase, 7½", hndl.	85.00
Bowl, 9½", hndl., serving bowl	42.50		Plate, 16", torte	110.00		Vase, 8", flip, #2660	100.00
Bowl, 9½", oval, serving bowl	45.00		Platter, 12"	95.00		Vase, 8", ftd., bud, #5092	85.00
Bowl, 10", oval, hndl.	48.00		Preserve, w/cover, 6"	70.00		Vase, 8½", oval	85.00
Bowl, 10½", salad	50.00		Relish, 7⅜", 2-part	20.00		Vase, 10", ftd., #2470	140.00
Bowl, 10¾", ftd., flared	50.00		Relish, 11⅛", 3-part	32.50			
Bowl, 11, ftd., rolled edge	55.00		Salt and pepper, 3⅛", pr.	50.00			
Bowl, 11¼", lily pond	50.00		Salver, 12¼", ftd. (like cake stand)	75.00			
Bowl, 12", flared	60.00		Saucer	4.50			
Butter, w/cover, ¼ lb.	75.00		Stem, #6037, 4", 1 oz., cordial	45.00			
Candlestick, 4½"	25.00		Stem, #6037, 4", 4½ oz., oyster				
Candlestick, 7", double	40.00		cocktail	16.00			
Candlestick, 7¾", triple	60.00		Stem, #6037, 4¾", 7 oz.,			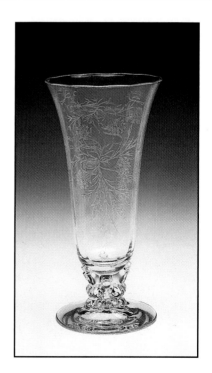	
Candy, w/cover, 7"	55.00		low sherbet	14.00			
Comport, 2¾", cheese	25.00		Stem, #6037, 5", 4 oz., cocktail	18.00			
Comport, 4⅜"	30.00		Stem, #6037, 6⅛", 6 oz., parfait	25.00			
Cracker plate, 10¾"	30.00		Stem, #6037, 6⅜", 9 oz.,				
Creamer, 4¼"	20.00		low goblet	28.00			
Creamer, individual	15.00		Stem, #6037, 6", 4 oz.,				
Cup, 6 oz., ftd.	17.00		claret-wine	30.00			
Ice bucket	75.00		Stem, #6037, 6", 7 oz., saucer				
Mayonnaise, 3 pc.	40.00		champagne	16.00			
Mayonnaise, 4 pc., div. w/2 ladles	50.00		Stem, #6037, 7⅞", 9 oz., goblet	26.00			
Mustard, w/spoon, cover	35.00		Sugar, 4", ftd.	20.00			
Oil, w/stopper, 5 oz.	50.00		Sugar, individual	15.00			
Pickle, 8¾"	30.00		Tidbit, 8⅛", 3-ftd., upturned edge	30.00			
Pitcher, 6⅛", 16 oz.	110.00		Tidbit, 10¼", 2-tier, metal hndl.	50.00			
Pitcher, 7⅛", 48 oz.	225.00		Tray, 7⅛", for ind. sug/cr.	17.50			
Plate, 6", bread/butter	7.00		Tray, 9½", hndl., muffin	33.00			
Plate, 7½", crescent salad	50.00		Tray, 9⅛", hndl., utility	45.00			
Plate, 7½", salad	10.00		Tray, 11½", center hndl.	37.50			

HEIRLOOM, FOSTORIA GLASS COMPANY, 1959 – 1970

Colors: blue, green, pink and yellow opalescent, orange, and red

Heirloom is another Fostoria pattern that is usually misidentified as an opalescent Duncan and Miller pattern. You will find most collectors seek the opalescent colors, but there are admirers for red and orange which Fostoria called Bittersweet. Not all pieces were made in each color; but pricing is so similar right now, I am going to list only one price. If necessary, I can expand the pricing in the future.

I might point out the yellow opalescent tri-candle in the top row on page 102 is technically not a part of this line; but it is collected to go with it so I have put it here. As shown, it consists of an 8" peg vase, three floral/snack bowls and a trundle candle arm which is always crystal. Pricing is obtained by adding the sum of the parts.

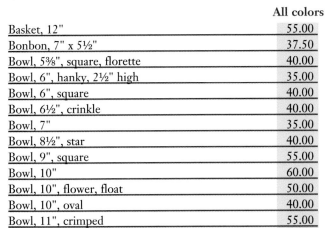

	All colors			All colors
Basket, 12"	55.00		Candle, 3⅞", flora	35.00
Bonbon, 7" x 5½"	37.50		Candle, 6"	50.00
Bowl, 5⅜", square, florette	40.00		Epergne, 6½" high x 5" wide	150.00
Bowl, 6", hanky, 2½" high	35.00		Epergne, 9½" high x 16" wide	225.00
Bowl, 6", square	40.00		Plate, 8"	30.00
Bowl, 6½", crinkle	40.00		Plate, 11"	55.00
Bowl, 7"	35.00		Plate, 17"	75.00
Bowl, 8½", star	40.00		Trindle candle arm (crystal)	25.00
Bowl, 9", square	55.00		Vase, 4½", handled	100.00
Bowl, 10"	60.00		Vase, 6"	25.00
Bowl, 10", flower, float	50.00		Vase, 8", peg	35.00
Bowl, 10", oval	40.00		Vase, 9", pitcher	100.00
Bowl, 11", crimped	55.00		Vase, 10", candle	75.00
Bowl, 11", shallow	50.00		Vase, 11"	40.00
Bowl, 12", oval centerpiece	60.00		Vase, 11", winged	135.00
Bowl, 15", oblong	75.00		Vase, 18"	150.00
Bowl, 16", oval, centerpiece	110.00		Vase, 20"	150.00
Candle, 3" x 5" flora/snack bowl	25.00		Vase, 24"	200.00
Candle, 3½"	25.00			

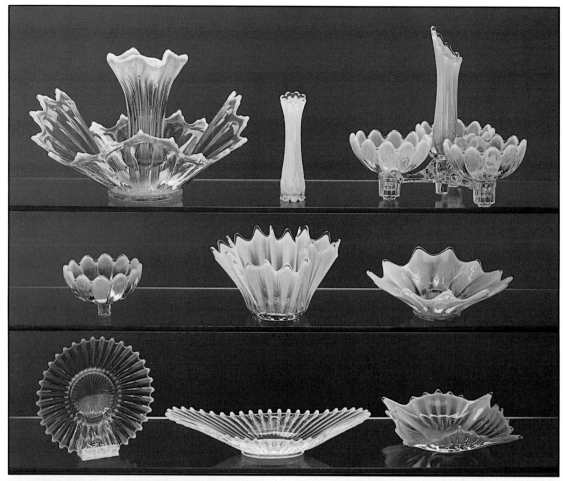

HERITAGE, FEDERAL GLASS COMPANY, 1940 – 1955

Colors: crystal, some pink, blue, green, and cobalt

Heritage is a smaller pattern that has captivated some collectors. It was advertised as late as 1954 in several women's magazines. Right now, prices for crystal creamers, sugars, and 8½" berry bowls have slowed. These are the most frustrating pieces to find. For some reason, the sugar materializes with more consistency than the creamer.

Reproduction berry bowls from several years ago are so crudely made that they are presenting little trouble for collectors. McCrory's and similar stores marketed reproductions of Heritage bowls in the late 1980s. These were made in amber, crystal, and green. Many are marked "MC" in the center. I say "many" because not all reports from readers have mentioned this mark. A recent letter stated his bowl had an "N" mark so possibly these were also made for someone else. In any case, the smaller berry bowls sold three for $1.00 and the larger for $1.59 each. The pattern on these pieces is crude and should not fool anyone. Sparsely designed hobs on the reproductions are easy to see when compared to the fully designed hobs on the original. The green reproduction is much darker and closer to the 1970s avocado green. Notice the Depression green of the original bowl in the photo. Federal never made Heritage in amber.

Authentic pink, blue, and green berry bowls remain in short supply. These are indisputably rare. It is a shame that only berry bowl sets were made in these colors. The cobalt blue bowl is the only one of that color known.

Crystal Heritage sets can be amassed more easily than many other patterns given that there are so few pieces. There are only ten separate objects to find. The only limitation you have is how many place settings you wish to own. Thankfully, you only have to find one creamer and one 8½" berry bowl no matter how many place settings you collect. Some collectors are buying several of the larger fruit bowls and ignoring the harder to find smaller berry bowl all together.

Refer to "Daisy" (page 50) for an explanation of Indiana's green Heritage pattern.

	Crystal	Pink	Blue Green
Bowl, 5", berry	8.00	80.00	90.00
Bowl, 8½", large berry	35.00	210.00	295.00
Bowl, 10½", fruit	16.00		
Cup	6.00		
Creamer, footed	25.00		
Plate, 8", luncheon	7.00		
Plate, 9¼", dinner	12.00		
Plate, 12", sandwich	15.00		
Saucer	2.00		
Sugar, open, footed	22.50		

white

Enjoy this large collection of Fenton's Hobnail which was graciously made available to us to photograph by collectors from Illinois. This wonderful lady's husband is always protesting (tongue in cheek) how much he dislikes it — though he's bought pieces for the collection. So, when we spotted a plastic Hobnail kitchen clock at a market which looked something like this pattern, we gave it to him as a gag gift and much hilarity ensued. In any case, lending wonderful collections such as this for photography purposes is greatly appreciated.

Measurements were taken as we photographed this collection and not all these agree with catalog listings. Watch for this Fenton's Hobnail is gathering new devotees all the time and right now, you can find this at markets, often for less than its worth. Do check for damage to the pieces, however, since it is frequently found with some.

Item	Price
Apothecary jar, 11", w/cover, #3689	135.00
Ashtray, 3¼" x 4½", rectangular, #3693	10.00
Ashtray, 3½", round, #3972	6.00
Ashtray, 4", ball, #3648	35.00
Ashtray, 4", octagon, #3876	10.00
Ashtray, 5", round, #3973	10.00
Ashtray, 5", square, #3679	17.50
Ashtray, 5¼", octagon, #3877	10.00
Ashtray, 6½", octagon, #3878	12.00
Ashtray, 6½", pipe w/center flower, #3773	55.00
Ashtray, 6½", round, #3776	10.00
Basket, 4" x 6", 4-ftd., oval, #3634	25.00
Basket, 4½", #3834	17.50
Basket, 5½" x 5½", double crimped, #3735	15.50
Basket, 5¾", 1¾" base, #3336	22.00
Basket, 6½" x 4½", oval, two-hndl., #838	25.00
Basket, 6½" x 7½", double crimped, #3736	27.50
Basket, 7" x 7", deep, #3637	65.00
Basket, 7½" x 7", #3837	27.50
Basket, 8" x 7¾", 3" base, #3032	30.00
Basket, 8", 2¼" diameter base, #3335	30.00
Basket, 8½", double crimped, #3638	30.00
Basket, 10", #3830	50.00
Basket, 10½" x 11½", deep, #3734	55.00
Basket, 13" x 7", oval, #3839	65.00
Bell, 5½", #3645	15.00
Bell, 6", #3667	25.00
Bell, 6¾", #3067	18.00
Bonbon, 5" x 2½", two-hndl., #3935	20.00
Bonbon, 5" x 2", #3630	15.00
Bonbon, 5" x 2¾", star, #3921	12.00
Bonbon, 6" x 1⅝", double crimped, #3926	10.00
Bonbon, 7" x 2½", two-hndl., #3937	15.00
Bonbon, 8" x 2¼", #3716	18.00
Bonbon, 8" x 5½", #3706	20.00
Boot, 4", #3992	14.00
Bottle, vanity, 5⅜", w/stopper, #3865	50.00
Bowl, 4", berry, square, #3928	18.00
Bowl, 4", candle orifice, #3873	22.50
Bowl, 5", cereal, 2" high, #3719	80.00
Bowl, 5½" x 6¾", candy, ribbon top, #3730	90.00
Bowl, 5½", rose, #3022	20.00
Bowl, 6" x 6", octagonal, peanut, #3627	18.50
Bowl, 6½", candle orifice, #3872	17.50

Item	Price
Bowl, 7", double crimped, #3927	12.50
Bowl, 7½", candle, ftd., 5" high, #3971	60.00
Bowl, 8", 3-toed, #3635	22.00
Bowl, 8", candle, double crimped, #3771	27.50
Bowl, 8", double crimped, #3639	30.00
Bowl, 8", oval, #3625	25.00
Bowl, 8½", console, rippled top, #3724	70.00
Bowl, 9", cupped, #3735	135.00
Bowl, 9", double crimped, 5" high, #3924	22.50
Bowl, 9", oval, ftd., #3621	60.00
Bowl, 9", scalloped/flared, #3626	60.00
Bowl, 9", square, #3929	65.00
Bowl, 9½", chip n' dip candle, #3924	25.00
Bowl, 10", ftd., double crimped, #3731	40.00
Bowl, 10¼", shallow, #3622	55.00
Bowl, 10½", #3623	85.00
Bowl, 10½", double crimped, #3624	30.00
Bowl, 10½", ftd., crimped, #3723	35.00
Bowl, 11", 3 holes for hanging, #3705	145.00
Bowl, 12" x 5", banana, #3620	40.00
Bowl, 12" x 7", banana, #3720	45.00
Bowl, 12", double crimped, #3938	25.00
Butter and cheese, 4¼", w/8" plate, cover, #3677	160.00
Butter, ¼ lb., oval, 7¾" x 3¾", #3777	35.00
Butter, ¼ lb., rectangular, 7½" x 2⅛", #3977	30.00
Cake plate, 12⅞" x 5", pie crust crimped edge, #3913	50.00
Candleholder, 2" x 5", pr., #3670	28.00
Candleholder, 2¾" x 4¼", ftd., pr., #3673	45.00
Candleholder, 3", flat, ruffled edge, pr., #3974	30.00
Candleholder, 3½", cornucopia, pr., #3971	70.00
Candleholder, 3½", hndl., pr., #3870	50.00
Candleholder, 3½", rounded, flared top, pr., #3974	30.00
Candleholder, 3½", single, ruffled edge, pr., #3770	90.00
Candleholder, 5½", 2-light, pr., #3672	125.00
Candleholder, 6½", cornucopia, pr., #3874	57.50
Candleholder, 6", pr., #3674	30.00
Candleholder, 7", #3745	40.00
Candleholder, 8", crescent, pr., #3678	175.00
Candleholder, 10", pr., #3774	65.00
Candy box, 5¼", shoe w/cover, #3700	35.00
Candy box, 6", w/cover, #3600	35.00
Candy box, 6", w/cover, 6" diameter, #3984	60.00
Candy box, 6¾", w/cover, #3886	35.00
Candy box, 8⅛", w/cover, ftd., #3784	45.00
Candy dish, 6½" x 4¾", #3668	45.00
Candy dish, 6½" x 6½", #3668	45.00
Candy dish, 6½", heart, #3033	22.50
Candy jar, 5¼", w/cover, #3883	32.00
Candy jar, 6½", w/cover, 4½" wide, #3688	45.00
Candy jar, 7½", w/cover, #3688	45.00
Candy jar, 8½", ftd., w/pointed knob cover, #3885	38.50
Candy jar, 8½", ftd., w/rounded knob cover, #3887	35.00
Celery, 12", #3739	100.00
Chip n' dip, 12¼" x 3¼" bowl w/division, #3922	250.00
Comport, #3703	45.00
Cigarette box, 4¼", sq., #3685	35.00
Cigarette lighter 2¼", cube, #3692	25.00
Comport, 3¾", double crimped, #3727	17.50
Comport, 5½", double crimped, #3920	86.00
Comport, 5¼", double crimped, #3728	16.00
Comport, 6" x 5½", octagonal stem, #3628	18.00
Cookie jar, 11", w/lid, #3680	110.00
Creamer, 2⅛", plain hndl. and edge, #3900	10.00
Creamer, 3½", plain hndl., #3901	10.00
Creamer, 3½", scalloped edge, #3708	17.50
Creamer, 3", beaded hndl. and edge, #3665	20.00
Creamer, 3", beaded hndl. and ruffled edge, #3702	25.00
Creamer, 3", star shaped edge, #3906	12.50
Creamer, 4", #3606	10.00
Creamer, 4¾", scalloped edge, #3902	22.50
Cruet, 7¾", #3863	50.00
Cup, child's, #489	60.00
Decanter, 12", hndl., w/stopper, #3761	250.00
Egg cup, 4", #3647	65.00
Epergne candle, 2" high x 5" wide, petite, #3671	40.00
Epergne candle, 6" wide, for 7" candleholder, #3746	70.00
Epergne set, 6½", 2-pc., 7" horn, #3704	75.00
Epergne set, 6½", 4-pc., 6" tri-horns, #3801	50.00
Epergne set, 9½", 4-pc., 8" tri-horns, #3701	50.00
Epergne set, 9", 5-pc. (#3920 comport, frog, 5" tri-horns), #3800	200.00
Fairy light, 4½", 2-pc., #3608	15.00
Fairy light, 8½", 3-pc., #3804	85.00
Goblet, 3⅞", 3 oz., wine, #3843	15.00
Goblet, 4½", 4 oz., wine, #3843	14.00
Goblet, 5⅝", 8 oz., water, #3845	12.50
Hat, 2⅝", burred, #3991	15.00
Hat, 2⅝", plain, #3991	25.00
Jam & jelly set, 2 4¾" jars, lid, ladle, double crimped chrome hndl. tray, #3915	45.00
Jam set, 4 pc., 4¾" jar, lid, label, and 6" crimped saucer, #3903	50.00
Jar, 5", jam w/spoon and lid, #3601	35.00
Jar, 7¼", honey, round, ftd., w/cover, #3886	65.00
Jardiniere, 4½", scalloped, #3994	12.00
Jardiniere, 5½", scalloped, #3898	35.00
Jardiniere, 6", scalloped, 6" diameter, #3898	35.00
Jelly, 5½" x 4½", #3725	30.00
Kettle, 2½", 3-toed, 3" diameter, #3990	14.00
Lamp, 8", hurricane, hndl. base, scalloped top, #3998	65.00
Lamp, 9", courting, electric, crimped top, #3713	135.00
Lamp, 9", courting, oil, crimped top, #3713	135.00
Lamp, 11", hurricane, crimped top, #3713	115.00
Lamp, 19", student, crimped top, #3707	250.00
Lamp, 21", student, double crimped top, #3807	225.00
Lamp, 22", Gone with the Wind, #3808	250.00
Lamp, 22½", student, w/prisms, #1174	235.00
Lamp, 26", double crimped, pillar, #3907	210.00
Lavabo, 3-pc. (urn w/lid and basin), #3867	120.00
Margarine tub, 5¼", #3802	22.00
Mayonnaise set, 3-pc., bowl, 6" ruffled saucer, ladle, #3803	30.00
Mustard jar, 3½", w/spoon and lid, #3605	35.00
Mustard jar, 3½", w/spoon and lid, #3889	18.00
Mustard, 3⅝", kettle, #3979	20.00
Napkin ring, 2" diameter, #3904	35.00
Nut dish, 2½" x 4¾", #3650	58.00
Nut dish, 2½" x 5", #3729	45.00
Nut dish, 2¾" x 4", ftd., #3631	35.00
Nut dish, 5" x 3¼", oval, #3732	20.00
Nut dish, 5" x 5½", ftd., #3629	17.00
Nut dish, 7" x 3½", oval, #3633	14.00
Oil, 4¾", w/stopper, #3869	15.00
Oil, 8", w/stopper, #3767	55.00
Pickle, 8" x 4", oval, #3640	15.00
Pitcher, 5¼", squat, 4" diameter top, #3965	40.00
Pitcher, 7", #3365	32.00
Pitcher, 7¾", 80 oz., no ice lip (fat neck), #3967	130.00
Pitcher, 8", 54 oz., no ice lip (fat neck), #3764	70.00

HOBNAIL

Item	Price
Pitcher, 9½", w/ice lip, 70 oz., #3664	60.00
Pitcher, 11", #3360	65.00
Planter, 4½", square, scalloped top, #3699	14.00
Planter, 8½" long, scalloped top, #3690	20.00
Planter, 8", crescent, 4-ftd., #3798	30.00
Planter, 9½" long, scalloped top, #3690	32.00
Planter, 9" wall, #3836	57.50
Planter, 10" long, rectangular box, #3799	30.00
Planter, 10", crescent, 4-ftd., #3698	50.00
Plate, 8½", round, pie crust crimped edge, #3912	28.00
Plate, 8¼", round, pie crust crimped edge, #3816	28.00
Plate, 13½", crimped edge, #3714	55.00
Plate, 16", torte, #3817	70.00
Powder box, 6½", round w/lid, #3880	60.00
Puff box, 4½", round, #3885	75.00
Punch base, 3¾" x 8½", #3778	100.00
Punch bowl, 10½" x 5¼", plain edge, #3827	260.00
Punch bowl, 11¼" x 6½", octagon, #3820	465.00
Punch bowl, 15" x 7½", crimped edge, #3722	325.00
Punch cup, 2½" x 3", octagonal, #3840	20.00
Punch cup, 2¼" x 2¾", #3847	15.00
Punch ladle, #9520	55.00
Punch ladle (crystal), #9527	30.00
Relish, 5¼" x 7½", 3-part, #3607	35.00
Relish, 7½", 3-sections, #3822	16.00
Relish, 7½", non divided, #3822	50.00
Relish, 7½", scalloped, 3-sections, #3822	16.00
Relish, 8½", heart-shaped, #3733	25.00
Relish, 12⅜", 3-sections, #3740	35.00
Salt & pepper, 3", flat, pr., #3806	20.00
Salt & pepper, 3¾", pr., #3609	25.00
Salt & pepper, 4¼", pr., #3602	40.00
Salt dip, 2⅜" x 2¼" x ⅜", shell shape, #9496	45.00
Server, 10", two-tier, 12" bowl & 3-section top, #3709	50.00
Shaker, 4¾", cinnamon sugar, #3797	135.00
Sherbet, 4", #3825	15.00
Slipper, 5", kitten head and paws, #3995	10.00
Spoon holder, 7¼" long, #3612	115.00
Stein, 6¾", 14 oz., #3646	110.00
Sugar, 2⅛", plain handle and edge, #3900	10.00
Sugar, 3", beaded handle and edge, #3665	20.00
Sugar, 3", beaded handle and ruffled edge, #3702	25.00
Sugar, 3", star-shaped edge, #3906	12.50
Sugar, 3½", plain handle, #3901	10.00
Sugar, 3½", scalloped edge, #3708	17.50
Sugar, 4¾", scalloped edge, #3902	22.50
Sugar, 5¾", w/lid, #3606	12.50
Syrup pitcher, 5¼", 12 oz., #3660	35.00
Syrup pitcher, 5¾", 12 oz., #3762	30.00
Tidbit, two-tier, 13½" and 8½", #3794	55.00
Toothpick, 2¾", #3895	40.00
Toothpick, 3", #3795	12.00
Tray, 7½" x 3¾", oil/mustard, #3715	15.00
Tray, 7¾", chrome handle, #3879	25.00
Tray, 12½" x 7", vanity, #3775	100.00
Tray, 13½" sandwich w/metal handle, #3791	55.00
Tumbler, 3½", 5 oz., flat, #3945	12.00
Tumbler, 4¾", 9 oz. flat, #3949	15.00
Tumbler, 5", 12 oz., iced tea, #3942	18.50
Tumbler, 5", 12 oz., iced tea, barrel shape, #3947	37.50
Tumbler, 5¾", iced tea, ftd., #3842	38.50
Tumbler, 6", 16 oz., flat, #3946	50.00
Urn, 11", covered, #3986	185.00
Vanity bottle, 7⅛", 3-pc., #3986	235.00
Vase, 2¼", violet, ribbon crimped, #3754	35.00
Vase, 3", crimped, #3855	12.50
Vase, 3¾", double crimped, #3850	10.00
Vase, 4", 3¾" diameter, #3952	10.00
Vase, 4", 4¾" diameter, #3775	50.00
Vase, 4", fan, pie crust edge, #3953	12.50
Vase, 4½", double crimped, #3854	15.00
Vase, 5", 3-toed, #3654	12.50
Vase, 5", double crimped, #3850	17.50
Vase, 5", scalloped, #3655	17.50
Vase, 5½", double crimped, #3656	30.00
Vase, 5½", ivy ball, ruffled, ped. ft., #3726	20.00
Vase, 5¾", ivy, ribbed, ped. ft., #3757	20.00
Vase, 6", double crimped, #3856	20.00
Vase, 6", double crimped, #3954	25.00
Vase, 6", ftd., swung, handkerchief, #3651	40.00
Vase, 6", hand, #3355	30.00
Vase, 6¼", 3" diameter base, fan, #3957	22.00
Vase, 6¼", 5" diameter, double crimped, #3954	25.00
Vase, 6½", ftd., swung, handkerchief, #3651	50.00
Vase, 6½", swung, handkerchief, #3750	22.50
Vase, 7½", handkerchief, #3657	22.50
Vase, 8", 4" diameter base, fan, #3959	40.00
Vase, 8", bud, ftd., swung, #3756	18.00
Vase, 8", double crimped, 3½" diameter, #3859	55.00
Vase, 8", double crimped, 6½" diameter, #3958	28.00
Vase, 8", double crimped, 6¼" diameter, #3858	50.00
Vase, 8½" fan, #3852	150.00
Vase, 8½", Jack in the Pulpit, #3356	28.00
Vase, 9", #3659	55.00
Vase, 9", swung, #3755	50.00
Vase, 10", swung, ftd., bud, #3950	15.00
Vase, 10", swung, handkerchief, #3855	40.00
Vase, 11", double crimped, #3752	40.00
Vase, 12", 3-toed, #3658	175.00
Vase, 12", swung, ftd., 2½" diameter, #3758	25.00
Vase, 12", swung, ftd., 3¼" diameter, #3753	27.50
*Vase, 14", swung, handkerchief, #3755	50.00
*Vase, 14", swung, pitcher, 3¼" diameter, #3750	50.00
Vase, 18", ftd., 3¼" diameter, #3753	47.50
Vase, 24", swung, #3652	37.50

* size varies upward

Colors: Pink, iridescent; some Shell Pink and crystal

Holiday, or "Buttons and Bows" as many collectors still refer to it, can be a frustrating pattern to collect due to all the mould variations made by Jeannette. There are three styles of cup and saucer. One style cup and saucer has plain centers. These are easy to match. Two other cup styles have a rayed center. You cannot mix these since one cup's base size of 2" will only fit a 2⅛" cup ring and the 2⅜" cup base will only fit a 2½" saucer ring. Two styles of 10 ounce tumblers occur. One is flat bottomed and the other has a small raised foot and is narrower at the bottom. Two styles of sherbets are known. One has a rayed foot while the other is plain. Two distinct sherbet plates have 2¾" centers, but one has a beaded effect in the center, while the other has a center ring with a diamond effect. Mould variations occur in nearly all patterns, but Holiday's variations are especially unsettling for collectors. It is okay to mix styles.

Holiday was a well liked pattern in the late 1940s, and well used, judging by the wealth of damaged pieces I have found in sets over the years. Be sure to examine the underside of the edges. Pointed edges are prone to chips, nicks, and "chigger bites," an auction term that varies from place to place. A small chip to one person is a giant chip to someone else. Remember that damaged glass cannot be "almost mint." Prices listed here are for mint condition glassware.

I remember when $10.00 seemed like a high price for the Holiday 6" footed tumblers and now $165.00 is the asking price. They were not easily found when they were $10.00, but today's prices deter many collectors from owning them. There is a crystal tumbler out there sporting an enlarged version of this design that might suffice should you be able to find enough of them. Holiday cake plates, candlesticks, and console bowls remain tricky items to grab. Many of these have been chipped and chunked over the years. If you are flabbergasted by how such recently manufactured (relatively speaking) glassware could have so many hard-to-find pieces, we now know the iced teas went to the Philippines and some to Australia. One came free with a six pack of a famous chocolate candy bar sold to soldiers in the Philippines; and a pretty glass, even a free one, is not exactly what a soldier would want to keep toting in his gear.

Some collectors, to enhance their sets, buy iridescent pieces of Holiday. Only four different iridized pieces were made; and only the sandwich tray is not pictured.

	Pink	Crystal	Iridescent
Bowl, 5⅛", berry	12.50		
Bowl, 7¾", soup	60.00		
Bowl, 8½", large berry	35.00		
Bowl, 9½", oval vegetable	30.00		
*Bowl, 10¾", console	145.00		
Butter dish and cover	50.00		
Butter dish bottom	10.00		
Butter dish top	40.00		
Cake plate, 10½", 3-legged	135.00		
Candlesticks, 3" pr.	130.00		
Creamer, footed	10.00		
Cup, three sizes	7.00		
Pitcher, 4¾", 16 oz., milk	70.00	15.00	25.00
Pitcher, 6¾", 52 oz.	40.00		

	Pink	Crystal	Iridescent
Plate, 6", sherbet	6.00		
Plate, 9", dinner	20.00		
Plate, 13¾", chop	125.00		
Platter, 11⅜", oval	20.00		12.50
Sandwich tray, 10½"	15.00		15.00
Saucer, 3 styles	4.00		
Sherbet, 2 styles	8.00		
Sugar	10.00		
Sugar cover	18.00		
Tumbler, 4", 10 oz., flat	25.00		
Tumbler, 4", footed, 5 oz.	52.50		10.00
Tumbler, 4¼", footed, 5¼ oz.		8.00	
Tumbler, 6", footed	165.00		

* Shell Pink $45.00

HOLLY, CUTTING #815, FOSTORIA GLASS COMPANY, 1942 – 1980

Color: crystal

Holly was made for almost 40 years, ample evidence that many brides chose this Fostoria pattern over Navarre and Meadow Rose. That choice has today's collectors searching to complete partial family sets or simply purchasing it because they, too, love the pattern. Holly cuttings are found on many of Fostoria's mould blanks as you can see from the listing. Its cut band is distinctive and easily identified. If you are trying to find a full set, you will have two sizes of tumblers and eight different stems to contend with; and those are the more easily found items. As with virtually all elegant patterns of that time, stemware was purchased to accent china patterns so more stems are found today. "Food just looks better on solid, colored dishes than it does on crystal," said an older, elegantly dressed lady recently when I asked if she had any pieces other than stemware in her Fostoria pattern. She informed me that she never wanted any glass dishes to go with her Bavarian china. Basic Holly dinnerware and serving items are scarce now because of this. As with many Fostoria patterns, the dinner plates are only 9½" and some collectors frown on that small size for serving. There are no service plates, as in Cambridge wares, to use for a large dinner. The 11" sandwich would be too large unless there are teenagers involved; and then that size would be about right.

Fostoria referred to the Holly double candlestick as a duo. I asked one lady what she collected as she perused books at my table and she replied, "Interesting miniature pieces, which don't take up much room in my display cabinet." You can see the #2364 ashtray and cigarette holder pictured in Buttercup. They would fit her collecting criteria. These little items are rarely found, but increasingly sought by collectors of ashtrays or smoking items, or by a growing cadre of miniature item collectors. By the way, some companies used ashtray as one word and others as two. I am trying to be consistent with catalog listings and not inconsistent in spellings within the book.

That individual creamer and sugar on the Contour blank are rarely found with Holly cutting.

Ashtray, #2364, 2⅝", individual	22.00	Plate, #2337, 8½", luncheon	12.50
Bowl, #1769, finger	30.00	Plate, #2337, 9½", dinner	35.00
Bowl, #2364, 5", fruit	12.00	Plate, #2364, 11", sandwich	30.00
Bowl, #2364, 8", rimmed soup	35.00	Plate, #2364, 14", torte	50.00
Bowl, #2364, 9", salad	30.00	Plate, #2364, 16", torte	85.00
Bowl, #2364, baked apple	15.00	Plate, #2364, cracker	28.00
Bowl, #6023, 9", ftd.	55.00	Relish, #2364, 8¼", two-part	20.00
Bowl, #2364, 12", flared	35.00	Relish, #2364, 10", three-part	25.00
Bowl, #2364, 12", lily pond	35.00	Saucer, #2350	3.00
Bowl, #2364, 13", fruit	40.00	Shaker, #2364, 2⅝", individual pr.	45.00
Candlestick, #2324, 4"	20.00	Shaker, #2364, 3¼", pr.	45.00
Candlestick, #6023, 5½", duo	30.00	Stem, #6030, 3⅞", 1 oz., cordial	38.00
Celery, #2364, 11"	25.00	Stem, #6030, 3¾", 4 oz., oyster cocktail	14.00
Cheese comport, #2364, ftd.	22.00	Stem, #6030, 4⅜", 6 oz., low sherbet	10.00
Cigarette holder, #2364, 2" high	30.00	Stem, #6030, 5¼", 3½ oz., cocktail	11.00
Comport, #6030, 5"	25.00	Stem, #6030, 5⅝", 6 oz., high sherbet	11.00
Comport, #2364, 8"	35.00	Stem, #6030, 6", 3½ oz., claret/wine	24.00
Cream, #2350½, 3¼"	15.00	Stem, #6030, 6⅜", 10 oz., low goblet	16.00
Cream, #2666, ind.	20.00	Stem, #6030, 7⅞", 10 oz., water goblet	22.00
Cup, #2350½	10.00	Sugar, #21350½, 3⅛"	15.00
Ladle, mayonnaise	10.00	Sugar, 2666, ind.	20.00
Mayonnaise, #2364, 5"	30.00	Tray, #2364, 11¼", center hndl.	33.00
Pickle, #2364, 8", oval	22.00	Tray, #2666, individual sug/cr (no cutting)	15.00
Pitcher, #2666, 32 oz.	85.00	Tumbler, #6030, 4⅝", 5 oz., juice, ftd.	15.00
Pitcher, #6011, 53 oz., 8⅞", ftd. jug	225.00	Tumbler, #6030, 6", 12 oz., iced tea, ftd.	20.00
Plate, #2337, 6", dessert	5.00	Vase, #2619½, 6"	65.00
Plate, #2364, 6¾", mayonnaise	10.00	Vase, #2619½, 7½"	90.00
Plate, #2337, 7½", salad	10.00	Vase, #2619½, 9½"	125.00

HORIZON, #2650 LINE, FOSTORIA GLASS COMPANY, 1951 – 1958

Colors: crystal, Cinnamon, Spruce Green

Horizon was only made for eight years by Fostoria and it is beginning to gather some notice from collectors. It is beguilingly 50s-looking, with its wavy form and earthy tones. The brown and green colors were called Cinnamon and Spruce Green by the manufacturer.

Merchandise from the 50s is trendy, today, as people recall their childhood memories; and though I don't know the particular designer for Horizon, many of the wares from this time period were designed by persons who are now very familiar names to the art world. If this vaguely ultramodern styling is your forte, you'd better collect it before the supply runs out.

	All colors
Bowl, #5650, 2⅝" high, dessert/finger	10.00
Bowl, 4½", fruit	7.00
Bowl, 5", cereal	13.00
Bowl, 8½", salad	20.00
Bowl, 10½", salad	25.00
Bowl, 11½", four-part, server	25.00
Bowl, 12", two-handled, server	32.00
Candy, 5", w/cover	28.00
Coaster	10.00
Cream, 3½"	12.00
Cup, 8½ oz.	10.00
Mayonnaise, 3-pc. set	25.00

	All colors
Plate, 7", salad	8.00
Plate, 10", dinner	17.00
Plate, 11", sandwich	18.00
Plate, 14", torte	22.00
Platter, 12", oval	25.00
Relish, 12", three-part	25.00
Saucer	2.00
Sugar, 3⅛"	12.00
Tumbler, #5650, 3⅜", juice/cocktail	6.00
Tumbler, #5650, 3⅜", sherbet/old fashioned	8.00
Tumbler, #5650, 5", water/scotch & soda	9.00
Tumbler, #5650, 6", iced tea/highball	12.00

IRIS, "IRIS AND HERRINGBONE," JEANNETTE GLASS COMPANY, 1928 – 1932; 1950s;

Colors: Crystal, iridescent; some pink and green; recently bi-colored red/yellow and blue/green combinations, and white

The reproduction shysters are thumping our much-loved Iris. Don't panic; as has happened with other patterns, this, too, shall pass. Reproduced dinner plates and iced teas from Taiwan hit the market two years ago. Since then, coasters and flat tumblers have been remade and there are constant reports, right now, of cereal and soup bowls turning up. I have not been able to confirm either of these last items being remade, but it wouldn't surprise me. All the new crystal is exceedingly clear. If you place old crystal Iris on a white tablecloth or paper, it will look gray or even slightly yellow. The new is very crystal without a tinge of color of any sort. The flat tumblers have no herringbone on the bottom — just Iris. The coaster is more than half full of glass when you look from the side. These repros (with photos) are discussed in detail in the reproduction section of *Collector's Encyclopedia of Depression Glass*.

Would you believe a bright yellow Iris sugar bowl to go with the pink and green are found occasionally? One was found and brought into a Texas show recently. I first thought it was sprayed on yellow, but it is not. Most interesting is where it was found — Australia. I wasn't fond of the price, but I had to own it for future books.

Original crystal production for Iris began in 1928. Some was made in the late 1940s and 1950s; candy bottoms and vases appeared as late as the 1970s. Iridescent Iris belongs lock, stock, and barrel within the time makeup of this book. Jeannette made crystal candy bottoms and flashed them with two-tone colors such as red and yellow or blue and green in the 1970s. Many of these were sold as vases; and, over time, the colors have peeled off or been purposely stripped to make them crystal candy bottoms once more. These later pieces have no rays on the foot. Similarly, white vases were made and sprayed outside with green, red, and blue. Opaque white vases sell in the ballpark of $15.00. Yes, the colors can be removed. These are not rare. I have seen a pink painted over white vase in an antique mall for $90.00 marked as rare pink Iris. Rare Iris is transparent pink. Good transparent pink coloring will bring the price below, but lightly colored pink will not.

The 11" flat fruit bowl is turning up with several variations of rolled edges depending upon how far the edge was rolled downward.

Prices for crystal Iris have finally stabilized though somewhat softened due to the furor created by the first reproductions. This is especially true for iced teas, dinner plates, coasters, and flat tumblers. We have been through this with other patterns over the years and it will take a while for collectors to adjust. Prices plateau or drop slightly for a while, and then they start an upward march again. As prices increase, collectors who have sets observe these higher prices and begin to sell their wares and rare items once again appear for sale. Right now, some dealers are stocked with hard-to-find cereals, soups, and demitasse sets, which they rushed to buy from the last spiral. These are not selling well in the newer price zone. Bargains might be obtained on these.

The Internet has opened up a world that has both good and bad aspects to collecting. Bad is that the reproduced items get on there first, being represented as old wares and a few people pay high prices before word flashes worldwide in collecting circles. The good side is that there are many people auctioning pieces that collectors rarely see. An Internet address where the merchandise is guaranteed is best if you are worried about your purchases. I suggest www.glassshow.com as one of the best for dealers who stand behind their merchandise and will not sell known reproductions as old.

The 8 ounce water goblet, 5¾", 4 ounce goblet, 4" sherbet, and the demitasse cup and saucer are the most difficult pieces to find in iridescent. The 5¾" four ounce goblet is shown in the *Very Rare Glassware of the Depression Era, 4th Series*. Recently two more of these rare goblets (that were originally found at a yard sale south of Houston) were sold. Three iridescent 4" sherbets were also found in Texas. That may be the place to go to find rare iridescent Iris.

Note the odd Iris berry bowl pictured. Somebody forgot to ruffle one side while it was hot, so it is smooth on one side and ruffled on the other.

IRIS, "IRIS AND HERRINGBONE"

	Crystal	Iridescent	Green/ Pink
Bowl, 4½", berry, beaded edge	40.00	8.00	
Bowl, 5", ruffled, sauce	10.00	22.00	
Bowl, 5", cereal	110.00		
Bowl, 7½", soup	155.00	60.00	
Bowl, 8", berry, beaded edge	80.00	25.00	
Bowl, 9½", ruffled, salad	14.00	13.00	200.00
Bowl, 11½", ruffled, fruit	15.00	14.00	
Bowl, 11", fruit, straight edge	60.00		
Butter dish and cover	47.50	45.00	
Butter dish bottom	12.50	12.50	
Butter dish top	35.00	32.50	
Candlesticks, pr.	42.50	45.00	
Candy jar and cover	185.00		
*** Coaster	90.00		
Creamer, ftd.	12.00	12.00	150.00
Cup	15.00	14.00	
* Demitasse cup	45.00	150.00	
* Demitasse saucer	145.00	250.00	
Fruit or nut set	110.00	150.00	
Goblet, 4", wine		25.00	

	Crystal	Iridescent	Green/ Pink
Goblet, 4½", 4 oz., cocktail	22.00		
Goblet, 4½", 3 oz., wine	15.00		
Goblet, 5½", 4 oz.	24.00	395.00	
Goblet, 5½", 8 oz.	24.00	295.00	
** Lampshade, 11½"	90.00		
Pitcher, 9½", ftd.	40.00	42.50	
Plate, 5½", sherbet	13.00	11.00	
Plate, 8", luncheon	100.00		
*** Plate, 9", dinner	48.00	45.00	
Plate, 11¾", sandwich	35.00	30.00	
Saucer	8.00	9.00	
Sherbet, 2½", ftd.	26.00	15.00	
Sherbet, 4", ftd.	24.00	295.00	
Sugar	11.00	11.00	150.00
Sugar cover	12.00	12.00	
*** Tumbler, 4", flat	130.00		
Tumbler, 6", ftd.	18.00	18.00	20.00
*** Tumbler, 6½", ftd.	26.00		
Vase, 9"	30.00	25.00	225.00

*Ruby, blue, amethyst priced as iridescent
**Colors: $65.00
***Has been reproduced

JAMESTOWN, FOSTORIA GLASS COMPANY, 1958 – 1982

Colors: amber, amethyst, blue, brown, crystal, green, pink, and red

My record of pieces came from a couple of different Fostoria catalogs. The line numbers on each stem in those catalogs have two diverse dimensions and capacities listed. That is one of the many things that creates something of a conundrum writing a book. Which statistics do you use? I have recorded both stem listings for the perfectionists. Either someone measured incorrectly one year or the sizes were actually changed. I don't believe those half ounces and eighth inches are going to make much difference in the overall scheme of things. I have referred to this problem before in the measurements section of the *Collector's Encyclopedia of Depression Glass*. Accordingly, your measurements could differ from those I have listed, so don't be too shocked.

Stems are available in Jamestown; serving pieces are scarcely found. Amber or brown Jamestown is not hunted by many collectors. Fostoria did not produce serving items for the same manufacturing span as the stemware line; that leaves both collectors and dealers scrounging for those. I have finally determined that not every piece was made in each color. I have grouped colors into three pricing groups based upon sales information. You may find prices for amber and brown even less than those listed. If you are looking for either of those colors, ask dealers for them and you might get a real bargain.

In the middle pricing group, crystal is most in demand, but green is beginning to close the gap. You might find some good buys in amethyst Jamestown since it sometimes is mistaken for Moroccan Amethyst.

Ruby Jamestown has always sold well, but there is not a complete line of Ruby. Pink and blue Jamestown are selling better than Ruby at the present. A distasteful note for collectors is that Ruby stemware has once again been made. Newer stems were selling for $16.00 each in outlet stores, which has caused prices to adjust on older Ruby Jamestown stemware. Unhappily, there is little distinction between the old and newly made items. Both older stems and newer ones have three mould lines which I overheard someone touting as a point of distinction. Now that Viking has gone out of business, this problem may be solved since Viking was making this Ruby for Lancaster Colony who bought the Fostoria moulds.

JAMESTOWN

	Amber/Brown	Amethyst/Crystal/Green	Blue/Pink/Ruby
Bowl, 4½", dessert, #2719/421	8.50	14.00	20.00
Bowl, 10", salad, #2719//211	21.00	40.00	55.00
Bowl, 10", two hndl. serving, #2719/648	21.00	50.00	70.00
Butter w/cover, ¼ pound, #2719/300	24.00	45.00	65.00
Cake plate, 9½", hndl., #2719/306	16.00	35.00	45.00
Celery, 9¼", #2719/360	18.00	32.50	40.00
Cream, 3½", ftd., #2719/681	11.00	17.50	25.00
Jelly w/cover, 6⅛", #2719/447	32.50	57.50	80.00
Pickle, 8⅜", #2719/540	21.00	40.00	45.00
Pitcher, 7⁵⁄₁₆", 48 oz., ice jug, #2719/456	50.00	100.00	145.00
Plate, 8", #2719/550	8.50	16.00	23.00
Plate, 14", torte, #2719/567	26.00	42.50	65.00
Relish, 9⅛", 2-part, #2719/620	16.00	32.00	37.50
Salad set, 4-pc. (10" bowl, 14" plate w/wood fork & spoon), #2719/286	55.00	85.00	135.00
Salver, 7" high, 10" diameter, #2719/630	60.00	**130.00	145.00
Sauce dish w/cover, 4½", #2719/635	18.00	35.00	40.00
Shaker, 3½", w/chrome top. pr., #2719/653	26.00	40.00	50.00
Stem, 4⁵⁄₁₆", 4 oz., wine, #2719/26	10.00	20.00	24.00
*Stem, 4¼", 6½ oz., sherbet, #2719/7	6.50	14.00	18.00
*Stem, 4⅛", 7 oz., sherbet, #2719/7	6.50	14.00	18.00
*Stem, 5¾", 9½ oz., goblet, #2719/2	10.00	16.00	18.00
*Stem, 5⅞", 10 oz., goblet, #2719/2	10.00	18.00	18.00
Sugar, 3½", ftd., #2719/679	11.00	17.50	25.00
Tray, 9⅜", hndl. muffin, #2719/726	26.00	45.00	65.00
Tumbler, 4¼", 9 oz., #2719/73	9.00	21.00	25.00
Tumbler, 4¾", 5 oz., juice, #2719/88	9.50	21.00	26.00
Tumbler, 5⅛", 12 oz., #2719/64	9.00	21.00	26.00
Tumbler, 6", 11 oz., ftd. tea, #2719/63	10.00	21.00	25.00
Tumbler, 6", 12 oz., ftd. tea, #2719/63	10.00	21.00	25.00

*Made in recent years
**Green $250.00

KING'S CROWN, THUMBPRINT, LINE NO. 4016, U.S. GLASS (TIFFIN) COMPANY, LATE 1800s – 1960s; INDIANA GLASS COMPANY, 1970s

Colors: crystal, crystal with ruby or cranberry flash, crystal with gold or platinum

I have an e-mail from a reader who says that over 25 different companies made some form of King's Crown pattern and look-alike wares during the past 100 or so years. I doubt a really complete listing will ever be finished. Originally issued as Thumbprint Line No. 4016 by U. S. Glass in the late 1800s, this glassware was still being made by Tiffin in the early 1960s. The Tiffin catalog reprint shown is from 1955. Indiana bought the Tiffin moulds and changed the design somewhat. This listing is mainly concerned with the Tiffin and Indiana wares made after 1940.

You will find additional items, but please realize that many of those could be from an earlier time or a different company. The Tiffin plates seem to have starred designs in the center while the Indiana ones appear to be plain. I have discovered no hard, fast rules in researching this confounding pattern. One of the exhilarating things about King's Crown is that you never know what piece is available around the next corner. Collectors seem to like it all.

King's Crown has been one of the fastest selling patterns that I stock as long as I stay away from the multitude of stems that are available. Unfortunately, stems are what I keep running into and I have had to learn to control buying them no matter how reasonable they are. Buy any of the serving pieces you can find.

Most collectors prefer the deeper red shade of flashing to the lighter shade called cranberry. Cranberry can be seen on the bottom of page 120 with a variety of other colors of King's Crown items that I have found. The pitcher and other purple pieces are Tiffin's Mulberry. There are pieces flashed with gold, platinum, blue, green, yellow, cranberry, or ruby. Most flashed colors are selling for less than ruby, although gold trimmed are not far behind.

Demand makes ruby the desired color. For crystal without flashed-on colors, subtract fifty percent of the prices listed. Gold and platinum decorated products were also made at Indiana.

Take into consideration that amber, avocado green, and iridized carnival colors are all Indiana's production of the late 1970s and 1980s. In 1976, they also made a blue for the Bicentennial. I believe they called it Colonial Blue.

The price on the punch bowl set has doubled in the last few years. Demand for these is almost unimaginable. The 24" plate listed as the party server measures 22½" to 23" on the ones I have measured.

Long-drawn-out thumbprint designs are from the original Tiffin moulds. Some elongated thumbprint styles may have been made at Indiana before they changed the moulds; but if the pieces you have show rounded thumbprints, you definitely have King's Crown made by Indiana. Most Tiffin-made tumblers are flared at the top while Indiana's are straight. Expect to pay less than the prices below for the more recently issued Indiana tumblers. You alone can decide what price you are willing to pay.

KING'S CROWN, THUMBPRINT

	Ruby Flashed		Ruby Flashed
Ashtray, 5¼", square	35.00	Plate, 5", bread/butter	8.00
Bowl, 4", finger	25.00	Plate, 7⅜", mayonnaise liner	12.50
Bowl, 5", mayonnaise	50.00	Plate, 7⅜", salad	14.00
Bowl, 5", divided mayonnaise	70.00	Plate, 9¾", snack w/indent	15.00
Bowl 5¾"	22.00	Plate, 10", dinner	40.00
Bowl, 6", diameter, ftd., wedding or candy	75.00	Plate, 14½", torte	100.00
Bowl, 8¾", 2-hndl., crimped bonbon	100.00	Plate, 24", party	225.00
Bowl, 9¼", salad	85.00	Plate, 24", party server (w/punch ft.)	325.00
Bowl, 10½", ftd., wedding or candy, w/cover	175.00	Punch bowl foot	185.00
Bowl, 11½", 4½" high, crimped	135.00	Punch bowl, 2 styles	775.00
Bowl, 11¼", cone	90.00	Punch cup	15.00
Bowl, 12½", center edge, 3" high	115.00	Punch set, 15-pc., w/foot	1,275.00
Bowl, 12½", flower floater	85.00	Punch set, 15-pc., w/plate	1,050.00
Bowl, crimped, ftd.	115.00	Relish, 14", 5-part	125.00
Bowl, flared, ftd.	100.00	Saucer	8.00
Bowl, straight edge	80.00	Stem, 2 oz., wine	9.00
Cake salver, 12½", ftd.	85.00	Stem, 2¼ oz., cocktail	12.50
Candleholder, sherbet type	30.00	Stem, 4 oz., claret	14.00
Candleholder, 2-lite, 5½"	115.00	Stem, 4 oz., oyster cocktail	14.00
Candy box, 6", flat, w/cover	65.00	Stem, 5½ oz., sundae or sherbet	9.00
Cheese stand	35.00	Stem, 9 oz., water goblet	14.00
Compote, 7¼", 9¾" diameter	65.00	Sugar	22.50
Compote, 7½", 12" diameter, ftd., crimped	135.00	Tumbler, 4 oz., juice, ftd.	12.00
Compote, small, flat	28.00	Tumbler, 4½ oz., juice	14.00
Creamer	22.50	Tumbler, 8½ oz., water	13.00
Cup	8.00	Tumbler, 11 oz., iced tea	14.00
Lazy Susan, 24", 8½" high, w/ball bearing spinner	395.00	Tumbler, 12 oz., iced tea, ftd.	20.00
Mayonnaise, 3-pc. set	85.00	Vase, 9", bud	125.00
Pitcher	215.00	Vase, 12¼", bud	135.00

United States Glass Company
TIFFIN, OHIO
KINGS CROWN
Also known as No. 4016 Thumbprint

Sugar

Cream

5" Bread and Butter Plate

Cup and Saucer

10" Dinner Plate

AVAILABLE PLAIN CRYSTAL, DECORATED CRANBERRY OR RUBY

KINGS CROWN

Goblet 9 oz.

Wine 2 oz.

Juice 4 oz.

Claret 4 oz.

Cocktail 2¼ oz.

Oyster Cocktail 4 oz.

Sundae 5½ oz.

Footed Ice Tea 12 oz.

Ice Tea Tumbler 11 oz.

Water Tumbler 8½ oz.

Juice Tumbler 4½ oz.

Finger Bowl 4″ Diameter

7⅜″ Salad Plate

KINGS CROWN

Center Edge Bowl 12½" Diameter 3" High

2-Lite Candle Holder 5½" High

Footed Fruit Compote 9¾" Diameter 7¼" High

Crimped Bowl 11½" Diameter 4½" High

Cone Bowl 11¼" Diameter 4¾" High

Page 2   AVAILABLE PLAIN CRYSTAL, DECORATED CRANBERRY OR RUBY

KINGS CROWN

Wedding Bowl and Cover
6" Diameter 10½" High

Flower Floater 12½" Diameter

Torte Plate 14" Diameter

Ash Tray 5¼" Square

Footed Cake Salver
12½" Diameter 4¾" High

LIDO, PLATE ETCHING #329, FOSTORIA GLASS COMPANY, 1937 – 1960

Color: crystal, Azure

Fostoria's Lido is collected mostly in crystal. It is not that collectors shun the blue; it's that the Azure is rarely seen and is quite expensive when it is found. You can see an Azure tumbler and an ice bucket on the bottom of page 127 as pattern shots. One collector confided in me that he didn't believe the blue existed until he saw a photo in my book. He had over 150 pieces in crystal, but had never seen the blue. Unless you are extremely fortunate, that picture might be all you ever see in Azure. The tumbler was sold shortly after the photography session, but I have had several collectors inquire about buying it. (By the time you see a picture in the book, it has been a minimum of nine months since that picture was taken. Pictures are just the first step in the book process. It's similar to having a baby time-wise.) Azure was discontinued during World War II. Blue fetches up to double the prices for crystal on hard-to-find items; but basic pieces sell for only a little more than crystal since there are fewer collectors searching for it.

My wife, Cathy, thinks this design looks like fireworks exploding overhead; actually, it's a stemmed plant.

All things considered, this is a sensibly priced Fostoria pattern; but do notice the rarely found, but costly, pitcher in the photo.

All items without a line number listed below are found on Baroque blank #2496. You may find other Lido items than those listed here. Please let me know what you find or own that isn't listed.

	Crystal
Bowl, 4", one hndl., square	14.00
Bowl, 4⅜", one hndl.	14.00
Bowl, 4⅝", one hndl., 3 cornered	14.00
Bowl, 5", one hndl., flared	13.00
Bowl, 6¼", 3 ftd., cupped	22.00
Bowl, 7⅜" 3 ftd., bonbon	17.00
Bowl, 8½", 2 hndl.	40.00
Bowl, 10½", 2 hndl.	45.00
Bowl, 12", flared	50.00
Bowl, 12½", oval, #2545 "Flame"	55.00
Bowl, finger, #766	25.00
Candlestick, 4½", duo	35.00
Candlestick, 4"	20.00
Candlestick, 5½"	22.00
Candlestick, 6¾", duo, #2545 "Flame"	47.50
Candy w/cover, 6¼", 3-part	90.00
Celery, 11"	25.00
Comport, 3¼", ftd. cheese	25.00
Comport, 4¾"	22.00
Comport, 5½"	30.00
Comport, 5¾"	35.00
Creamer	10.00
Creamer, individual	11.00
Cup, ftd.	15.00
Ice bucket	85.00
Jelly w/cover, 7½"	55.00
Mayonnaise, 3-pc. set, #2496½	45.00
Oil bottle w/stopper, 3½ oz.	95.00
Pickle, 8"	17.50
Pitcher, #6011, 8⅞", 53 oz., ftd.	195.00
Plate, 6"	6.00
Plate, 7", #2337	9.00
Plate, 7½"	9.00
Plate, 8½"	12.50
Plate, 9½", small dinner	35.00

	Crystal
Plate, 10", hndl. cake	35.00
Plate, 10¼", dinner	50.00
Plate, 11", cracker	30.00
Plate, 14", torte	55.00
Relish, 6", square, 2-part	17.50
Relish, 10", 3-part	30.00
Saucer	4.00
Shaker, 2¾"	30.00
Stem, #6017, 3⅝", 4 oz., oyster cocktail	18.00
Stem, #6017, 3⅞", ¾ oz. cordial	45.00
Stem, #6017, 4½", 6 oz., low sherbet	12.00
Stem, #6017, 4⅞", 3½ oz., cocktail	15.00
Stem, #6017, 5½", 3 oz., wine	25.00
Stem, #6017, 5½", 6 oz., high sherbet	16.00
Stem, #6017, 5⅞", 4 oz., claret	27.50
Stem, #6017, 7⅜", 9 oz., water	22.50
Sugar	9.00
Sugar, individual	10.00
Sweetmeat, 6", square, 2 hndl.	17.50
Tidbit, 8¼", 3-ftd., flat	20.00
Tray, 6½" ind. sug/cr., #2496½	12.00
Tumbler, #4132, 2⅛", 1½ oz., whiskey	30.00
Tumbler, #4132, 3½", 4 oz., sham	14.00
Tumbler, #4132, 3⅛", 7½ oz., old fashioned	16.00
Tumbler, #4132, 3¾", 5 oz., sham	14.00
Tumbler, #4132, 3¾", 9 oz., sham	15.00
Tumbler, #4132, 4⅛", 7 oz., sham	14.00
Tumbler, #4132, 4⅞", 12 oz., sham	18.00
Tumbler, #4132, 5⅜", 14 oz., sham	20.00
Tumbler, #6017, 4¾", 5 oz., ftd. juice	14.00
Tumbler, #6017, 5½", 9 oz., ftd. water	18.00
Tumbler, #6017, 6", 12 oz., ftd. iced tea	25.00
Tumbler, #6017, 6½", 14 oz., ftd.	30.00
Vase, 5"	75.00

Colors: green; recently iridized, spray painted, and crystal

Some pieces from this line have surfaced quite recently, indicating Indiana has once again put old moulds in use. However, pieces I've seen have been crystal plates, iridized vegetable bowls, and various sprayed colors of oval pickle dishes. The older Depression green wares haven't yet been remade. You may well have trouble finding the sugar and creamer. We did. We had a couple of sets before deciding to include this small line, but sold them. Then we looked high and low and couldn't find any for the picture. Because the pieces look like flowers, they're always noticed and collected.

	Green	Other colors		Green	Other colors
Bowl, 6½" ftd. bonbon	15.00	6.00	Sherbet/fruit cocktail, flat	15.00	5.00
Bowl, 7" deep nappy	25.00	10.00	Plate, 6" leaf dessert	12.00	5.00
Bowl, 7" shallow preserve	20.00	8.00	Plate, 8" salad	15.00	6.00
Bowl, 8½" pickle	20.00	6.00	Sugar, open	25.00	
Creamer	25.00				

LODESTAR, PATTERN #1632, A.H. HEISEY & CO. c. 1950s

Color: Dawn

Lodestar is the Heisey pattern pictured, but it is only known as Lodestar in this Dawn color. Crystal pieces of the same design are called Satellite and prices for crystal drop off dramatically. Each piece has the star-like shape for its base. Dawn is costly as you can see by the prices listed below; but these are reasonable selling prices, not wished for prices.

Ashtray	85.00
Bowl, 4½", sauce dish, #1626	40.00
Bowl, 5", mayonnaise	85.00
Bowl, 6¾", #1565	60.00
Bowl, 8"	70.00
Bowl, 11", crimped	100.00
Bowl, 12", deep floral	100.00
Bowl, 14", shallow	130.00
Candleblock, 2¾" tall, 1-lite star, #1543, pr. (Satellite)	275.00
Candlestick, 2" tall, 1-lite centerpiece, pr.	140.00
Candlestick, 5¾" tall, 2-lite, pr.	600.00
Candy jar, w/cover, 5"	225.00
Celery, 10"	60.00
Creamer	50.00
Creamer, w/handle	70.00
Jar, w/cover, 8", #1626	160.00
Pitcher, 1 qt., #1626	150.00
Plate, 8½"	65.00
Plate, 14"	90.00
Relish, 7½", 3-pt.	70.00
Sugar	50.00
Sugar, w/handles	70.00
Tumbler, 6 oz., juice	40.00
Vase, 8", #1626	200.00
Vase, 8", crimped, #1626	210.00

MANHATTAN, LINE #15078, U.S. GLASS COMPANY, C. 1902; ANCHOR HOCKING #0-5078, C. 19[...]
BARTLETT-COLLINS, C. 1970S

Colors: crystal, and with ruby or gold; avocado and amber, c. 1970s

    Manhattan was a popular U.S. Glass pattern for years. Anchor Hocking produced a punch bowl look-alike in the 1950s. However, it had different dimensions from the older ware and was not a part of their Manhattan pattern. Hocking's punch bowl is 13½" in diameter with a 23" underliner plate. The older, more closed, rose bowl shape was only 12" across and the liner only measured 21½", according to Fred Bickenheuser. He also said the Hocking cups had a more open handle than the older version. In the 1970s Bartlett-Collins produced some items in crystal, avocado, and amber; however their large berry bowls had straight rims, rather than scalloped ones; and they called the pattern St. Genevieve.

	Crystal		Crystal
Bowl, 4½", berry	4.00	Goblet, 6 oz., low sherbet	5.00
Bowl, 6", cereal	10.00	Goblet, 10 oz., water	11.00
Bowl, 7", flat edge	10.00	Goblet, 12 oz. tea	13.00
Bowl, 8½", large berry	10.00	Plate, 6"	5.00
Celery, 9½"	15.00	Plate, 11", serving	12.00
Cup	4.00	Punch bowl	50.00
Compote, 9½"	12.00	Punch cup	3.00
Compote, 10½"	15.00	Saucer	2.00
Creamer	6.00	Sugar	6.00
Goblet, 4 oz., cocktail	9.00	Tumbler, 8 oz., flat water	18.00

MAYFLOWER, PLATE ETCHING #332, FOSTORIA GLASS COMPANY, 1938 – 1954

Color: crystal

Fostoria's Mayflower pattern has a curving, cornucopia of flowers as the focal point of its design. Sporadically, this is confused with Fostoria's Corsage. On page 44 you can scrutinize the cone-shaped floral etching that is the Corsage design. You might have been able to combine these two patterns had Fostoria chosen to etch them on the same mould blank; but alas, they did not.

Mayflower is mostly etched on Fostoria's #2560 blank known as Coronet. Notice that there are three gently sloping lines around the top of each Coronet blank. You can spot these easily on the relish, comport, two-handled bowl, creamer, and sugar. The rope appearing handles on the sugar and creamer are an absolute indication of blank #2560.

The stems are depicted on line #6020, which is the only stemware line that you will find in Mayflower. Note its twisted rope appearance.

Fostoria's "Flame" #2545 blank is shown on the oval bowl in the second row and a single candlestick on the right of the bottom row. Only a few pieces of Mayflower will be found on this blank. Speaking of candlesticks, there are mounting numbers of collectors searching for these throughout the country. Many of these are shown in my book, *Glass Candlesticks of the Depression Era*. I've met one collector who now has over 4,000.

The tall vase pictured first on the bottom row is the #5100 blank. The large vase following it stands 8" tall, but looks even larger due to its opening. This is the #2430 vase in the listing. Vases are infrequently found in Fostoria crystal patterns, contrary to what you see displayed. It took thousands of miles of travel to garner these for your perusal.

Any unlisted pieces you find, feel free to drop me a postcard so we can get them documented.

Bowl, finger, #869	27.50	Plate, 6¼", hndl., lemon, #2560	8.00
Bowl, 5", hndl., whip cream, #2560	22.50	Plate, 7½", #2560	10.00
Bowl, 5½", hndl., sweetmeat, #2560	20.00	Plate, 8½", #2560	15.00
Bowl, 5¾" x 6¼", hndl., bonbon, #2560	20.00	Plate, 9½", #2560	40.00
Bowl, 7¼", 3-ftd., bonbon, #2560	22.50	Plate, 10½", hndl. cake, #2560	35.00
Bowl, 8½", hndl., #2560	50.00	Plate, 14", torte, #2560	60.00
Bowl, 10", salad, #2560	50.00	Relish, 6½", hndl., 2-part, #2560	20.00
Bowl, 10½", hndl., #2496	50.00	Relish, 10" x 7¾", 3-part, #2560	32.50
Bowl, 11", hndl., #2560	60.00	Salt & pepper, pr.	75.00
Bowl, 11½", crimped, #2560	65.00	Saucer, #2560	5.00
Bowl, 12", flared, #2560	55.00	Stem, #6020, 3¾", 1 oz., cordial	45.00
Bowl, 12½", oval, #2545 "Flame"	55.00	Stem, #6020, 3¾", 4 oz., oyster cocktail	16.00
Bowl, 13", fruit, #2560	60.00	Stem, #6020, 4⅝", 6 oz., low sherbet	12.00
Candlestick, 4", #2560½	27.50	Stem, #6020, 4⅞", 3½ oz., cocktail	16.00
Candlestick, 4½", #2545 "Flame"	37.50	Stem, #6020, 5⅜", 3½ oz., wine	25.00
Candlestick, 4½", #2560	25.00	Stem, #6020, 5½", 6 oz., saucer champagne	16.00
Candlestick, 5", duo, #2496	35.00	Stem, #6020, 5¾", 4½ oz., claret	30.00
Candlestick, 5⅛", duo, #2560	40.00	Stem, #6020, 6⅛", 5½ oz., claret	30.00
Candlestick, 6¾", duo, #2545 "Flame"	60.00	Stem, #6020, 7¼", 9 oz., water	25.00
Celery, 11", #2560	35.00	Sugar, #2560	11.00
Comport, 5½"	30.00	Sugar, individual, #2560	12.00
Creamer, #2560	12.00	Tray, 7½", individual cr./sug., #2560	15.00
Creamer, individual, #2560	12.50	Tray, 10" x 8¼", hndl., muffin, #2560	32.50
Cup, ftd., #2560	17.00	Tumbler, #6020, 4⅞", 5 oz., ftd. juice	16.00
Mayonnaise set, 3-pc., #2560	40.00	Tumbler, #6020, 5¾", 9 oz., ftd. water	18.00
Olive, 6¾", #2560	20.00	Tumbler, #6020, 6⅜", 12 oz., ftd. ice tea	23.00
Pickle, 8¾", #2560	25.00	Vase, 3¾", #2430	65.00
Pitcher, 7½,", 60 oz., flat, #4140	275.00	Vase, 8", #2430	115.00
Pitcher, 9¾", 48 oz., ftd., #5000	275.00	Vase, 10", ftd., #2545 "Flame"	150.00
Plate, 6", #2560	6.00	Vase, 10", ftd., #5100	125.00

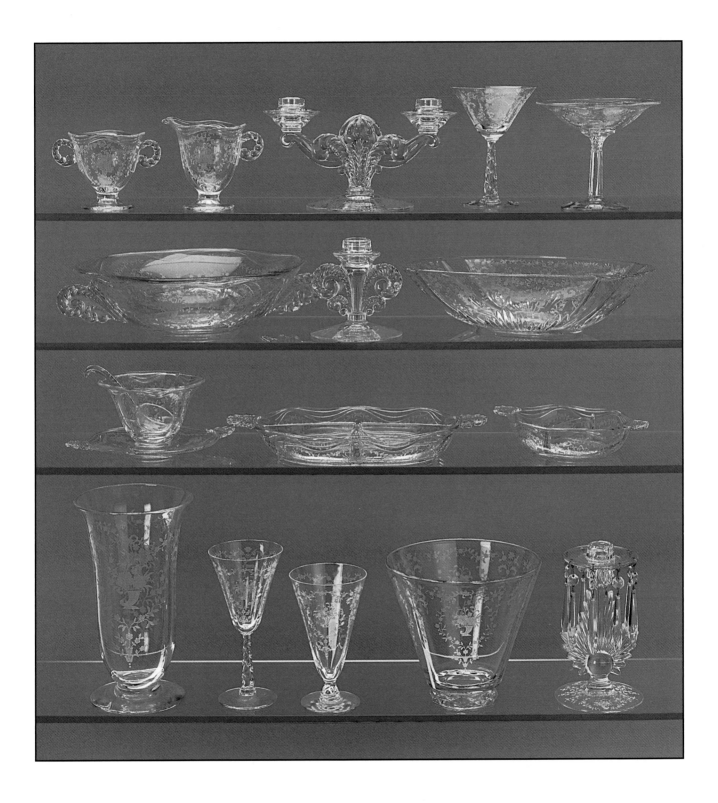

MEADOW ROSE, PLATE ETCHING #328, STEM BLANK #6016, FOSTORIA GLASS COMPANY, 1936 – 1982

Colors: crystal and Azure

Meadow Rose was one of Fostoria's enduring lines. For glass patterns to remain on the market for over 40 years says something for the designer of this ware. Since the addition of Meadow Rose to this book, there has been less confusion between it and Fostoria's Navarre, yet another of their top-selling bridal ware lines.

The center of the Meadow Rose medallion is open; but it is filled in for Navarre. See the catalog reprint of Navarre on page 160. Matching stemware service was available until 1982. Prices for Meadow Rose are edging upward toward those of Navarre, though numerous items sell for less. Meadow Rose collectors are still outnumbered by those pursuing Navarre; but the gap is closing.

I have had difficulty in finding Azure to photograph. Were I collecting this pattern, I would be buying the blue. I've been told that Azure in all Fostoria patterns was discontinued during World War II owing to the materials not being available. Pieces found in Azure will fetch an additional 35% to 50%. Thanks for all those who have sent lists of what they have in Azure which are indicated by an asterisk in the listing below.

If there is no mould blank number listed then the item is #2496 or the Baroque blank that has the raised fleur-de-lis. Any other mould blanks are listed with the item.

	Crystal		Crystal
Bowl, 4", square, hndl.	14.00	Plate, 9½", dinner	45.00
Bowl, 4½", #869, finger	40.00	Plate, 10", hndl., cake	47.50
Bowl, 4⅝", tri-cornered	15.00	Plate, 11", cracker	30.00
Bowl, 5", hndl., flared	24.00	Plate, 14", torte	65.00
Bowl, 6", square, sweetmeat	20.00	Plate, 16", torte, #2364	100.00
Bowl, 7⅜", 3-ftd., bonbon	27.50	Relish, 6", 2-part, square	32.50
Bowl, 8½", hndl.	45.00	Relish, 10" x 7½", 3-part	40.00
Bowl, 10", oval, floating garden	50.00	Relish, 13¼", 5-part, #2419	75.00
Bowl, 10½", hndl.	60.00	Salad dressing bottle, #2083, 6½"	295.00
*Bowl, 12", flared	65.00	Salt & pepper, #2375, 3½", ftd., pr.	95.00
Bowl, 12", hndl., ftd.	65.00	*Sauce dish liner, 8", oval	30.00
Bowl, #2545, 12½", oval, "Flame"	75.00	Sauce dish, 6½" x 5¼"	125.00
Candlestick, 4"	25.00	*Sauce dish, div. mayo., 6½"	45.00
Candlestick, 4½", double	35.00	Saucer	6.00
Candlestick, 5½"	32.00	*Stem, #6016, ¾ oz., cordial, 3⅞"	50.00
Candlestick, 6", triple	55.00	*Stem, #6016, 3¼ oz., wine, 5½"	35.00
Candlestick, #2545, 6¾", double, "Flame"	65.00	*Stem, #6016, 3½ oz., cocktail, 5¼"	22.00
Candy, w/cover, 3-part	110.00	*Stem, #6016, 4 oz., oyster cocktail, 3⅝"	22.00
Celery, 11"	37.50	*Stem, #6016, 4½ oz., claret, 6"	35.00
Comport, 3¼", cheese	27.50	*Stem, #6016, 6 oz., low sherbet, 4⅜"	18.00
Comport, 4¾"	30.00	*Stem, #6016, 6 oz., saucer champagne, 5⅝"	20.00
*Creamer, 4¾", ftd.	18.00	*Stem, #6016, 10 oz., water, 7⅝"	28.00
Creamer, individual	17.50	*Sugar, 4½", ftd.	18.00
Cup	20.00	Sugar, individual	16.00
Ice bucket, 4⅜" high	100.00	Tidbit, 8¼", 3 ftd., turned-up edge	25.00
Jelly w/cover, 7½"	65.00	Tray, #2375, 11", center hndl.	35.00
Mayonnaise, #2375, 3-piece	55.00	Tray, 6½", 2496½, for ind. sugar/creamer	22.00
Mayonnaise, 2496½, 3-piece	55.00	*Tumbler, #6016, 5 oz., ftd., juice, 4⅝"	22.00
Pickle, 8"	30.00	*Tumbler, #6016, 10 oz., ftd., water, 5⅜"	22.00
Pitcher, #2666, 32 oz.	235.00	*Tumbler, #6016, 13 oz., ftd., tea, 5⅞"	28.00
*Pitcher, #5000, 48 oz., ftd.	350.00	Vase, #4108, 5"	85.00
Plate, 6", bread/butter	11.00	Vase, #4121, 5"	85.00
*Plate, 7½", salad	15.00	Vase, #4128, 5"	85.00
Plate, 8½", luncheon	20.00	Vase, #2470, 10", ftd.	165.00

*Indicates items made in Azure which will bring an additional 35% to 40%

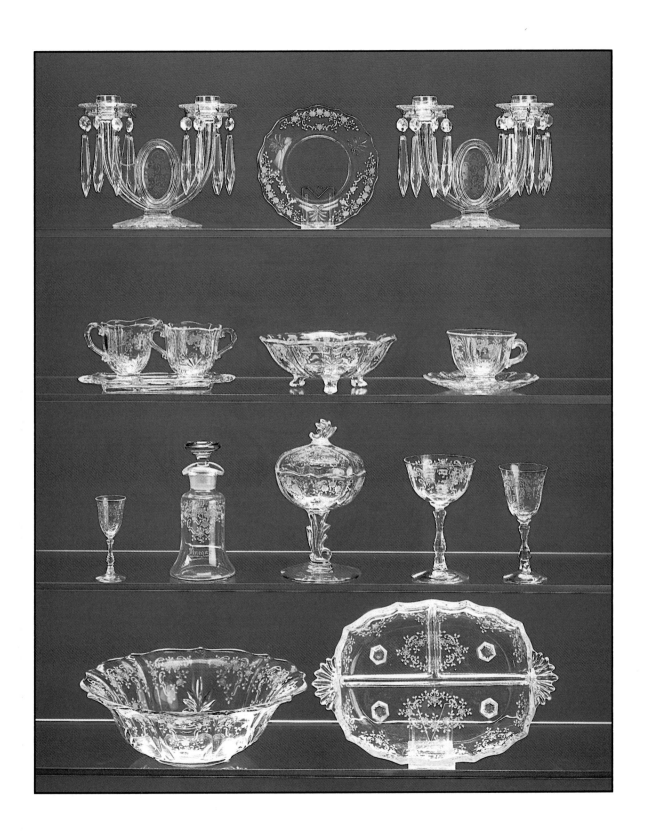

MODERNTONE PLATONITE, HAZEL ATLAS GLASS COMPANY, 1940 – EARLY 1950S

Colors: Platonite pastel, white, and white decorated

Blue and red decorated Platonite Moderntone is eye-catching. I have had several e-mails in the last few months from collectors searching for anything decorated with blue deco lines or the red and blue Willow. It has never been plentiful. The dealer who sold the blue wares pictured here tried to sell me all the settings she had. Like a dummy, I only bought one of each piece as I am prone to do for photography. A savvy collector bought all she had left. Unfortunately, there is little of either of these decorations being found today. I have bought every piece of Willow decorated Moderntone I have seen for sale and that is not a lot. The red Deco is found more frequently, but that is not to say it is commonly seen.

Platonite Moderntone, one of the more reasonably priced patterns from this era, has become a starting point for many young couples just beginning to buy collectible glass. You can still find pieces at garage and yard sales for a dollar or less. Not everyone is fond of this fired color ware; but if you are, buy it every chance you can. No one thought the supply of Jade-ite Fire-King would ever dwindle: but there are scores of collectors now kicking themselves for not buying more of certain items when the supply seemed inexhaustible.

At present, demand is insignificant for plain white Platonite Moderntone; but that may well change. One lady told me she was mixing pieces with her cobalt and was very well pleased with the effect. Many pieces of glass from this era were obtained by buying some product. Glassware packaged in a popular product of yesteryear is often commonly found today; but those not-so-popular items may well be treasures now. Glassware was the package itself for some products (spices, teabags, bath salts) or was the enclosed "gift/prize" in others (oats, flour).

Pastel colors are the lighter shades of blue, green, pink, and yellow. To date, there is no significant price difference between white interiors as opposed to those with colored interiors. I, personally, have found more demand for colored interiors than the white. It's a matter of preference. Buy what you like.

At the bottom of page 139 two distinct shades of pink are displayed. I have been assured by Moderntone collectors that this variation in shade is of no importance to them. It's notable to me.

Those four, 9 oz. tumblers shown on page 141 are fired-on Moderntone tumblers in color shades I had never seen before and were unusual enough that I had to buy them. They are fired over crystal and not white Platonite. Do you happen to own any other piece that's been fired over crystal? The seller had them labeled Swanky Swigs, but these are larger. The light blue one does not fit the known Swanky Swigs color scheme. Speaking of the Swigs, Moderntone collectors often buy the Fiesta colored Swigs to use as juice tumblers with their Platonite Moderntone.

Platonite Moderntone bowls come with or without rims. Bowls without rims are more difficult to find, but those with rims tend to have more inner roughness, which is a deterrent to collectors. Pastel pink 8" bowls with or without rims and yellow 12" platters are easier to find than other pastel colors. I suspect they were a premium item at one time, which would account for their abundance. Other colored platters are rarely found. Children's dishes in this pattern are shown on pages 143 – 145.

	Pastel Colors	White or w/stripes	Deco/Red or Blue Willow
Bowl, 4¾", cream soup	6.50	4.00	25.00
Bowl, 5", berry, w/rim	5.00	3.00	17.50
Bowl, 5", berry, w/o rim	6.00		
Bowl, 5", deep cereal, w/white	7.50	4.00	
Bowl, 5", deep cereal, w/o white	10.00		
Bowl, 8", w/rim	*15.00	6.00	45.00
Bowl, 8", w/o rim	*22.00		
Bowl, 8¾", large berry		7.00	45.00
Creamer	4.00	4.00	25.00
Cup	3.50	2.50	25.00

	Pastel Colors	White or w/stripes	Deco/Red or Blue Willow
Mug, 4", 8 oz.		9.00	
Plate, 6¾", sherbet	4.00	2.50	11.00
Plate, 8⅞", dinner	6.00	3.50	30.00
Plate, 10½", sandwich	15.00	9.00	
Platter, 11", oval		12.50	40.00
Platter, 12", oval	**15.00	9.00	50.00
Salt and pepper, pr.	16.00	13.00	
Saucer	1.00	1.50	5.00
Sherbet	4.50	2.50	22.00
Sugar	4.00	4.00	25.00
Tumbler, 9 oz.	9.00		
Tumbler, cone, ftd.		6.00	

*Pink $9.00
* *Yellow $9.00

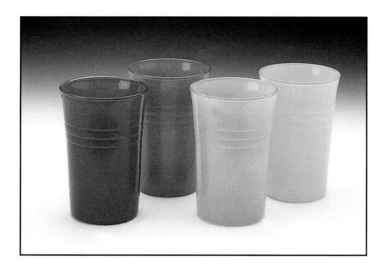

MODERNTONE PLATONITE, HAZEL ATLAS GLASS COMPANY, 1940 – EARLY 1950S (CONT.)

Colors: dark fired colors of cobalt, turquoise, yellow, orange, Chartreuse, Burgundy, green, gray, rust, gold

Collecting the darker, later colors of Moderntone Platonite will test your determination. Relative to the quantities of pastel, there are minuscule amounts of darker colors existing. Buy it whenever you find it.

The price listing below separates colors into two price groups based upon *demand* and *availability*. The first group consists of cobalt blue, turquoise green, lemon yellow, and orange. All these colors can eventually be collected in sets with a little effort. This group can be gathered with white or colored interiors. White interiors are more plentiful. Most collectors will take anything they can find.

Assembling a set of any of the other colors, Chartreuse, Burgundy, green, gray, rust, or gold is questionable. Should you undertake it, you will find that none of the previous colors are found with white interiors. Collectors have incorrectly called the dark green "forest green" and the Burgundy "maroon." I have also heard the gold referred to as "butterscotch." As with the two pinks, some collectors consider gold merely a variation of lemon yellow and not a separate color.

Several pieces listed under pastel have not been found in the darker colors. To my knowledge, cream soups, bowls with rims, sandwich plates, and shakers have not turned up. Green (dark) tumblers, as pictured, are the only color I have seen in the later colors. If you see others, I'd appreciate your letting me know.

With the introduction of rainbow color collecting, many collectors are mixing all the colors available with great success. I suspect you'll have fun collecting and using this.

	Cobalt Turquoise Lemon Orange	Burgundy Chartreuse Green/Gray Rust/Gold		Cobalt Turquoise Lemon Orange	Burgundy Chartreuse Green/Gray Rust/Gold
Bowl, 4¾", cream soup	11.00		Plate, 6¾", sherbet	6.00	8.00
Bowl, 5", berry, w/rim	12.00		Plate, 8⅞", dinner	12.00	13.00
Bowl, 5", berry, w/o rim	8.00	12.00	Plate, 10½", sandwich	22.00	
Bowl, 5", deep cereal, w/white	12.00		Platter, 12", oval	22.00	32.00
Bowl, 5", deep cereal, w/o white		15.00	Salt and pepper, pr.	20.00	
Bowl, 8", w/rim	30.00		Saucer	4.00	5.00
Bowl, 8", w/o rim	30.00	40.00	Sherbet	7.00	9.00
Creamer	8.00	11.00	Sugar	8.00	11.00
Cup	7.00	8.00	Tumbler, 9 oz.	10.00	*30.00

*Green $16.00

MODERNTONE "LITTLE HOSTESS PARTY DISHES"

HAZEL ATLAS GLASS COMPANY, EARLY 1950s

Moderntone children's sets have seen a slight increase in prices for the harder to find colored sets. An all white set in the original box was found a few years ago. It is pictured in *Very Rare Glassware of the Depression Years, Fourth Series.* Occasionally, you will find a white cup and saucer, but other white pieces are exceptionally rare. Teapots are the most difficult pieces to find, with lids being harder to find than the bottoms. When buying Burgundy teapot tops or bottoms individually, you should be aware that Burgundy shades vary. The hues of color may not match unless you have the piece to match in hand.

The picture at the top of page 144 contains two sets, mixed. There are pieces from a pink and black set and a couple from an all-white set. I was trying to show several different sets in one photo to conserve space. Notice the souvenir cup and saucer at center which was yet another way these small wares have been dispersed.

You would be surprised by how many people come into a Depression glass show for the first time, see a piece of Moderntone children's dishes displayed and say, "I have some of those at home. I need a cup (or some missing piece) that got broken." Instantly, they're on the hunt for their missing piece. John Q. Public, as well as doll collectors and dealers, also want sets of children's dishes. Prices always increase due to demand. Nostalgia is one entrance to the collecting world.

The set pictured at the top of page 145 was a premium from Big Top peanut butter. If you sent in so many peanut butter labels, you could get a set of Little Hostess dishes. You can read more about the Big Top peanut butter story on page 13.

LITTLE HOSTESS PARTY SET
pink/black/white (top 144)

Cup, ¾", bright pink, white	17.50
Saucer, 3⅞", black, white	12.00
Plate, 5¼", black, bright pink, white	15.00
Creamer, 1¾", bright pink	22.50
Sugar, 1¾", bright pink	22.50
Teapot, 3½", bright pink	95.00
Teapot lid, black	95.00
Set, 16-piece	395.00

LITTLE HOSTESS PARTY SET
lemon/beige/pink/aqua
(bottom 144)

Cup, ¾", bright pink, aqua, lemon	17.50
Saucer, 3⅞", same	12.00
Plate, 5¼", same	15.00
Creamer, 1¾", pink	20.00
Sugar, 1¾", pink	20.00
Teapot, 3½", brown	95.00

Teapot lid, lemon	95.00
Set, 16-piece	410.00

LITTLE HOSTESS PARTY SET
gray/rust/gold
Turquoise (top 145)

Cup, ¾", gray, rust	12.00
Cup, ¾", gold, turquoise	12.00
Saucer, 3⅞", all four colors	7.00
Plate, 5¼", same	7.00
Creamer, 1¾", rust	14.00
Sugar, 1¾", rust	14.00
Teapot, 3½", turquoise	50.00
Teapot lid, turquoise	50.00
Set, 16-piece	235.00

LITTLE HOSTESS PARTY SET
green/gray/chartreuse/
burgundy (bottom 145 left)

Cup, ¾", green, gray, chartreuse	10.00

Cup, ¾", burgundy	13.00
Saucer, 3⅞", green, gray & burgundy, chartreuse	7.00
Plate, 5¼", burgundy	10.00
Plate, 5¼", green, gray, chartreuse	8.00
Creamer, 1¾", chartreuse	12.50
Sugar, 1¾", chartreuse	12.50
Teapot, 3½", burgundy	50.00
Teapot lid, burgundy	50.00
Set, 16-piece	230.00

LITTLE HOSTESS PARTY SET
pastel pink/green/blue
yellow (bottom 145 right)

Cup, ¾", all four colors	8.00
Saucer, 3⅞", same	6.00
Plate, 5¼", same	9.00
Creamer, 1¾", pink	15.00
Sugar, 1¾", pink	15.00
Set, 14-piece	100.00

MOON AND STAR, ADAMS & CO. C 1880; U.S. GLASS 1890s; L. G. WRIGHT, 1930s – 60s; FENTON GLASS CO. FOR L.G. WRIGHT; L.E. SMITH, 1940s AND MINIATURE CARNIVAL WARES FOR LEVAY DISTRIBUTING CO. 1970s; WEISHAR ENTERPRISES, ½ SIZE MINIATURES, 1990s, CURRENTLY JADITE

Colors: crystal; amber, amberina, amethyst, blue, blue satin, blue opalescent, brown, cranberry opalescent, green, green satin, mint, green opalescent, milk glass, ruby, ruby satin, pink, pink satin, vaseline, vaseline satin, vaseline opalescent, jadite

Collectors had been approaching me for years to include the Moon and Star pattern in my books. One of the reasons I had resisted adding it was the can of worms this pattern presents due to all the different manufactures, time periods involved, and the fact it is still being made. Before my last book came out, I was able to add jadite to this color listing. As I wrote about the pattern, jadite had not been released — at least where I was in Florida. When I went north in May, it was saturating every mall and flea market I attended.

New items and colors continue to be made; but that isn't deterring collectors. Many people are buying this as fast as it can be produced; so, I'm stuck with at least touching bases with the L.G. Wright and L.E. Smith production lines which mostly fit the time parameters for this book. L.G. Wright Company's forte in glass was built around remaking older company wares, either by purchasing the original moulds or by remaking moulds of discontinued lines. Their first foray into the Moon and Star pattern was some crystal items (goblets, dessert bowls, egg cups, miniature night lamps, etc.) in late 1930s to early 1940s. These wares were shinier and more polished than their antique ancestors, but sold well. This Palace design, as it was first called, with its plain, upper row of circles and its bottom row with center stars, has been attracting supporters since its first issue; so, why should today's collector feel any other way? Besides, some collectors enjoy that connection with the past as an added bonus to their collection — and they may own an inherited item from a previous manufacturer.

I have designated Smith items with "S" in the listings and Wright with "W." You will most definitely find additional pieces in these patterns, but they will have been made after 1969.

By the late 1960s, Wright had most of the items shown below for sale. A few weren't incorporated until the 1970s. We know as of the late 1990s, Moon and Star items were still being produced. Weishar Enterprises is making numerous pieces in the popular jadite color, a new color for Moon and Star as far as I know. Again, I tried to include only those items from the 40s, 50s, and 60s in this listing. All colored wares in this pattern have been made in the last 55 years, though crystal has been manufactured in that time period, also. Kemple Glass also made a variant Moon and Star pattern.

It seems that lamps in this pattern are big sellers. Every lamp I find sells almost immediately upon putting it up for sale.

	Amber/ Crystal/Green	Blue/Ruby/ Vaseline	Other colors		Amber/ Crystal/Green	Blue/Ruby/ Vaseline	Other colors
Ashtray, 4½" dia., 6-sided, S	10.00	12.50	11.00	Creamer, 3", individual, S	8.00	12.00	10.00
Ashtray, 5" dia., 6-sided, W	28.00	38.00	32.00	Creamer, W	15.00	25.00	20.00
Ashtray, 8" dia., 6-sided, S	15.00	20.00	25.00	Decanter, W	55.00	100.00	85.00
Ashtray, 8½" dia., 6-sided, W	20.00	30.00	25.00	Epergne, 8" high, S	25.00	45.00	35.00
Banana dish, folded sides, 9", S	25.00	38.00	30.00	Goblet, 9 oz., W	15.00	25.00	20.00
Banana dish, folded sides, 12", W	32.00	42.00	48.00	Goblet, 11 oz., S	15.00	25.00	20.00
Basket, 4", double twig hndl., scallop rim, S	20.00	25.00	22.50	Lamp, 10", miniature, w/shade, W	110.00	205.00	160.00
Bowl, 6" dia., ftd., crimped rim, W				Lamp, 12", oil, flat, bulbous, S	68.00	100.00	80.00
Bowl, 7½" dia., S				Lamp, 16" elec. metal base, S	110.00		
Bowl, 8" dia., console, low ft., W			35.00	Lamp, 24", table w/shade, S	165.00		
Bowl, 8" dia., flared, scalloped, S				Nappy, 6", crimped, W	15.00	30.00	
Butter dish & lid, 5¾" dia., W	40.00	55.00	45.00	Pitcher, 32 oz., tall, W	95.00	210.00	160.00
Butter dish & lid, 7" dia., S	35.00	50.00	40.00	Relish, 8", 3 pt., S	20.00	30.00	25.00
Cake stand, 11", high, skirt rim, 2-pc., S	50.00	65.00	60.00	Relish, 8", oval, boat, W	25.00	35.00	30.00
Cake stand, 11", low, no rim, S	45.00	60.00	55.00	Relish, 8", rectangular, W	35.00	60.00	45.00
Cake stand, 12", low, W	55.00	75.00	65.00	Relish, 8", triangular, W	35.00	60.00	45.00
Candlestick, 4⅝", S	12.00	22.50	15.00	Salt dip, S	12.50	25.00	20.00
Candlestick, 6", S	18.00	30.00	25.00	Salt dip, W	15.00	30.00	25.00
Candlestick, 6", W	18.00	30.00	25.00	Salt shaker, 4", W	15.00	25.00	20.00
Candy jar w/lid, 10", S	45.00	60.00	55.00	Salt shaker, 4", straight, S	15.00	25.00	20.00
Candy jar w/lid, 12", S	75.00	120.00	95.00	Sauce dish, 4½", round, ftd., W	15.00	25.00	20.00
Canister, 1 lb., S	10.00	15.00	12.50	Sherbet, 4½", 6 oz., flared, W	15.00	25.00	20.00
Canister, 2 lb., S	15.00	25.00	20.00	Sherbet, 6 oz., S	15.00	25.00	20.00
Canister, 3½ lb., S	15.00	25.00	20.00	Soap dish, 6", oval, W	18.00	30.00	25.00
Canister, 5 lb., S	20.00	30.00	25.00	Spoon holder, 5¼", W	25.00	45.00	35.00
Compote, 4" w/lid, ftd., W	30.00	45.00	40.00	Sugar shaker, 4½", W	25.00	45.00	35.00
Compote, 4½" w/lid, ftd., W				Sugar, 3", individual, S	8.00	12.00	10.00
Compote, 6" w/lid, ftd., W	35.00	50.00	45.00	Sugar, w/lid, W	18.00	30.00	25.00
Compote, 6½" crimped, S	15.00	25.00	20.00	Toothpick, 3", W	10.00	15.00	12.50
Compote, 8", flared, W	40.00	55.00	45.00	Toothpick, 3⅛", S	10.00	15.00	12.50
Compote, 8", ruffled, W	35.00	50.00	40.00	Tumbler, ftd., 5 oz. juice, W	15.00	25.00	20.00
Compote, 8", w/lid, S	55.00	90.00	65.00	Tumbler, ftd., 7 oz. water, W	20.00	30.00	25.00
Compote, 8", w/lid, W	65.00	100.00	75.00	Tumbler, 11 oz. flat, S	15.00	25.00	20.00
Compote, 10", rolled edge, S	45.00	60.00	50.00	Tumbler, ftd., 11 oz.	18.00	30.00	25.00
Compote, 10", scalloped, S	40.00	55.00	45.00	Urn, ftd., S	8.00	12.00	10.00
Compote, 10", scalloped, W	48.00	63.00	53.00	Vase, 6½" bud, S	15.00	25.00	20.00
Compote, 12", rolled edge, S	65.00	100.00	75.00	Wine, 2 oz., W	15.00	25.00	20.00
				Wine, 3 oz., S	10.00	15.00	12.50

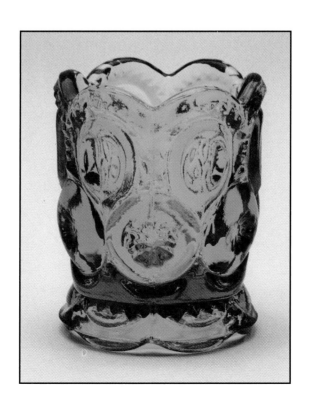

MOON GLOW, LINE #113, GREENBRIER, LINE #116, FEDERAL GLASS COMPANY, C. 1974

Color: rainbow iridescent hue

Moon Glow line with that pearl-like finish was packaged in three ways, as a 16-, 35- or 45-piece set. There were only 11 different pieces if you include the sugar bowl lid. Though we had little difficulty finding pieces of this to photograph, I would assume that the chop plate and vegetable bowl are going to be the harder to find items, and perhaps the sugar lid. It's quite attractive and it was advertised as oven-proof; so, it should be durable. This was made toward Federal's "last hurrah" period before going out of business.

Greenbrier was sold only as 16- and 45-piece sets. Green was described as "shimmering beauty." These two patterns are usually found in sets and often mislabeled carnival or even stretch glass. Prices vary greatly at the moment, perhaps because most have no idea what it is.

Bowl, 4⅞" dessert	4.00
Bowl, 6⅜" soup/cereal	8.00
Bowl, 8½" vegetable	12.00
Creamer	5.00
Cup	4.00
Plate, 7⅝" salad	4.00
Plate, 10" dinner	8.00
Plate, 11¼" chop	12.00
Saucer	1.00
Sugar w/cover	10.00

MOONSTONE, ANCHOR HOCKING GLASS CORPORATION, 1941 – 1946

Colors: crystal with opalescent hobnails and some green with opalescent hobnails; other experimental colors

Moonstone is an opalescent hobnail that truly caught on with War World II brides. Earliest records indicate it began production some time in 1941 and was made until a year after the war. This 1940s glassware still captivates collectors. Moonstone was predominately displayed in all the five-and-dime stores during the middle of the war; and it's very likely that someone from your past had a piece or two. Like Fire-King ovenware, it was a recognizable fixture in the homes of the 1950s even though production had ceased years before. My grandmother had a bottom to a puff box she kept bobbie-pins in and I noticed that Cathy's grandmother had a cloverleaf bowl. The photograph of a J. J. Newberry store window display on page 151 is one example of how this glassware was promoted.

A number of experimental pieces have shown up in Moonstone, including a 9½" dinner plate. Had that plate been a regular production item, this set would now gather even more collectors who tend to avoid sets without dinner plates. You can see the dinner plate, a toothpick, and a 7¾" divided relish without a crimped edge in *Very Rare Glassware of the Depression Years, Fifth Series*. New finds continue to surface. Most of the pieces pictured below and on page 150 are compliments of Anchor Hocking's morgue. (Discontinued or experimental items were stored in a place appropriately called a morgue.) Some of these wares used to find their way home with factory workers. One former employee explained to me that it wasn't *stealing* then, in fact it was encouraged as an overlooked kind of "bonus" for work well done. He said a lot of employees didn't even bother to take the pieces when they were offered. It wasn't something they wanted after working with it all the time. Back then, it "wasn't like it is now," he continued. "They track everything now."

The most distressing normal production pieces to find today are 5½" berry bowls (bottom of page 151) listed as M2775 in the Hocking brochure. There are none of those in the Newberry store photo. Admittedly, goblets and cups and saucers are also excluded in that store window display; and they are easily found today.

Ruffled 5½" bowls are more available than their straight-side counterparts; but even they are not as abundant as once believed. Even the brochure shows six ruffled bowls to one of the straight edge. The sandwich plate measures 10¾", but I have seen very few of these of late. Moonstone is a pattern that has gently slipped away into collections. Little is seen at shows and there are fewer quantities appearing in the market place in general, which is a serious problem for many collectible types of glassware.

Green Moonstone was issued under the name Ocean Green and was made in sets containing goblets, cups, saucers, plates, creamer, and sugar. Notice the pieces shown are somewhat different from the standard line in the catalog page.

Fenton Opalescent Hobnail pitchers and tumblers are good companion pieces to go with Anchor Hocking Moonstone sets since there are no pitchers, flat tumblers, or shakers found in Moonstone. Those found are Fenton and the hobs are more pointed. There is also no Moonstone cologne bottle, but the Fenton one goes well with this pattern. If you would like additional pieces that are similar to your pattern, buy them.

	Opalescent Hobnail		Opalescent Hobnail
Bowl, 5½", berry	19.00	Cup	7.00
Bowl, 5½", crimped, dessert	9.00	Goblet, 10 oz.	20.00
Bowl, 6½", crimped, handled	10.00	Heart bonbon, one handle	15.00
Bowl, 7¾", flat	11.00	Plate, 6¼", sherbet	5.00
Bowl, 7¾", divided relish	9.00	Plate, 8⅜", luncheon	13.00
Bowl, 9½", crimped	28.00	Plate, 10¾", sandwich	30.00
Bowl, cloverleaf	14.00	Puff box and cover, 4¾", round	25.00
Candle holder, pr.	20.00	Saucer (same as sherbet plate)	5.00
Candy jar and cover, 6"	28.00	Sherbet, footed	9.00
Cigarette box and cover	23.00	Sugar, footed	10.00
Creamer	10.00	Vase, 5½", bud	18.00

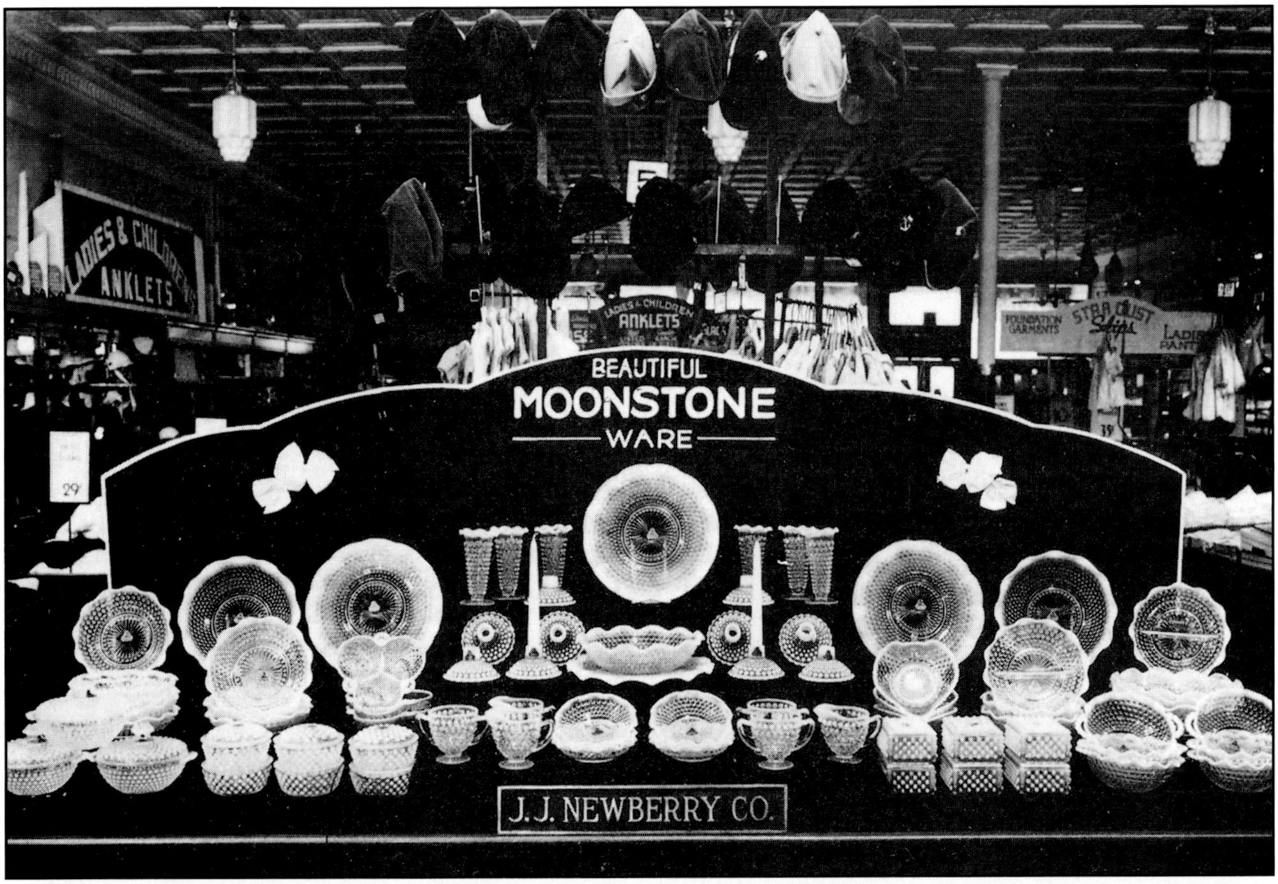
LADIES & CHILDREN'S
ANKLETS
LADIES & CHILDREN
ANKLETS
FOUNDATION GARMENTS
STAR DUST
Slips
BEAUTIFUL
MOONSTONE
WARE
J. J. NEWBERRY CO.

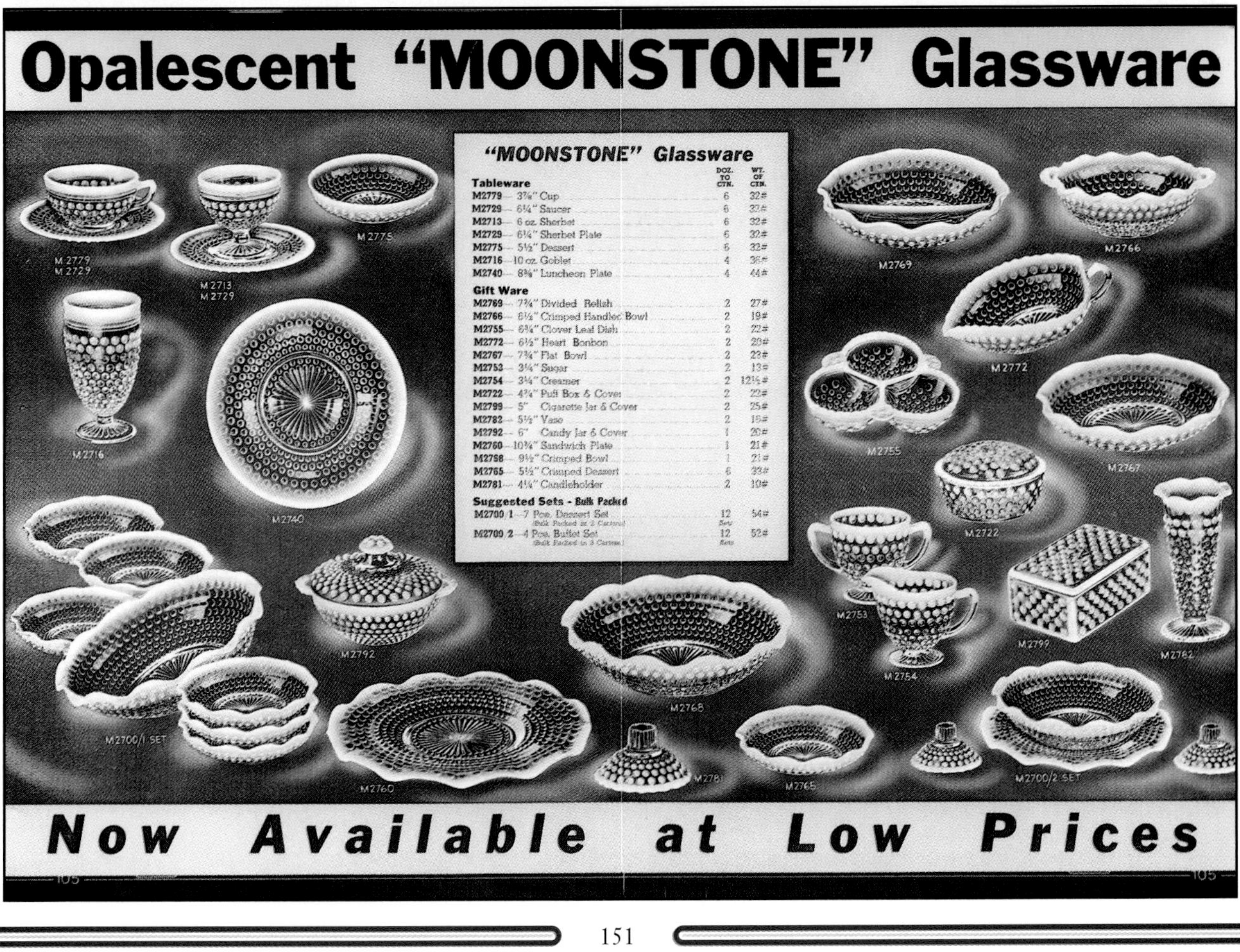
Opalescent "MOONSTONE" Glassware
M2779
M2729
M2713
M2729
M2775
M2716
M2740
M2792
M2700/1 SET
M2760
M2781
M2768
M2765
M2769
M2766
M2772
M2755
M2767
M2722
M2753
M2754
M2799
M2782
M2700/2 SET
Now Available at Low Prices

"MOONSTONE" Glassware

		DOZ. TO CTN.	WT. OF CTN.
Tableware			
M2779	3⅞" Cup	6	32#
M2729	6¼" Saucer	6	32#
M2713	6 oz. Sherbet	6	32#
M2729	6¼" Sherbet Plate	6	32#
M2775	5½" Dessert	6	32#
M2716	10 oz. Goblet	4	36#
M2740	8⅜" Luncheon Plate	4	44#
Gift Ware			
M2769	7¾" Divided Relish	2	27#
M2766	6½" Crimped Handled Bowl	2	19#
M2755	6¾" Clover Leaf Dish	2	22#
M2772	6½" Heart Bonbon	2	20#
M2767	7¾" Flat Bowl	2	23#
M2753	3¼" Sugar	2	13#
M2754	3¼" Creamer	2	12½#
M2722	4¾" Puff Box & Cover	2	22#
M2799	5" Cigarette Jar & Cover	2	25#
M2782	5½" Vase	2	16#
M2792	6" Candy Jar & Cover	1	20#
M2760	10¾" Sandwich Plate	1	21#
M2768	9½" Crimped Bowl	1	21#
M2765	5½" Crimped Dessert	6	33#
M2781	4¼" Candleholder	2	10#
Suggested Sets - Bulk Packed			
M2700/1	7 Pcs. Dessert Set (Bulk Packed in 2 Cartons)	12 Sets	54#
M2700/2	4 Pcs. Buffet Set (Bulk Packed in 3 Cartons)	12 Sets	52#

Color: Amethyst

Moroccan Amethyst brings back memories in our household. When Cathy and I were married in 1964, we received a set of eight iced teas. Cathy's sorority's color was purple and one of her "sisters" gave us the tumblers as a wedding gift. We used them until Chad started walking. He would grab hold of the table cover to hold on and these tumblers would fall over and roll spilling contents as they rolled. We sold them at our first garage sale for a dime each. The 35 cent Nippon vase and my white shirts that had to be ironed went for a nickel, but that's another story.

Just as colors of today will define our era, this rich, purple color could be identified with the 1960s. Numerous glassware companies had wares of this hue. Hazel Ware called all their wares in this delightful shade of purple, Moroccan Amethyst; and these goods have found a loyal following with collectors. Not everyone likes amethyst; but those who do are quite zealous about it. Since real names have not been found, the various designs have acquired names based upon shapes as has been done in Capri. (Think about it. No collector wants to say he collects W4221. He wants a *name* to present.) Square or rectangular based pieces are being called Colony as they are in Capri. Moroccan also has a Swirl just as in Capri. There are octagonal and pentagonal shape names which are self explanatory. One interesting shape is the apple inspired salad bowl with an apple blossom in the bottom (pictured on the bottom of page 154). You may find this bowl in fired Platonite, usually in Chartreuse or green; however the blossom design is missing from the bottom of those. There is a floral design in the bottom of the 4½" square ashtray, but it is covered by an original Moroccan Amethyst sticker which I wouldn't let the photographer remove. The 4½" star candle is desirable.

Pieces of Moroccan Amethyst that are beginning to disappear from markets include the ice bucket, 8 ounce old fashioned tumbler, cocktail shaker, and the short, covered candy dish. You can find the tall candy without much difficulty. The lids to these candy jars are interchangeable. This was another case of economy in mould usage.

An amethyst and white punch bowl set, called Alpine by the factory, can be seen on the bottom of page 154. The punch cups have open handles to hang onto the side of the punch bowl. A "Seashell" snack set in the same two colors was also labeled "Alpine."

Crystal and white stemware are being found that match the Moroccan stems. You will find swirled bowls in green, amber, and white, sometimes with matching small bowls suggesting these were marketed as salad sets. These are usually reasonably priced. I imagine that they are a later production made to go with the 1970s Avocado and Harvest Gold colors. These items were

made from the same moulds as Moroccan; actual names for these colors are lacking. Crystal, amber, and green pieces made from these moulds may someday be desirable; but they don't attract much collector attention at the moment.

A "Magic Hour" four-piece cocktail set was shown in the previous edition. You will find two- and three-tier tidbit trays made from assorted pieces (bowls, plates, ashtrays). A boxed set of iced tea tumblers was discovered recently which also contained coasters in white with 14 juts surrounding the edge. They also have the embossed apple blossom design in the center. These are 3¾" outside to outside, with 3¼" outside ring diameter and an opening for the glass of 2⅝". I'd seen these ashtrays before in markets, but I didn't imagine them to have played a role in the Moroccan Amethyst collection.

Ashtray, 3¼", triangular	5.50	Goblet, 4⅜", 5½ oz., juice	9.00
Ashtray, 3¼", round	5.50	Goblet, 5½", 9 oz., water	10.00
Ashtray, 6⅞", triangular	9.50	Ice bucket, 6"	38.00
Ashtray, 8", square	13.00	Plate, 5¾"	4.50
Bowl, 4¾", fruit, octagonal	8.00	Plate, 7¼", salad	7.00
Bowl, 5¾", deep, square	10.00	Plate, 8", square	12.00
Bowl, 6", round	12.00	Plate, 8", square, snack	10.00
Bowl, 7¾", oval	16.00	Plate, 9¾", dinner	9.00
Bowl, 9¾", rectangular	14.00	Plate, 10", fan shaped, snack w/cup rest	7.00
Bowl, 9¾", rectangular, w/metal handle	18.00	Plate, 12", round	15.00
Bowl, 10¾"	30.00	Plate, 12", sandwich, w/metal /handle	17.50
Candle, star shape, 4½"	35.00	Saucer	1.50
Candy w/lid, short	38.00	Tumbler, 4 oz., juice, 2½"	8.50
Candy w/lid, tall	38.00	Tumbler, 8 oz., old fashioned, 3¼"	12.00
Chip and dip, 10¾" & 5¾" bowls in metal holder	40.00	Tumbler, 9 oz., water	10.00
Cocktail w/stirrer, 6¼", 16 oz., w/lip	32.00	Tumbler, 11 oz., water, crinkled bottom, 4¼"	10.00
Cocktail shaker w/lid	30.00	Tumbler, 11 oz., water, 4⅝"	10.00
Cup	5.00	Tumbler, 16 oz., iced tea, 6½"	15.00
Goblet, 4", 4½ oz., wine	10.00	Vase, 8½", ruffled	35.00
Goblet, 4¼", 7½ oz., sherbet	8.00		

Colors: blue, crystal, pink, and Shell Pink

Most recent National finds include the iced teas in sprayed on colors and the blue and white sugar and creamer on a tray that is shown below. Notice the bi-colored, blue/crystal candy. That crystal top has an intriguing color-coordinated blue knob. Notice, too, the red decorated wheat design given the shallow bowl at the center of the photo. Sprays of wheat were common decorations on glassware from this time frame.

If you have ever eaten in a restaurant you may recognize the pitchers from National being used by the servers. National is a Jeannette pattern recognized by sight, but rarely by name. It is a heavy, bold pattern which more and more collectors are regarding favorably. They are particularly charmed by the log-like handles on the cup, creamer, and sugar, which are reminiscent of early pattern glass.

Two pieces of National are more familiar to collectors of Shell Pink than anyone else. Found in Shell Pink are the candy bottom, which is seen frequently, and the "heavy bottomed" 9" vase which is not. That vase is one of the harder to find items in Shell Pink. Many National crystal candy dishes are gold trimmed and were probably promoted separately from the other wares.

When patterns are relatively new to a book, I always try to find as many colors and pieces and get as many items listed as possible, a formidable task. Complete listings (sometimes, even with company catalogs) are nearly impossible. I am always appreciative of your help in adding to these listings and I have said so on many occasions.

Writing today has been especially difficult as I spent sixteen hours driving yesterday to attend the funeral of John Davis. He was one of the founders of the Peach State Depression Glass Club and a driving force behind getting our Depression glassware recognized by the Smithsonian, as well as photographed and shown to beginning collectors in my earlier books. He was a friend and mentor — to all of us. His presence will be solely missed; but his legacy is very much alive.

	Crystal			Crystal
Ashtray, small	3.00		Punch bowl stand	15.00
Ashtray, large	4.00		Punch cup	3.00
Bowl, 4½", berry	4.00		Punch set, 15-pc.	90.00
Bowl, 8½", large berry	15.00		Relish, 13", 6-part	17.50
Bowl, 12", flat	15.00		Saucer	1.00
Candle, three ftd.	17.50		Shakers, pr.	9.00
*Candy, ftd., w/cover	22.50		Sugar	5.00
Celery, 9½"	15.00		Tray, 8", hndl., sug/cr	5.00
Cigarette box	12.50		Tray, 12½", hndl.	15.00
Creamer	5.00		Tumbler, 3¼", ftd.	8.00
Cup	3.00		Tumbler, 5¾", flat	8.00
Jar, relish	12.50		**Tumbler, 7⅛", ftd.	12.00
Lazy Susan	45.00		***Vase, 9"	20.00
Pitcher, 20 oz., milk	18.00			
Pitcher, 64 oz.	28.00			
Plate, 8", salad	5.00			
Plate, 15", serving/punch liner	17.50			
Punch bowl, 12"	25.00			

*Shell Pink bottom only, $10.00
**Flashed colors, $20.00
***Shell Pink, $150.00

NAVARRE, PLATE ETCHING #327, FOSTORIA GLASS COMPANY, 1937 – 1982

Colors: crystal; some blue, pink stems; rare in green and red w/gold etch

Fostoria's Navarre pattern was one of their three top selling etched patterns of all time and was nationally advertised as found "at better stores everywhere." Chintz and Meadow Rose were the other two. Most Navarre was sold after 1940, although it was first launched in 1937. This is the only overlapping pattern from *Elegant Glassware* in this *Collectible Glassware of the 40s, 50s, 60s....*

An assortment of (now hard to find) pieces were made near the end of Fostoria's reign (late 1970s and early 1980s). A greater part of these pieces were signed "Fostoria" with acid etching on the base; a small number had only a sticker. Factory "seconds" that sold through the outlet stores were rarely signed. Quality signed pieces were run through the outlets only when those stores ran short of seconds. Shown on page 160 are a few of the later made pieces of Navarre in the catalog strip taken from a 1982 Fostoria catalog. The price on many of these items has really ballooned to the point that some collectors are doing without or just buying one as an example instead of six, eight, or even twelve. They were already too pricey for many Navarre collectors to own, but they are more so now. You will find that assembling a crystal set of Navarre will be a time-consuming chore, but it can still be done with patience. Possibly only well-heeled collectors can afford to build a set with all pieces.

Some Navarre stems were made with pink and blue bowls from 1973. Lenox Company bought the molds for this line from Fostoria and made and signed them Lenox. Usually the pink made by Lenox is a very washed-out pink or even tends to shade toward a light purple rather than pink. These are difficult to match unless you stick to buying just Lenox or just Fostoria. Sometimes, however, you have to buy what you can find. Besides, as glass supplies dwindle, collectors are being a great deal more tolerant of aberrations such as color hues than they once were.

NAVARRE

	Crystal	Blue/Pink
Bell, dinner	75.00	95.00
Bowl, #2496, 4", square, hndl.	12.00	
Bowl, #2496, 4⅜", hndl.	12.00	
Bowl, #869, 4½", finger	85.00	
Bowl, #2496, 4⅝", tri-cornered	25.00	
Bowl, #2496, 5", hndl., ftd.	25.00	
Bowl, #2496, 6", square, sweetmeat	30.00	
Bowl, #2496, 6¼", 3 ftd., nut	25.00	
Bowl, #2496, 7⅜", ftd., bonbon	50.00	
Bowl, #2496, 10", oval, floating garden	80.00	
Bowl, #2496, 10½", hndl., ftd.	75.00	
Bowl, #2470½, 10½", ftd.	75.00	
Bowl, #2496, 12", flared	62.50	
Bowl, #2545, 12½", oval, "Flame"	75.00	
Candlestick, #2496, 4"	25.00	
Candlestick, #2496, 4½", double	35.00	
Candlestick, #2472, 5", double	55.00	
Candlestick, #2496, 5½"	30.00	
Candlestick, #2496, 6", triple	60.00	
Candlestick, #2545, 6¾", double, "Flame"	75.00	
Candlestick, #2482, 6¾", triple	65.00	
Candy, w/cover, #2496, 3-part	125.00	
Celery, #2440, 11½"	50.00	
Comport, #2496, 3¼", cheese	35.00	
Comport, #2400, 4½"	35.00	
Comport, #2496, 4¾"	35.00	
Cracker, #2496, 11" plate	42.50	
Creamer, #2440, 4¼", ftd.	20.00	
Creamer, #2496, individual	20.00	
Cup, #2440	20.00	
Ice bucket, #2496, 4⅜" high	125.00	
Ice bucket, #2375, 6" high	150.00	
Mayonnaise, #2375, 3-piece	75.00	
Mayonnaise, #2496½, 3-piece	75.00	
Pickle, #2496, 8"	33.00	
Pickle, #2440, 6½"	37.50	
Pitcher, #2666, 32 oz.	265.00	
Pitcher, #5000, 48 oz., ftd.	350.00	
Plate, #2440, 6", bread/butter	11.00	
Plate, #2440, 7½", salad	15.00	
Plate, #2440, 8½", luncheon	22.50	
Plate, #2440, 9½", dinner	52.50	
Plate, #2496, 10", hndl., cake	55.00	

	Crystal	Blue/Pink
Plate, #2440, 10½" oval cake	55.00	
Plate, #2496, 14", torte	80.00	
Plate, #2364, 16", torte	150.00	
Relish, #2496, 6", 2-part, square	32.50	
Relish, #2496, 10" x 7½", 3-part	47.50	
Relish, #2496, 10", 4-part	75.00	
Relish, #2419, 13¼", 5-part	100.00	
Salt & pepper, #2364, 3¼", flat, pr.	85.00	
Salt & pepper, #2375, 3½", ftd., pr.	125.00	
Salad dressing bottle, #2083, 6½"	465.00	
Sauce dish, #2496, div. mayo., 6½"	50.00	
Sauce dish, #2496, 6½" x 5¼"	80.00	
Sauce dish liner, #2496, 8", oval	35.00	
Saucer, #2440	5.00	
Stem, #6106, ¾ oz., cordial, 3⅞"	53.00	
Stem, #6106, 3¼ oz., wine, 5½"	40.00	
Stem, #6106, 3½ oz., cocktail, 6"	25.00	
Stem, #6106, 4 oz., oyster cocktail, 3⅝"	28.00	
Stem, #6106, 4½ oz., claret, 6"	55.00	85.00
Stem, #6106, 5 oz., continental champagne, 8⅛"	150.00	165.00
Stem, #6106, 6 oz., cocktail/sherry, 6³⁄₁₆"	75.00	
Stem, #6106, 6 oz., low sherbet, 4⅜"	24.00	
Stem, #6106, 6 oz., saucer champagne, 5⅝"	24.00	40.00
Stem, #6106, 6½ oz., large claret, 6½"	50.00	65.00
Stem, #6106, 10 oz., water, 7⅝"	35.00	55.00
Stem, #6106, 15 oz., brandy inhaler, 5½"	130.00	
Stem, #6106, 16 oz., magnum, 7¼"	175.00	195.00
Sugar, #2440, 3⅝", ftd.	20.00	
Sugar, #2496, individual	20.00	
Syrup, #2586, Sani-cut, 5½"	465.00	
Tidbit, #2496, 8¼", 3-ftd., turned up edge	30.00	
Tray, #2496½, for ind. sugar/creamer	35.00	
Tumbler, #6106, 5 oz., ftd., juice, 4⅝"	25.00	
Tumbler, #6106, 10 oz., ftd., water, 5⅜"	25.00	
Tumbler, #6106, 12 oz., flat, highball, 4⅞"	110.00	
Tumbler, #6106, 13 oz., flat, double old fashioned, 3⅝"	100.00	
Tumbler, #6106, 13 oz., ftd., tea, 5⅞"	32.00	60.00
Vase, #4108, 5"	110.00	
Vase, #4121, 5"	110.00	
Vase, #4128, 5"	110.00	
Vase, #2470, 10", ftd.	250.00	

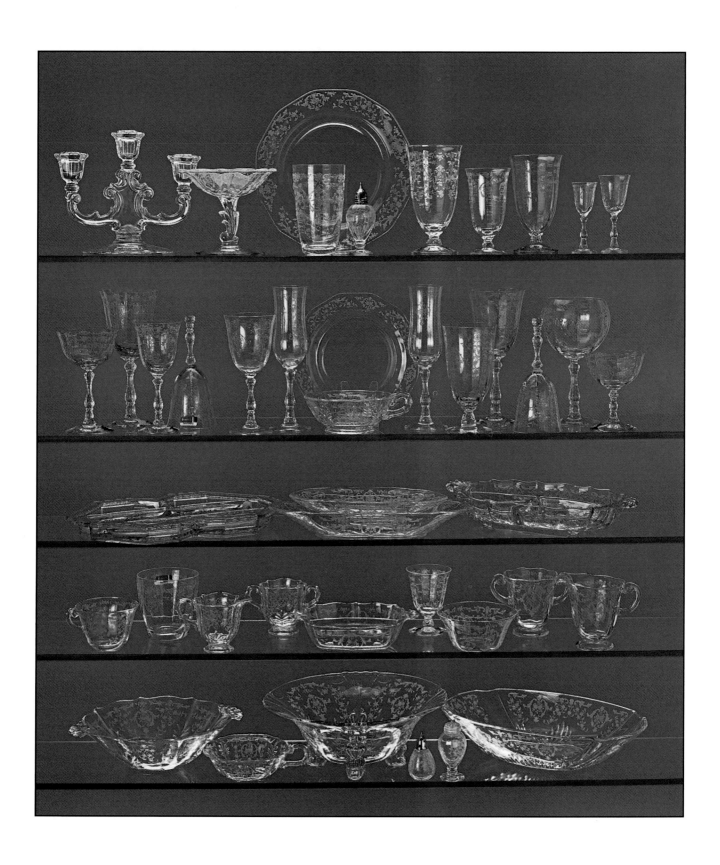

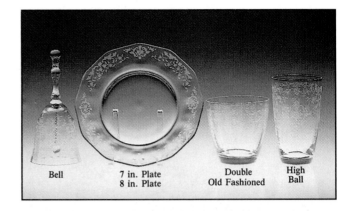

Bell   7 in. Plate / 8 in. Plate   Double Old Fashioned   High Ball

Wilma Blue — Goblet   Wilma Crystal — Goblet   Navarre Crystal — Goblet   Low Dessert/Champagne   High Dessert/Champagne

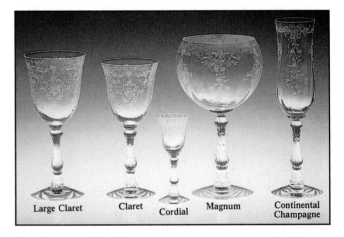

Large Claret   Claret   Cordial   Magnum   Continental Champagne

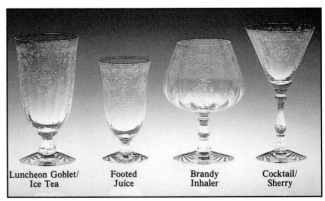

Luncheon Goblet/Ice Tea   Footed Juice   Brandy Inhaler   Cocktail/Sherry

NEW ERA #4044, A.H. HEISEY CO., 1934 – 1941; 1944 – 1957 (STEMS, CELERY TRAY, AND CANDLESTICKS)

Colors: crystal, frosted crystal, some cobalt with crystal stem and foot

New Era was introduced in 1934 as Modern Line. In 1935, it was renamed New Era. This modern linear look was a reflection of its time. Art Deco buffs often seek New Era because it exemplifies the Art Moderne movement. New Era stemware can be used with a variety of patterns, old or new. It has a wonderful, timeless appeal.

Occasionally, New Era stems and tumblers can be found with cobalt bowls atop crystal stems. Four are pictured. Any New Era piece with a cobalt bowl will fetch a minimum of $125.00. All are rare and desirable. Keep that in the mind on your outings. Crystal stems are sometimes found with Venus, Sea Glade, Stardust, or Tahiti etches. A prized pilsner may carry the Tally Ho etch. Some New Era can also be found with beautiful cuttings.

The double-branched candelabra with the New Era bobeches is very appealing and may be found higher priced than my listing. My price is acceptable to Heisey collectors because they understand how commonly found these candelabra are. This mould was purchased from Heisey when the plant closed and reissued by Imperial for quite a few years. Seeing these highly priced definitely does not mean they are selling for those prices.

New Era serving pieces are exceptionally difficult to find. Dinner plates without scratches in that plain, flat center, as well as after-dinner cups and saucers will keep you shopping for a long time unless you are very lucky. Remember though, searching is part of the enjoyment in collecting.

That decanter pictured below is rarely seen; watch for it. The hunting scene is admired more by male collectors. You will find New Era pieces with the borders or stems satinized (frosted). These tend to enhance the pattern, but can go unrecognized as New Era. I admit to once leaving six such plates for $10.00 each. Three weeks later they had been sold twice more and were priced "out of sight" even by today's standards.

	Crystal
Ashtray or indiv. nut	30.00
Bottle, rye, w/stopper	150.00
Bowl, 11", floral	45.00
Candelabra, 2-lite w/2 #4044 bobeche & prisms	120.00
Creamer	37.50
Cup	10.00
Cup, after dinner	62.50
Pilsner, 8 oz.	27.50
Pilsner, 12 oz.	32.50
Plate, 5½" x 4½", bread & butter	15.00
Plate, 9"x 7", luncheon	25.00
Plate, 10" x 8", dinner	45.00
Relish, 13", 3-part	25.00
Saucer	5.00
Saucer, after dinner	12.50
Stem, 1 oz., cordial	35.00
Stem, 3 oz., wine	25.00
Stem, 3½ oz., high, cocktail	12.00
Stem, 3½ oz., oyster cocktail	12.00
Stem, 4 oz., claret	18.00
Stem, 6 oz., sherbet, low	12.50
Stem, 6 oz., champagne	13.00
Stem, 10 oz., goblet	16.00
Sugar	37.50
Tray, 13", celery	30.00
Tumbler, 5 oz., ftd., soda	10.00
Tumbler, 8 oz., ftd., soda	11.00
Tumbler, 10 oz., low, ftd.	11.00
Tumbler, 12 oz., ftd., soda	18.00
Tumbler, 14 oz., ftd., soda	20.00

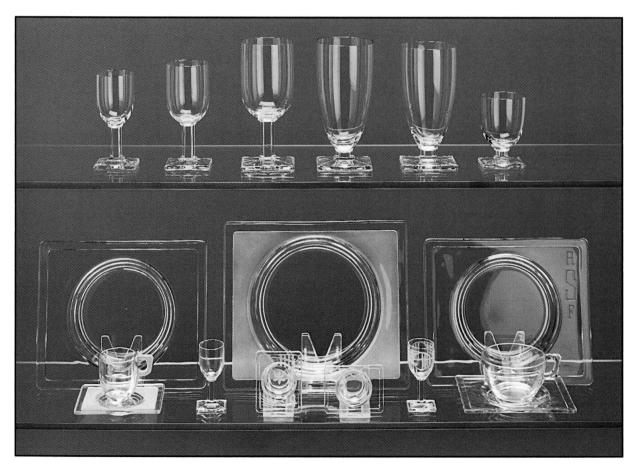

NEWPORT, "HAIRPIN," HAZEL ATLAS GLASS COMPANY, 1940 – EARLY 1950s

Colors: Platonite white and fired-on colors

Newport is one pattern divided between this book and my *Collector's Encyclopedia of Depression Glass* book. Platonite Newport was made during the time structure for this book since Hazel Atlas made it until the early 1950s. The transparent colors of cobalt blue, pink, and amethyst were made entirely before 1940 which is the beginning time for this book. I received quite a few positive comments about the beauty of the colors of Newport chosen for the back cover of the last 50s book. It would look just as fantastic at your table.

Platonite (opaque) white and white with fired-on colors were popular lines for Hazel Atlas around the 1940s and beyond. Newport is a pattern that easily lends itself to the concept of rainbow collecting. The colors are abundant as you can see from the photographs and blending those will work well.

Observe the white edge on the fired-on pink plate in the rear. The edges and back of this plate are white. The color decorates only the top. Evidently, the first colors manufactured all had white interiors or exteriors, depending on the piece. However, the turquoise blue bowl and dark green plate have colors fired both front and back. One collector mentioned that she bought the darker colors in both Newport and Moderntone. Since Hazel Atlas made both these, the colors do match. Blending patterns is also an emerging trend. Many are making their tables bloom with setting from various patterns, either ensemble or having each guest served from a separate design or color.

There are nine tumblers in different colors illustrated. Have you seen any other? I doubt that only nine colors were made. That is an odd number and production modes were mostly in even numbers.

White Platonite comes in two distinct hues. One is opalescent white and probably dates from very early production in the late 1930s; the other is a flat white similar to milk glass, which is the ware seen by the late 30s and early 40s when they "got this color act together" so to speak. Milk glass was popular and so each company contributed patterns. The Newport white shaker is often used by Petalware collectors for their pattern since there are no shakers in the MacBeth-Evans set. It is not unprecedented for novice collectors to be fooled into thinking these shakers really are Petalware.

	White	Fired-on colors		White	Fired-on colors
Bowl, 4¾", berry	3.50	7.50	Plate, 11½", sandwich	10.00	18.00
Bowl, 4¾", cream soup	5.50	12.00	Platter, 11¾", oval	12.00	22.00
Bowl, 8¼, large berry	9.50	20.00	Salt and pepper, pr.	18.00	25.00
Cup	3.50	6.00	Saucer	.75	1.00
Creamer	4.50	7.50	Sherbet	3.50	6.00
Plate, 6", sherbet	1.00	1.50	Sugar	4.50	7.50
Plate, 8½", luncheon	3.00	5.00	Tumbler	8.00	25.00

OAK CUTTING, WABASH CUTTING COMPANY (INDIANA), LATE 1940s – EARLY 1950s

Color: crystal

One of the more entertaining aspects of researching glass comes from finding the same cut pattern on different companies' blanks.

The Oak cutting here is an extreme example, but one I felt compelled to show to confirm why there is sometimes difficulty identifying a cutting using just the company blank. Because the blank is recognized as Heisey or Fostoria does not mean the cutting came from that factory.

Pictured are groups of Fostoria Glass Company items including nine different pieces of Century Blank #2630, one piece of Baroque Blank #2496, and a #2482 trindle candlestick. That is 11 pieces of Fostoria on three different blanks. Oak is cut on two different Heisey blanks including Lariat #1540 stems and Queen Ann #1509 mould blank. Viking Glass is represented by three different pieces including a butter dish and #5247 creamer and sugar. There are six unidentified pieces although I feel sure the two tumblers are Libbey due to their characteristic safety edged rim. I have priced items by what uncut pieces bring and what I had to pay to get this glass to illustrate this point.

FOSTORIA GLASS COMPANY

CENTURY BLANK #2630 Line

Bonbon, 7¼", 3-ftd.	25.00
Bowl, 9½", 2 hdld.	40.00
Creamer, individual	12.50
Mayonnaise	25.00
Mayonnaise liner	10.00
Relish, 11⅛", 3-part	30.00
Sugar, individual	12.50
Tidbit, 8⅛", 3-ftd.	25.00
Tray, 7⅛", individual sugar/creamer	17.50

BAROQUE BLANK #2496

Bowl, 10", hdld.	45.00

BLANK #2482

Trindle candlestick, 6¾" high	65.00

A. H. HEISEY GLASS COMPANY

LARIAT BLANK #1540

Stem, 9 oz., pressed water goblet	25.00
Stem, 5½ oz., pressed saucer champagne	20.00

QUEEN ANN BLANK #1509

Relish, 10", triplex	35.00

VIKING GLASS COMPANY

Creamer, # 5247	15.00
Sugar, #5247	15.00
Butter dish, ¼ pound	40.00

UNIDENTIFIED COMPANIES

Paperweight, rectangular	35.00
Pitcher, 16 oz.	20.00
Pitcher, 32 oz.	30.00
Salt dip w/spoon	20.00
Tumbler, juice (possibly Libbey)	10.00
Tumbler, water (possibly Libbey)	12.50

ORANGE BLOSSOM, LINE # 619, INDIANA GLASS COMPANY, C. 1957

Color: Milk white

During the 1950s and early 1960s, milk glass production by glass companies was very big news. Everybody was making wares as fast as they could in milk colored glass. Indiana had produced a pattern in the 1930s in a custard color which collectors now refer to as "Indiana Custard." They pulled the moulds from that prior production and re-issued it as Orange Blossom in milk glass. I have included this information in the past Depression glass books I've written. However, in the last two or three years, people have been specifically asking me at shows if I have any Orange Blossom. Thus, I assume it's time it has its own place in this book about 50s wares. This pattern is quite small since it was presented only as a luncheon set.

Bowl, 5½", dessert	5.00
Creamer, ftd.	5.00
Cup	4.00
Plate, 5¾", sherbet	3.00
Plate, 8⅞", lunch	8.00
Saucer	1.00
Sugar, ftd.	5.00

ORCHID, ETCHING #1507 ON WAVERLY BLANK #1519 AND QUEEN ANN BLANK #1509,

A.H. HEISEY & CO., 1940 – 1957

Colors: crystal

Orchid is generally found etched on two major Heisey blanks. Blank #1509, or Queen Ann, is pictured below and Blank #1519, known as Waverly, is illustrated on page 170. Originally, most collectors did not mix these two lines, but some of the new breed do not seem to follow conventional collecting modes and are pleased to acquire any piece that they do not have.

Orchid tumblers, stemware, and other Heisey mould lines with Orchid etching are pictured on page 171. The pitcher and vases shown are rarely seen today unless you go to a show specializing in Heisey glassware. The Internet has brought masses of Heisey stemware out of every storage place known to man and Orchid has been extremely well represented. Evidently, Orchid stems were purchased by thousands to be used with china sets.

Today, serving pieces and flatware items are continuing to rise in price. Orchid dinner plates without scuffs and scrapes are difficult to acquire. I picked up a "priceless dinner plate" (no price sticker) at a recent show and the dealer said he could make me a great price on those hardly used plates. Evidently hardly used in the west means the owners only got out chain saws for special occasions to cut the meat. Hardly used in the east means light scuffing and rubbing at most. I expect this enormous supply of stemware from the Internet to diminish in time. If you need Orchid stems, consider this is the time to acquire it.

Ashtray, 3"	30.00
Basket, 8½", LARIAT	1,200.00
Bell, dinner, #5022 or #5025	135.00
Bottle, 8 oz., French dressings	175.00
Bowl, finger, #3309 or #5025	90.00
Bowl, 4½", nappy, QUEEN ANN	37.50
Bowl, 5½", ftd., mint, QUEEN ANN	45.00
Bowl, 6", jelly, 2 hndl., QUEEN ANN.	37.50
Bowl, 6" oval, lemon, w/cover, QUEEN ANN	310.00
Bowl, 6", oval, lemon, w/cover, WAVERLY	695.00
Bowl, 6½", ftd., honey, cheese, QUEEN ANN	60.00
Bowl, 6½", ftd., jelly, WAVERLY	60.00
Bowl, 6½", 2 pt., oval, dressings, WAVERLY	55.00
Bowl, 7", lily, QUEEN ANN	125.00
Bowl, 7", salad	60.00
Bowl, 7", 3 pt., rnd., relish	55.00
Bowl, 7", ftd., honey, cheese, WAVERLY	55.00
Bowl, 7", ftd., jelly	45.00
Bowl, 7", ftd., oval, nut, WAVERLY	90.00
Bowl, 8", mint, ftd., QUEEN ANN	65.00
Bowl, 8", nappy, QUEEN ANN	70.00
Bowl, 8", 2 pt., oval, dressings, ladle	55.00
Bowl, 8", pt., rnd., relish	62.50
Bowl, 8½", flared, QUEEN ANN	67.50
Bowl, 8½", floral, 2 hndl., ftd., QUEEN ANN	65.00
Bowl, 9", 4 pt., rnd., relish	75.00
Bowl, 9", ftd., fruit or salad	135.00
Bowl, 9", gardenia, QUEEN ANN	65.00
Bowl, 9", salad, WAVERLY	195.00
Bowl, 9½", crimped, floral, QUEEN ANN	75.00
Bowl, 9½", epergne	525.00
Bowl, 10", crimped	72.50
Bowl, 10", deep salad	150.00
Bowl, 10", gardenia	75.00
Bowl, 10½", ftd., floral	115.00
Bowl, 11", shallow, rolled edge	70.00
Bowl, 11", 3-ftd., floral, seahorse ft.	165.00
Bowl, 11", 3-pt., oblong, relish	70.00
Bowl, 11", 4-ftd., oval	125.00
Bowl, 11", flared	135.00
Bowl, 11", floral	70.00
Bowl, 11", ftd., floral	115.00
Bowl, 12", crimped, floral, WAVERLY	95.00
Bowl, 13", floral	95.00
Bowl, 13", crimped, floral, WAVERLY	95.00
Bowl, 13", gardenia	70.00
Butter, w/cover, ¼ lb., CABOCHON	325.00
Butter, w/cover, 6", WAVERLY	150.00
Candleholder, 6", deep epernette, WAVERLY	1,000.00
Candlestick, 1-lite, MERCURY	45.00
Candlestick, 1-lite, QUEEN ANN, w/prisms	150.00
Candlestick, 2-lite, FLAME	180.00
Candlestick, 5", 2-lite, TRIDENT	60.00
Candlestick, 2-lite, WAVERLY	65.00
Candlestick, 3-lite, CASCADE	85.00
Candlestick, 3-lite, WAVERLY	100.00
Candy box, w/cover, 6", low ft.	175.00
Candy, w/cover, 5", high ft., WAVERLY	250.00
Candy, w/cover, 6", bow knot finial	175.00
Cheese (comport) & cracker (11½") plate	135.00
Cheese & cracker, 14", plate	155.00
Chocolate, w/cover, 5", WAVERLY	220.00
Cigarette box, w/cover, 4", PURITAN	140.00
Cigarette holder, #4035	85.00
Cigarette holder, w/cover	195.00
Cocktail icer, w/liner, UNIVERSAL, #3304	250.00
Cocktail shaker, pt., #4225	240.00
Cocktail shaker, qt., #4036 or #4225	225.00

Comport, 5½", blown	95.00
Comport, 6", low ft., WAVERLY	85.00
Comport, 6½", low ft., WAVERLY	80.00
Comport, 7", ftd., oval	165.00
Creamer, individual	35.00
Creamer, ftd.	28.00
Cup, WAVERLY or QUEEN ANN	38.00
Decanter, oval, sherry, pt.	250.00
Decanter, pt., ftd., #4036	700.00
Decanter, pt., #4036½	375.00
Ice bucket, ftd., QUEEN ANN	200.00
Ice bucket, 2 hndl., WAVERLY	425.00
Marmalade, w/cover	235.00
Mayonnaise and liner, #1495, FERN	250.00
Mayonnaise, 5½", 1 hndl.	55.00
Mayonnaise, 5½", ftd.	55.00
Mayonnaise, 5½", 1 hndl., div.	50.00
Mayonnaise, 6½", 1 hndl.	65.00
Mayonnaise, 6½", 1 hndl., div.	65.00
Mustard, w/cover, QUEEN ANN	145.00
Oil, 3 oz., ftd.	195.00
Pitcher, 73 oz.	475.00
Pitcher, 64 oz., ice tankard	550.00
Plate, 6"	11.00
Plate, 7", mayonnaise	18.00
Plate, 7", salad	18.00
Plate, 8", salad, WAVERLY	20.00
Plate, 10½", dinner	150.00
Plate, 11", demi-torte	62.50
Plate, 11", sandwich	65.00
Plate, 12", ftd., salver, WAVERLY	250.00
Plate, 12", rnd., sandwich, hndl.	70.00
Plate, 14", ftd., cake or salver	265.00
Plate, 14", torte, rolled edge	65.00
Plate, 14", torte, WAVERLY	90.00
Plate, 14", sandwich, WAVERLY	80.00
Plate, 15", sandwich, WAVERLY	75.00
Plate, 15½", QUEEN ANN	110.00
Salt & pepper, pr.	75.00
Salt & pepper, ftd., pr., WAVERLY	70.00
Saucer, WAVERLY or QUEEN ANN	10.00
Stem, #5022 or #5025, 1 oz., cordial	135.00
Stem, #5022 or #5025, 2 oz., sherry	115.00
Stem, #5022 or #5025, 3 oz., wine	75.00
Stem, #5022 or #5025, 4 oz., oyster cocktail	60.00
Stem, #5025, 4 oz., cocktail	35.00
Stem, #5022 or #5025, 4½ oz., claret	135.00
Stem, #5022 or #5025, 6 oz., saucer champagne	26.00
Stem, #5022 or #5025, 6 oz., sherbet	22.00
Stem, #5022 or #5025, 10 oz., low water goblet	36.00
Stem, #5022 or #5025, 10 oz., water goblet	38.00
Sugar, individual	35.00
Sugar, ftd.	28.00
Tray, indiv., creamer/sugar, QUEEN ANN	90.00
Tray, 12", celery	60.00
Tray, 13", celery	60.00
Tumbler, #5022 or #5025, 5 oz., fruit	50.00
Tumbler, #5022 or #5025, 12 oz., iced tea	55.00
Vase, 4", ftd., violet, WAVERLY	140.00
Vase, 6", crimped top	125.00
Vase, 7", ftd., fan, lariat	110.00
Vase, 7", ftd., fan	185.00
Vase, 7", crimped top, LARIAT	120.00
Vase, 8", ftd., bud	215.00
Vase, 8", sq., ftd., bud	225.00
Vase, 10", sq., ftd., bud	295.00
Vase, 12"	375.00
Vase, 14"	695.00

Colors: Green, black, white Platonite, and white with trimmed or fired-on colors in 1950s

I recently had contact with a collector of Ovide who said he had over 40 different patterns and designs on this Hazel Atlas mould blank. I was only aware of about 20 or so. Ovide production began in the Depression mostly in transparent colors; yet, production lasted well into the 1950s with opaque Platonite. Collectors are buying this economically priced glassware to use as their daily dishes. According to these users, Ovide works well in both the microwave and the dishwasher. It would seem that Hazel Atlas did a better job of adhering their designs to the surface than did some of the other glass companies.

Pattern names (Sierra Sunrise and Informal pictured below and on page 175) have surfaced for some of the pastel-banded Platonite that was used in restaurants and competed with Anchor Hocking's Jade-ite and white Restaurant Ware lines. Only a few of the combination colors pictured here are found in quantity today. Evidently, they were not as profusely distributed as Hocking's Fire-King wares.

I once received an 18-piece set of dark "Moderntone" colors expecting to receive the Moderntone pattern. I obtained Moderntone Ovide, but the original box stated it only as Moderntone. Evidently, Moderntone at the factory may have referred to the colors and not the pattern. You will find Ovide pieces in the 50s Moderntone colors of Burgundy, Chartreuse, Green, and Gray. That Green is the actual color designation by Hazel Atlas in spite of collectors calling it forest or dark green. This colored Ovide ware appears to be Hazel Atlas Glass Company's answer to the popular 50s Fiesta dinnerware.

Colors shown at the bottom of page 173 have been hard for me to find. It's taken almost 15 years to accumulate what is shown. I have never found a platter in any color other than the "butterscotch." Platters in all Hazel Atlas's Platonite patterns seem to rule in that one color. All basic pieces should be found in all colors; but serving pieces may only be "butterscotch." Let me know if you find something different.

Page 174 shows a variety of the decorated white Ovide. You can gather sets in any of the patterns illustrated. The black floral and leaf crosses over into kitchenware items with refrigerator jars, kitchen shakers, and even a reamer pitcher set. In most cases, you have a wide choice of Ovide to select from without having to obtain a second mortgage to buy it.

	White w/trims	Designs Decorated on White	Fired-on Colors	Art Deco
Ashtray, square			4.00	
Bowl, 4¾", berry	3.50	8.00	5.50	
Bowl, 5½", cereal, deep		12.00		
Bowl, 8", large berry			18.00	
Creamer	4.50	9.00	4.00	110.00
Cup	3.50	11.00	4.50	75.00
Plate, 6", sherbet	1.50	2.50		
Plate, 8", luncheon	2.50	12.00	4.00	50.00
Plate, 9", dinner	3.50		8.00	
Platter, 11"	7.50	25.00		
Refrigerator stacking set, 4-pc.		47.50		
Salt and pepper, pr.	13.00			
Saucer	1.00	2.00	2.00	20.00
Sherbet	5.50	3.00		65.00
Sugar, open	4.50	9.00	4.00	110.00
Tumbler		17.00		110.00

Colors: white and white w/decorations, and some mint green in 1979

Paneled Grape is one of three Westmoreland patterns that almost all collectors have learned to identify. Della Robbia and English Hobnail are familiar, but not everyone seems to know that Westmoreland made them as well. Maybe that WG marking on the bottom of Paneled Grape facilitated learning.

Production of Pattern #1881 (Paneled Grape) began in 1950 and continued for nearly 30 years. Westmoreland listed this pattern with both designations (#1881 and Paneled Grape) as you can see from the catalog copies on the following pages. Catalog pages from 1973 are depicted on pages 179 – 190. Company pictures and descriptions are always helpful. (Pieces shown on the catalog sheets as line #1884 are called Beaded Grape by collectors and are not priced in the Paneled Grape listing below.)

Paneled Grape isn't everyone's cup of tea; but its devotees are passionate about their regard for it.

Mint green Paneled Grape can be found, but there are few buyers at present for this 1979 production. Westmoreland collectors are close-mouthed about values on their glass and no one I talked to wanted to price green other than to say it was hard to sell right now. Since it was a very limited run, collectors may be missing the mark here. Notice the Christmas decorated plate on page 178. I bought it, photographed it, and sold it at the first show afterward. It is the only such Paneled Grape piece I'd seen, but there may be a whole selection of Christmas-themed pieces.

To answer a question frequently asked about vases in this pattern, swung vases are actually swung while hot to extend their shape and therefore, their sizes vary. Very rarely do two measure the same; that is why I list "size varies" on prices of swung vases.

Rarely found pieces of Paneled Grape have continued to rise in price, albeit slowly. Prices for basic pieces remain steady or with only a slight dip or two. Produced for so long, #1881 has been able to keep up with present collector demand. Were more collectors enchanted by milk glass, the rarities in this pattern would skyrocket in price due to short supply.

Punch sets and the triple candelabra are, apparently, not quite as hard to acquire as once thought. We have sold four complete punch sets, two partial sets, and five candelabra in the last few years, although there are collectors still searching for them.

	White w/decorations
Appetizer or canapé set, 3 pc. (9" three-part relish, round fruit cocktail, ladle)	65.00
Basket, 5½", ruffled	55.00
Basket, 6½", oval	25.00
Basket, 8"	75.00
Basket, 8", ruffled	75.00
Bonbon, 8", ruffled, w/metal handle	50.00
Bottle, 5 oz., toilet	60.00
Bottle, oil or vinegar, w/stopper, 2 oz.	23.00
Bowl, pedestal base, 5" (used w/12" – 12½" lipped, 10" rnd. bowls & epergne)	65.00
Bowl, 4", crimped	22.00
Bowl, 6", crimped, stemmed	30.00
Bowl, 6", ruffled edge, stemmed	30.00
Bowl, 6½" x 12½", 3⅛" high	125.00
Bowl, 6½", oval	23.00
Bowl, 8", cupped	38.00
Bowl, 8½", shallow	55.00
Bowl, 9", ftd., 6" high, skirted base	50.00
Bowl, 9", ftd., w/cover	80.00
Bowl, 9", lipped	110.00
Bowl, 9", lipped, ftd.	115.00
Bowl, 9", square, w/cover	50.00
Bowl, 9½", bell-shaped	45.00
Bowl, 9½", ftd., bell-shaped	110.00
Bowl, 10", oval	45.00
Bowl, 10½", round	77.50
Bowl, 11", oval, lipped, ftd.	125.00
Bowl, 11½", oval, ruffled edge	80.00
Bowl, 12", lipped	120.00
Bowl, 12" ftd., banana	175.00
Bowl, 12½", bell-shaped	135.00
Bowl, 13", punch, bell or flared	325.00
Bowl, 14", shallow, round	150.00
Bowl, ftd., ripple top	85.00
Butter w/cover, ¼ pound	25.00
Cake salver, 10½"	70.00
Cake salver, 11", round ftd., w/skirt	75.00
Canapé or set, 3 pc. (12½" canapé tray, 3½" cocktail, ladle)	120.00
Candelabra, 3-lite, ea.	165.00
Candle holder, 4", octagonal	15.00

	White w/decorations
Candle holder, 5", w/colonial hndl.	37.50
Candle holder, 8", 2-lite (4 of these form a circular center piece)	40.00
Candy jar, 3-ftd., w/cover	32.50
Candy jar, 6¼", w/cover	25.00
Canister, 7"	165.00
Canister, 9½"	195.00
Canister, 11"	225.00
Celery or spooner, 6"	40.00
Cheese or old fashioned butter, 7", round, w/cover	57.50
Chocolate box, 6½", w/cover	55.00
Compote, 4½", crimped	30.00
Compote, 7" covered, ftd.	50.00
Compote, 9" ftd., crimped	80.00
Condiment set, 5-pc. (oil and vinegar, salt and pepper on 9" oval tray)	135.00
Creamer, 6½ oz.	16.00
Creamer, individual	11.00
Creamer, large (goes w/lacy edge sugar)	22.50
Creamer, small	15.00
Cup, coffee, flared	15.00
Cup, punch, cupped	15.00
Decanter, wine	165.00
Dresser set, 4-pc. (two) 5 oz. toilet bottles, puff box, and 13½" oval tray	250.00
Egg plate, 12"	85.00
Egg tray, 10", metal center handle	70.00
Epergne vase, 8½", bell	60.00
Epergne vase, pattern at top	250.00
Epergne set, 2-pc. (9" lipped bowl, 8½" epergne vase)	120.00
Epergne set, 2-pc. (11½" epergne flared bowl, 8½" epergne vase)	120.00
Epergne set, 2-pc. (12" epergne lipped bowl, 8½" epergne vase)	200.00
Epergne set, 2-pc. (14" flared bowl, 8½" epergne vase)	235.00
Epergne set, 3-pc. (12" epergne lipped bowl, 5" bowl base, 8½" epergne vase)	325.00
Epergne set, 3-pc. (14" flared bowl, 5" bowl base, 8½" epergne vase)	350.00
Flower pot	45.00
Fruit cocktail, 3½" w/6" sauce plate, bell-shaped	22.50

PANELED GRAPE

	White w/decorations		White w/decorations
Fruit cocktail, 4½" w/6" sauce plate, round	25.00	*Salt and pepper, 4¼", small, ftd., pr.	27.50
Ivy ball	45.00	Salt and pepper, 4½", large, flat, pr.	52.50
Jardiniere, 5", cupped and ftd.	28.00	Sauce boat	35.00
Jardiniere, 5", straight sided	25.00	Sauce boat tray, 9"	25.00
Jardiniere, 6½", cupped and ftd.	38.00	Saucer	8.50
Jardiniere, 6½", straight sided	35.00	Sherbet, 3¾", low foot	16.00
Jelly, 4½", covered	27.50	Sherbet, 4¾", high foot	17.50
Ladle, small	10.00	Soap dish	110.00
Ladle, punch	75.00	Stem, 2 oz., cordial or wine goblet	18.00
Lighter in 2 oz. goblet	26.50	Stem, 3 oz.	28.00
Lighter in tooth pick	28.00	Stem, 5 oz., wine goblet	28.00
Marmalade, w/ladle	57.50	Stem, 8 oz., water goblet	20.00
Mayonnaise set, 3-pc. (round fruit cocktail, 6" sauce plate, ladle)	35.00	Sugar w/cover, lacy edge on sugar to serve as spoon holder	35.00
Mayonnaise, 4", ftd.	27.50	Sugar, 6½"	14.00
Napkin ring	20.00	Sugar, small w/cover	18.00
Nappy, 4½", round	14.00	Tidbit or snack server, 2-tier (dinner and breakfast plates)	65.00
Nappy, 5", bell shape	22.00	Tidbit tray, metal handle on 8½" breakfast plate	27.50
Nappy, 5", round, w/handle	28.00	Tidbit tray, metal handle on 10½" dinner plate	47.50
Nappy, 7", round	30.00	Toothpick	25.00
Nappy, 8½", round	32.00	Tray, 9", oval	55.00
Nappy, 9", round, 2" high	42.00	Tray, 13½", oval	100.00
Nappy, 10", bell	45.00	Tumbler, 5 oz. juice	24.00
Oil bottle	25.00	Tumbler, 6 oz., old fashioned cocktail	27.50
Parfait, 6"	25.00	Tumbler, 8 oz.	20.00
Pedestal, base to punch bowl, skirted	95.00	Tumbler, 12 oz. iced tea	25.00
Pickle, oval	21.00	Vase, 4", rose	20.00
Pitcher, 16 oz.	40.00	Vase, 4½, rose, ftd., cupped, stemmed	32.00
Pitcher, 32 oz.	28.00	Vase, 6", bell shape	20.00
Planter, 3" x 8½"	35.00	Vase, 6½", or celery	35.00
Planter, 4½", square	40.00	Vase, 8½", bell shape	28.00
Planter, 5" x 9"	38.00	Vase, 9", bell shape	28.00
Planter, 6", small, wall	90.00	Vase, 9", crimped top	38.00
Planter, 8", large, wall	150.00	Vase, 9½", straight	35.00
Plate, 6", bread	4.00	Vase, 10" bud (size may vary)	20.00
Plate, 7" salad, w/depressed center	25.00	Vase, 11", rose (similar to bud vase but bulbous at bottom)	40.00
Plate, 8½", breakfast	22.00	Vase, 11½", bell shape	50.00
Plate, 10½", dinner	45.00	Vase, 11½", straight	38.00
Plate, 14½"	125.00	Vase, 12", hand blown	195.00
Plate, 18"	185.00	Vase, 14", swung (size varies)	28.00
Puff box or jelly, w/cover	30.00	Vase, 15"	32.00
Punch set, 15-pc. (13" bowl, 12 punch cups, pedestal and ladle)	545.00	Vase, 16", swung (size varies)	28.00
Punch set, 15-pc. (same as above w/11" bowl w/o scalloped bottom)	475.00	Vase, 18", swung (size varies)	30.00
Relish, 9", 3-part	40.00		
Salt and pepper, 4¼", small, ftd., pr.	22.50		

*All-over pattern

"Panel Grape"

GIFT SUGGESTIONS TO PLEASE THE DISCRIMINATING

1881
Bowl, Crimp.

1881 Bowl,
Lip. Ftd.

1881 Bowl,
Shallow

1881
Basket, Hld.

1881
Bowl, Lip.

1881
Bowl, Oval

1881/6½"
Basket

1881
Appetizer Set

1881
Bowl, Bell

1881
Bowl, Rose

1881
Butter

1881
Bon Bon

FAMOUS *"Panel Grape"* THE COLLECTORS FAVORITE

1881 Plates, 14½", 10½" & 8½"

1881
3 pc. Canister Set

1881
Jug, Qt.

1881
Salver, Skirted

1881
Salver, Ftd.

1881 Snack Server

1881
Egg Tray

1881
Ice Tea

1881
Goblet

1881
Sauce Boat/Tray

1881
Mayonnaise

1881
Condiment Set

1881
Salt/Pepper,
Lg.

1881
Oil

1881
Salt/Pepper
(Min. 3 Sets)

1881
Candy

1881
Dish, 3 Ftd.

1881
Puff Box/
Jelly

1881
Chocolate Box

1881
Candy, Crimp.

1881
Pickle

1881
Starter Set

1881
Candlestick

1881
Mayo
Set

1881
Cup/Saucer

1881
Dish, Oval

4

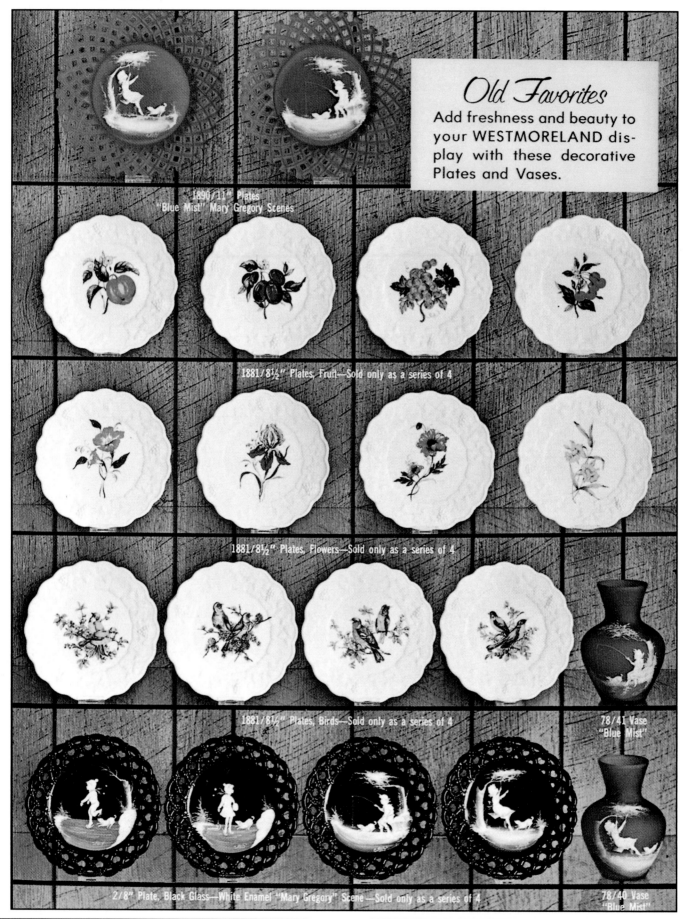

Old Favorites

Add freshness and beauty to your WESTMORELAND display with these decorative Plates and Vases.

1890/11" Plates
"Blue Mist" Mary Gregory Scenes

1881/8½" Plates, Fruit—Sold only as a series of 4

1881/8½" Plates, Flowers—Sold only as a series of 4

78/41 Vase
"Blue Mist"

1881/8½" Plates, Birds—Sold only as a series of 4

2/8" Plate, Black Glass—White Enamel "Mary Gregory" Scene—Sold only as a series of 4

78/40 Vase
"Blue Mist"

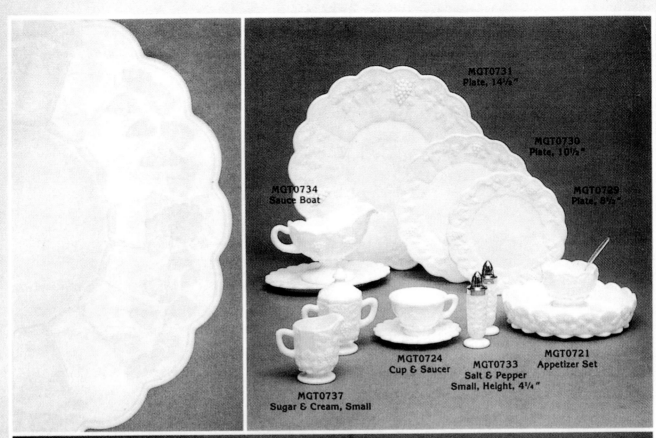

MGT0731
Plate, 14½"

MGT0730
Plate, 10½"

MGT0729
Plate, 8½"

MGT0734
Sauce Boat

MGT0724
Cup & Saucer

MGT0733
Salt & Pepper
Small, Height, 4¼"

MGT0721
Appetizer Set

MGT0737
Sugar & Cream, Small

MGT0726
Jug, 1 Qt.

MGT0725
Goblet

MGT0736
Sugar & Cream,
Large

MGT0722
Butter

MGT0732
Salt & Pepper
Large, Height, 4½"

MGT0739
Wine

MGT0738
Tid Bit Tray

Milk Glass Tableware

1881
Sauce Boat/Tray

1881
Goblet
8 oz.

1881
Sugar/Cream, Lg.

1881
Jug, Qt.

1881 Salt/Pepper

small

large

small

1881 Oil, 2 oz.

1881 Sugar/Cream

1881
Appetizer
Set

1881
Marmalade
W/Ladle

1881
Snack
Server

1881
Tid Bit
Tray

1881 Plate, 14½"

1881 Plate, 10½"

1881 Plate, 8½"

1881
Cheese

1881 Butter

1881 Cup/Saucer

...Kitchen & Table
Accessories

29

109
Cookie Jar

Collector's items from the vast "Paneled Grape" pattern

1881/9" Bowl, Sq.

1881/9" Compote, Crimped

1881 Compote, Crimped

1881/7" Compote

1881 Candy Jar

1881 Decanter

1881 Celery/Vase

1881 Dish, 3 Ftd.

1881 Chocolate Box

1881 Candleholder

1881 Cocktail, Fruit

1881 Cheese

1881/9" Bowl, Bell

1881/¼# Butter

1881 Cup/Saucer

1881 Candle

1881 Dish

1881/12" Bowl, Lipped

1881 Bowl, Banana

1881 Bowl, Oval Lpd.

PANELED GRAPE

Excellent Gift Suggestions in a treasured pattern

1881/14½" Plate

1881/10½" Plate

1881/8½" Plate

1881/6" Plate

1881 Mayonnaise

1881/2 oz. Oil

1881/4½" Nappy

1881 Ice Tea

1881 Goblet

1881/1 Pt. Jug

1881/1 Qt. Jug

1881/6½" Jardiniere

1881/5" Jardiniere

1881 Pickle

1881 Mayo Set

1881 Puff Box/Jelly

1881 Flower Pot

1881 Planter, Oblong

1881 Planter, Window

1881 Planter, Sq.

1881 Ivy Ball

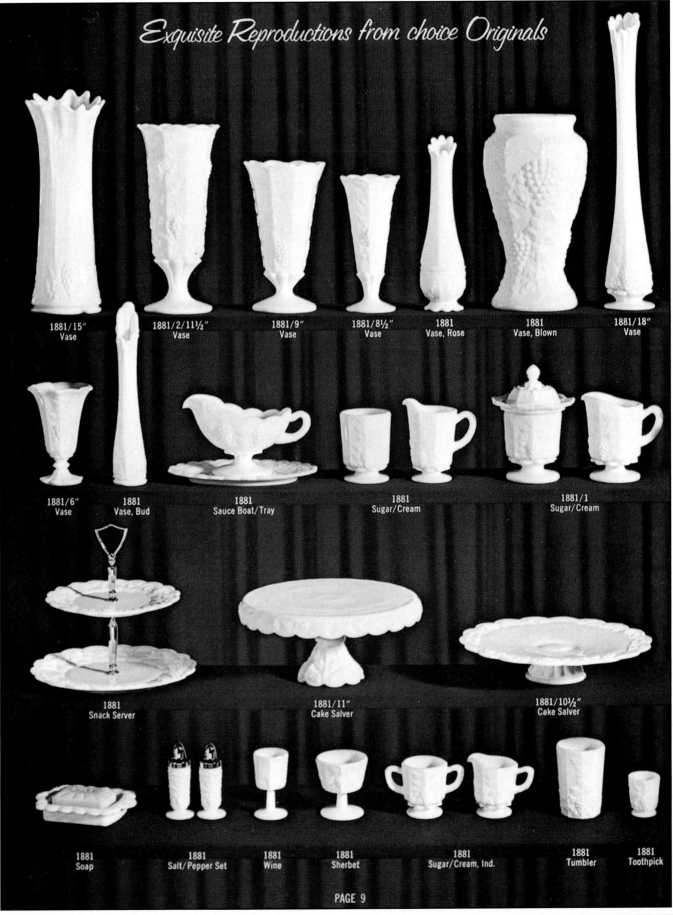

Exquisite Reproductions from choice Originals

1881/15"
Vase

1881/2/11½"
Vase

1881/9"
Vase

1881/8½"
Vase

1881
Vase, Rose

1881
Vase, Blown

1881/18"
Vase

1881/6"
Vase

1881
Vase, Bud

1881
Sauce Boat/Tray

1881
Sugar/Cream

1881/1
Sugar/Cream

1881
Snack Server

1881/11"
Cake Salver

1881/10½"
Cake Salver

1881
Soap

1881
Salt/Pepper Set

1881
Wine

1881
Sherbet

1881
Sugar/Cream, Ind.

1881
Tumbler

1881
Toothpick

PANELED GRAPE

1881
Jug, Pt.

1881
Jug, Qt.

1881
Dish, 3 Ftd.

1881/9"
Compote, Crimp.

1881
Decanter

1881/4½"
Compote, Crimp.

1881
Goblet

1881
Ice Tea

1881
Compote

1881
Candy

1881
Celery/Vase

1881
Flower Pot

1881
Candlestick

1881
Condiment Set

1881
Candy, Crimp.

1881
Canape Server

1881
Cheese

1881
Choc. Box

1881 Dish, Oval

1881 Wine

1881 Cup/Saucer

1881 Cocktail, Fruit

13

1881
15 Pc. Punch Set
(Ind. Boxed)

1881
Pickle

1881
Snack Server

1881
Sauce Boat/Tray

1881
Oil

1881
Salt/Pepper, Lg.

1881
Cake Salver
(Ind. Boxed)

1881
Planter, Obl.

1881
Puff Box/Jelly

1881
Salt/Pepper
(Packed 3 Sets Per Box)

1881
Mayonnaise

1881
Mayo Set

1881/10½"
Plate
14½" Plate Also Available

1881/8½"
Plate

1881/6"
Plate

14

PANELED GRAPE

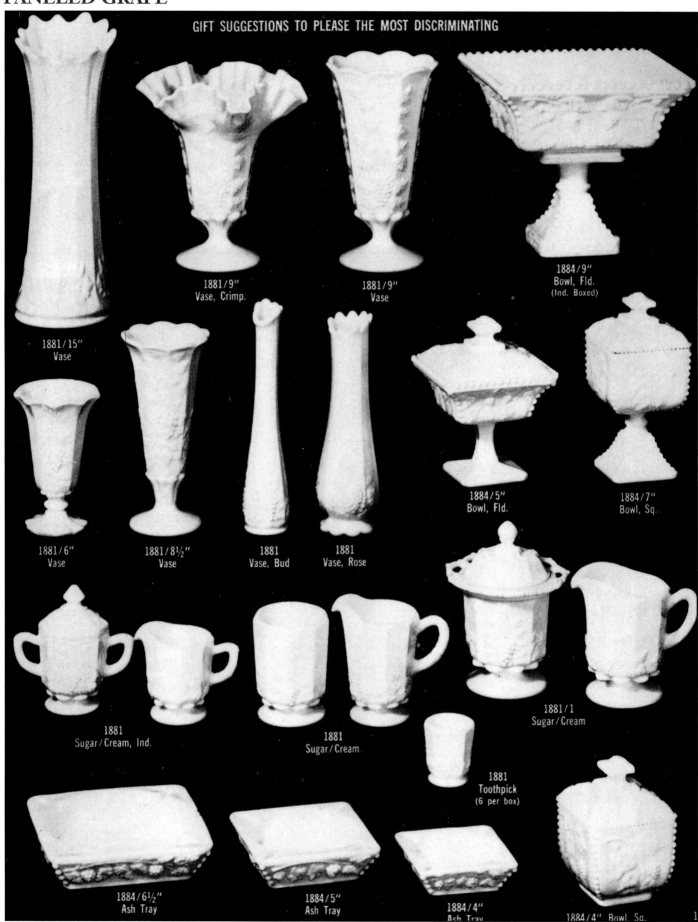

GIFT SUGGESTIONS TO PLEASE THE MOST DISCRIMINATING

1881/15"
Vase

1881/9"
Vase, Crimp.

1881/9"
Vase

1884/9"
Bowl, Fld.
(Ind. Boxed)

1881/6"
Vase

1881/8½"
Vase

1881
Vase, Bud

1881
Vase, Rose

1884/5"
Bowl, Fld.

1884/7"
Bowl, Sq.

1881
Sugar/Cream, Ind.

1881
Sugar/Cream

1881
Toothpick
(6 per box)

1881/1
Sugar/Cream

1884/6½"
Ash Tray

1884/5"
Ash Tray

1884/4"
Ash Tray

1884/4" Bowl, Sq.

PARK AVENUE, FEDERAL GLASS COMPANY, 1941 – EARLY 1970s

Colors: yellow, crystal, and crystal w/gold trim

Yellow is the color being sought by most collectors. I continue to have difficulty finding it as you can see by my one tumbler in the photo below. I keep finding sets of Federal's yellow Star in my travels, but not Park Avenue.

I separated the colors in the listing last book to better show that the demand for yellow has pushed those prices higher. I had several interesting letters saying I made buying more difficult with higher prices. I just try to reflect what the market is doing. Actually, I haven't run into it at any price because few dealers carry these smaller patterns to shows.

Crystal gold-trimmed pieces are difficult to find with strong gold decorations remaining. Gold wore off easily since it was a very soft 22K. If the gold is so worn that it looks awful, you can remove it with an art gum eraser or a *light* use of Soft Scrub®. Notice the emphasis is light as it will scratch the surface of glass if done vigorously. That is the voice of experience talking. A lemon-based soap in the dishwasher is another gold removing idea to try.

Apparently, crystal Park Avenue was circulated in the central Florida area. I found the bowl with the wire-hanging vases in this area. I doubt if it was factory made, but it does heighten the picture for the photographer. I have seen one other for sale.

You will find the Federal Glass Company trademark (F within a shield) embossed on the bottom of most of the pieces. No Park Avenue pitchers, per se, were made as far as catalog records indicate. Star pitchers shown on page 236 were often sold with tumblers from this set.

The small whisky tumbler (as well as other sizes of tumblers) in Park Avenue may be found with jelly labels still affixed to them. I'm told the smaller ones were distributed at restaurants like those plastic containers today stacked with tons of grape jelly and no other flavor in sight. Peach preserves were enclosed in one I found.

All pieces listed were made into the early 1960s except the whisky glass that was in production until the early 1970s. Before I get letters, let me point out that Federal's catalog used the British spelling of whisky without the "e"; so, it seemed appropriate here that I follow their lead.

	Yellow	Crystal
Ashtray, 3½", square		5.00
Ashtray, 4½", square		7.00
Bowl, 5", dessert	7.00	2.00
Bowl, 8½", vegetable	18.00	10.00
Candleholder, 5"		8.00
Tumbler, 2⅛", 1¼ oz., whisky		4.00
Tumbler, 3½", 4½ oz., juice	7.00	5.00
Tumbler, 3⅞", 9 oz.	10.00	5.00
Tumbler, 4¾", 10 oz.	12.00	6.00
Tumbler, 5⅛", 12 oz., iced tea	15.00	7.00

PRESSED TUMBLERS

Matching lines . . . such as the famed Park Avenue
on this page, or the Star Line on the next . . . new,
unusual shapes, and standard staples, are shown here in
Federal's selection of pressed tumblers. All are designed
and engineered for eye-appeal, serviceability, and
good value.

PARK AVENUE

TUMBLERS

1122 — 1¼ oz.
PARK AVENUE WHISKY
Ht. 2⅛″
Pkd. 12 doz. ctn. Wt. 16 lbs.

1122 — 4½ oz.
PARK AVENUE JUICE TUMBLER
Ht. 3½″
Pkd. 12 doz. ctn. Wt. 35 lbs.

1122 — 9 oz.
PARK AVENUE TUMBLER
Ht. 3⅞″
Pkd. 12 doz. ctn. Wt. 56 lbs.

1142 — 10 oz.
PARK AVENUE TUMBLER*
Ht. 4¾″
Pkd. 6 doz. ctn. Wt. 37 lbs.

1122 — 12 oz.
PARK AVENUE ICED TEA
Ht. 5⅛″
Pkd. 6 doz. ctn. Wt. 43 lbs.

*CK 1142—10 oz. PARK AVENUE TUMBLER IN CARRY-KITS
are available factory-packed: 6 tumblers to each
Carry-Kit, 12 kits to ctn. Wt. 40 lbs.

19

PETAL, LINE #2829, FEDERAL GLASS COMPANY 1954 – 1979

Colors: crystal, carnival iridescent, smoke, Aegean Blue, Sun Gold

This small, but increasingly popular line was a contemporary of Federal's Heritage and is shown in their #54 catalog on the page after Heritage. It continued to be listed and a full line was available in the #60 catalog, which attests to its popularity even then. As late as 1979, six pieces, including three bowls and three plates, were still being cataloged. At that time, it was pictured alongside the Madrid Recollection line which caused such a furor when it first appeared in the market. In 1974 a couple of new pieces were added in color. They included an 8" scalloped bonbon and a 4" bonbonnette.

I had a letter telling me of the various colored wares that one lady has been able to accumulate. She will be happy to see Petal finally listed in a book. Many pieces have been made from the basic listings including: 4¾" gold pedestal compote, 7¼" cherub pedestal snack tray, 3½" silver and crystal pedestal compote, 6⅜" gold marble pedestal compote, and jelly/nut in silver holder with spoon. What will you find?

Tidbits have been made in various combinations using two or three of the pieces listed. You may find two plates together, two bowls or even one or two of each.

	Crystal	All colors
Bonbonnette, 4", scalloped		12.00
Bonbon, 8¼", scalloped		15.00
Bowl, 5½"	4.00	6.00
Bowl, 8"	9.00	13.00
Bowl, 10¼", squared sides	12.00	16.00
Bowl, 10½	10.00	15.00
Candle w/handle & hurricane shade, 5½"	8.50	
Plate, 6½	1.25	2.50
Plate, 9½"	3.50	5.00
Plate, 12"	6.00	10.00
Snack tray w/metal handle	5.00	8.00
Tidbit (various combinations)	10.00 – 15.00	15.00 – 20.00

PINE CUTTING, NO. 835 FOSTORIA GLASS COMPANY, 1953 – 1972

Colors: Crystal w/cut

Pine Cutting was introduced in the 1953 Fostoria catalog and matching stemware was available as late as 1972. The good news about writing on 1950s glassware is that there usually are some factory catalogs from this time period whereas earlier paper goods were often destroyed or even donated to the paper drives of World War II. Collectors often wonder what comics or baseball cards went into those paper drives while I wonder what wonderful glassware catalogs and pamphlets were destroyed.

Pine is beginning to be noticed by collectors who like the modernistic lines of the Contour mould blank (#2666) on which most of this pattern is cut. The stemware is found on Blank #6052½ often referred to as Continental. If you like this pattern, start latching onto some before more collectors begin to notice it.

Bonbon , 6⅞"	12.50	Relish, 7⅜", 2-part	17.50
Bowl, finger	10.00	Relish, 10¾", 3-part	22.50
Bowl, 8¼", oval	20.00	Salver, 12¼", ftd.	50.00
Bowl, 10½", salad	25.00	Saucer	2.00
Butter & cover, ¼ lb.	35.00	Shaker, 3¼", pr.	35.00
Candle, 6", flora	17.50	Stem, 3⅛", 1¼ oz., cordial	35.00
Creamer, 3½"	8.50	Stem, 3⅞", 3¾ oz., cocktail	12.00
Creamer, individual	7.50	Stem, 3⅞", 4½ oz., oyster cocktail	12.50
Cup	10.00	Stem, 4⅜", 4¼ oz., claret-wine	17.50
Mayonnaise bowl	16.00	Stem, 4⅜", 6½ oz., sherbet	8.50
Mayonnaise plate	5.00	Stem, 5⅞", 9¾ oz., water	15.00
Pitcher, quart	100.00	Sugar, 2⅝"	8.50
Plate, 7"	5.00	Sugar, individual	7.50
Plate, 8"	8.00	Tray, sugar and creamer	15.00
Plate, 10", snack	12.00	Tumbler, 4⅞", 5½ oz., juice, ftd.	12.00
Plate, 14", serving	25.00	Tumbler, 9⅛", 13 oz., ice tea, ftd.	15.00

PIONEER, LINE #2806 ET AL. FEDERAL GLASS COMPANY, C. 1940

Colors: crystal, some pink and sprayed treatments

Pioneer was a fundamental Federal line which initially had a short run in pink. After that, crystal was all that was made; a few larger pieces continued to be made up until Federal went out of business in the late 70s. Some of the pieces came with intaglio fruit centers while others were left unadorned. At least one item (pictured in top row) was made having two intaglio Scottie dogs in the center which enchants collectors of those doggie trimmed wares. I have recently seen the smaller bowl with "Mr. Peanuts" embossing, not once or twice, but rather frequently, and I suspect someone is now making them. When glass businesses fold, the molds are sold at liquidation and they, subsequently may be used as found, or changed a bit by another company.

The 12" plate in the background of the top row was given the sprayed goofus treatment.

This is a sturdy, heavier design, harking back to star cut wares made around the turn of the century; and I would imagine the Pioneer name it was given was Federal's appreciation of that. It's a much prettier pattern than my photograph here shows.

Someone outside the factory probably made the handled tray in the top row. Often bowls or plates were sold to another manufacturer who "did their own thing" with the glass. Most glass factories did not add metal accoutrements to their wares.

	*Crystal	Pink/sprayed colors
Bowl, 5⅜", shallow nappy	8.00	12.00
Bowl, 7"	10.00	15.00
Bowl, 7¼", crimped	11.00	16.00
Bowl, 10½"	12.50	18.00
Bowl, 11", crimped	15.00	25.00
Plate, 8"	8.00	12.00
Plate, 12"	12.50	20.00

*Add 30 percent for intaglio fruit design and double price for Scottie.

Colors: crystal; rare in amber

The pineapple is a historical symbol of welcome. You find it on bed posts, over doors, in crochet handwork and yes, in glass-ware patterns. Plantation's pineapples continue to be picked by new buyers, escalating the prices of this Heisey ware. We sell Plantation faster than any other Heisey pattern that we stock, when we can find it. Not only are Plantation collectors charmed with it, but customers who have no idea what the pattern is succumb to it. I have had resistance in the past for buying pieces with the Ivy etch; but three times recently, I've had people ask me if I have any Plantation Ivy pieces, which may indicate a change in attitude toward those.

The pineapple hurricane lamp base measures 4½" wide and 5" tall. It was produced for less than five years, and some of those were made with a hole in the base for use as an electric lamp. A smaller pineapple candleblock was made through Heisey's production end in 1957 and measured 3". Years and careless use have made original #5080 shades with their plain rim and occasional etchings very hard to locate. The cigarette box shown is hard to come by; that pineapple knob gives away its identity to collectors.

You will have a major problem finding stems and tumblers in Plantation unlike many other Heisey patterns where stemware abounds. You can tell that they are not easily acquired by the prices listed. All flat tumblers are rare; do not pass them should you spot one.

The plate standing on the left in the bottom picture on page 198 pictures a lady with a pineapple on her head. This is known as a coupe plate that sells in the $500.00 range. They are rare and few collectors have one.

	Crystal
Ashtray, 3½"	35.00
Bowl, 9 qt., Dr. Johnson, punch	600.00
Bowl, 5", nappy	50.00
Bowl, 5½", nappy	55.00
Bowl, 6½", 2 hndl., jelly	50.00
Bowl, 6½", flared, jelly	80.00
Bowl, 6½", ftd., honey, cupped	75.00
Bowl, 8", 4-pt., rnd., relish	80.00
Bowl, 8½", 2-pt., dressing	70.00
Bowl, 9", salad	170.00
Bowl, 9½", crimped, fruit or flower	90.00
Bowl, 9½", gardenia	90.00
Bowl, 11", 3-part, relish	65.00
Bowl, 11½", ftd., gardenia	180.00
Bowl, 12", crimped, fruit or flower	100.00
Bowl, 13", celery	65.00
Bowl, 13", 2-part, celery	60.00
Bowl, 13", 5-part, oval relish	100.00
Bowl, 13", gardenia	90.00
Butter, ¼ lb., oblong, w/cover	110.00
Butter, 5", rnd. (or cov. candy)	150.00
Candelabrum, w/two #1503 bobeche & 10 "A" prisms	180.00
Candle block, hurricane type w/globe	200.00
Candle block, 1-lite	110.00
Candle holder, 5", ftd., epergne	130.00
Candlestick, 1-lite	100.00
Candlestick, 2-lite	85.00
Candlestick, 3-lite	125.00
Candy box, w/cover, 7" length, flat bottom	180.00
Candy, w/cover, 5", tall, ftd.	210.00
Cheese, w/cover, 5", ftd.	100.00
Cigarette box, w/cover	180.00
Coaster, 4"	60.00
Comport, 5"	60.00
Comport, 5", w/cover, deep	120.00
Creamer, ftd.	40.00
Cup	40.00

	Crystal
Cup, punch	30.00
Marmalade, w/cover	170.00
Mayonnaise, 4½", rolled ft.	65.00
Mayonnaise, 5¼", w/liner	55.00
Oil bottle, 3 oz., w/#125 stopper	160.00
Pitcher, ½ gallon, ice lip, blown	450.00
Plate, coupe (rare)	500.00
Plate, 7", salad	25.00
Plate, 8", salad	35.00
Plate, 10½", demi-torte	70.00
Plate, 13", ftd., cake salver	225.00
Plate, 14", sandwich	100.00
Plate, 18", buffet	175.00
Plate, 18", punch bowl liner	145.00
Salt & pepper, pr.	75.00
Saucer	8.00
Stem, 1 oz., cordial	125.00
Stem, 3 oz., wine, blown	65.00
Stem, 3½ oz., cocktail, pressed	40.00
Stem, 4 oz., fruit or oyster cocktail	35.00
Stem, 4½ oz., claret, blown	70.00
Stem, 4½ oz., claret, pressed	70.00
Stem, 4½ oz., oyster cocktail, blown	40.00
Stem, 6½ oz., sherbet/saucer champagne, blown	35.00
Stem, 10 oz., pressed	50.00
Stem, 10 oz., blown	50.00
Sugar, ftd.	40.00
Syrup bottle, w/drip, cut top	140.00
Tray, 8½", condiment, sugar & creamer	125.00
Tumbler, 5 oz., ftd., juice, pressed	60.00
Tumbler, 5 oz., ftd., juice, blown	40.00
Tumbler, 8 oz., water, pressed	125.00
Tumbler, 10 oz., pressed	90.00
Tumbler, 12 oz., ftd., iced tea, pressed	90.00
Tumbler, 12 oz., ftd., iced tea, blown	75.00
Vase, 5", ftd., flared	100.00
Vase, 9", ftd., flared	375.00

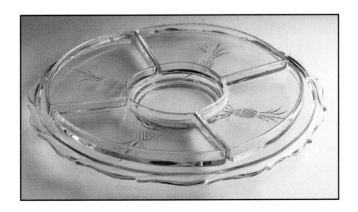

PRELUDE, NEW MARTINSVILLE & VIKING GLASS COMPANY, MID 1930s – 1950s

Color: crystal

Prelude was introduced at New Martinsville Glass Company in the mid-1930s and was a popular design as you can see from its longevity. Viking Glass Company continued Prelude production when they took over the New Martinsville Glass factory in 1943. I have included one page from an early 1950s Viking Glass catalog on 202, which illustrates the shakers. They have only flowers in the pattern. You may find that supposedly "like" pieces of Prelude are contrarily dissimilar on closer inspection. The capricious edged pieces were New Martinsville's production; items made at Viking were less precise and edges were more rounded to facilitate faster production. Pictured below is a cherub set making use of a Prelude bowl. You will find many patterns from the 1950s with similar embellishments not done at the glass factory.

Bonbon, 6", hndl.	20.00	Pitcher, 78 oz.	265.00	Stem, 1 oz., cordial	35.00
Bonbon, 6", 3-ftd.	22.00	Plate, 6", bread & butter	6.00	Stem, 1 oz., cordial, ball stem	40.00
Bowl, 7", cupped	25.00	Plate, 6½", hndl.	12.50	Stem, 3 oz., wine	22.00
Bowl, 8", crimped	35.00	Plate, 6½", lemon, 3-ftd.	14.00	Stem, 3 oz., wine, ball stem	25.00
Bowl, 8", 3-part, shrimp	70.00	Plate, 7"	8.00	Stem, 3½ oz., cocktail	15.00
Bowl, 9", 3-ftd., crimped	40.00	Plate, 7", lemon, 3-ftd.	15.00	Stem, 4 oz., cocktail, ball stem	15.00
Bowl, 9½", crimped, ftd.	40.00	Plate, 8", salad	10.00	Stem, 6 oz., low sherbet	12.00
Bowl, 10", crimped	45.00	Plate, 9"	20.00	Stem, 6 oz., sherbet, ball stem	12.00
Bowl, 10", 3-ftd.	40.00	Plate, 10", dinner	40.00	Stem, 6 oz., tall sherbet	15.00
Bowl, 10", shallow	35.00	Plate, 10", 3-ftd.	25.00	Stem, 9 oz., water	25.00
Bowl, 10½", nut, center hndl.	40.00	Plate, 11"	27.00	Sugar	12.50
Bowl, 11", 3 ftd.	55.00	Plate, 11", 3-ftd., cake	40.00	Sugar, 4-ftd.	15.00
Bowl, 12½", crimped	50.00	Plate, 11", cracker	22.50	Sugar, individual	12.00
Bowl, 13", oval	42.00	Plate, 13", hndl.	40.00	Tidbit, 2 tier, chrome hndl.	40.00
Bowl, 13", shallow	45.00	Plate, 14", flat or turned-up edge	45.00	Tray, 11", center hndl.	35.00
Bowl, 15", 3-ftd.	72.50	Plate, 16"	75.00	Tray, ind. cr./sug.	10.00
Butter dish, 6½", oval, w/cover	37.50	Plate, 16", 3-ftd.	75.00	Treasure jar, 8", w/cover	120.00
Butter dish, 8½", oval, w/cover	35.00	Plate, 18"	85.00	Tumbler, 5 oz., ftd. juice	16.00
Cake salver, 11", 5½" high	55.00	Platter, 14½"	65.00	Tumbler, 5 oz., juice, ball stem	17.50
Cake salver, 11", w/metal base	50.00	Relish, 6", 2-part	15.00	Tumbler, 10 oz., water,	
Candlestick, 4"	17.50	Relish, 6", 2-part, hndl.	18.00	ball stem	20.00
Candlestick, 4½"	20.00	Relish, 7", 2-part, hndl.	18.00	Tumbler, 12 oz., ftd., tea	20.00
Candlestick, 5", double	40.00	Relish, 7", 3-part, hndl.	15.00	Tumbler, 13 oz., tea, ball stem	25.00
Candlestick, 5½"	28.00	Relish, 10", 3-part, hndl.	32.00	Vase, 8"	40.00
Candlestick, 6", double	40.00	Relish, 13", 5-part	38.00	Vase, 10", bud	30.00
Candy box, 6", w/cover,		Salt and pepper, 3½" pr.,		Vase, 10", crimped	65.00
closed knob	60.00	2 styles	40.00	Vase, 11", crimped	70.00
Candy box, 6½", w/cover,		Saucer	5.00	Vase, 11", ftd.	75.00
open knob	65.00				
Candy box, 7", w/cover, 3-ftd.	65.00				
Celery, 10½"	30.00				
Cocktail shaker, w/metal lid	195.00				
Compote, cheese	15.00				
Compote, 5½" diameter, 3" high	30.00				
Compote, 6"	22.00				
Compote, 7", crimped	35.00				
Compote, 7½", flared	35.00				
Creamer	12.50				
Creamer, 4-ftd.	15.00				
Creamer, individual	12.00				
Cup	25.00				
Ensemble set, 13", bowl					
w/candle holder	145.00				
Ensemble set, 13", bowl					
w/flower epergne	175.00				
Lazy susan, 18", 3-pc. set (p. 192)	175.00				
Mayonnaise, 3-pc.	35.00				
Mayonnaise, divided, 4-pc.	40.00				
Nappy w/pc, 6", for candle	40.00				
Oil bottle, 4 oz.	45.00				

Prelude Etching

Magnificent expression of the designer's art in glass that is timeless and "right", with more than a touch of class.

5217
14" Plate

5201
13" Bowl

7539
8" Vase

5226
11" Cake Salver

5287
13" 5-pt. Relish

5223
13" 2-hdl. Plate

5238
10" 3-pt. Relish

5247
Cream & Sugar

13
Salt & Pepper

"PRETZEL," NO. 622, INDIANA GLASS COMPANY, LATE 1930s – 1980s

Colors: Crystal, teal, and avocado with more recent issues in amber and blue

"Pretzel" is the collector name for Indiana's No. 622 pattern. I have never heard anyone say that they collect No. 622. "Pretzel" was apropos for the design and just sticks in memory. A display of Pretzel was presented at one of the shows and people kept passing my table remarking how amazing they thought it looked with so much shown " together like that." Every now and then it's worth going to Depression glass shows just to see the table settings that are exhibited so creatively.

Has anyone found a teal saucer to go with the cup? I found this cup on the west coast seven years ago, which is not exactly, the place I would expect to find one. I have now confirmed three such saucer-less cups. This teal is Indiana's Terrace Green most likely from the Christmas Candy production run in the early 1950s.

After years of searching, I finally gathered the pitcher and all three sizes of tumblers. Sorry to say, the water tumbler didn't find its way to the photo session; but you can see the pitcher, juice, and iced tea. I took these beverage items to Michigan after we photographed last year and they flew off the table into another dealer's hands almost as soon as they hit the table.

Intaglio fruit centered and frosted crystal items are selling for 25% – 50% more than plain centered pieces.

The later made astrology and advertising pieces are the only colored pieces that are regularly turning up. Astrological bowls are selling in the $3.00 to $6.00 range although some have been found for pennies. I understand astrological sets of 12 have been discovered for as little as $20.00 and as much as $100.00. Most likely, these were a special order.

The 4½" fruit cup is being found on a 6" plate that has a 1¼" tab handle. Perhaps this was sold as a small snack set? Small, though it may be, it's a new set for those snack plate collectors to latch onto.

I have been told of a calendar plate with a side design of "Pretzel." If you have one, please send more details. Other pieces are being uncovered with dates indicating Indiana used this line for years to promote special events.

	Crystal
Bowl, 4½", fruit cup	4.50
Bowl, 7½", soup	10.00
Bowl, 9⅜", berry	16.00
Celery, 10¼", tray	1.50
Creamer	4.50
* Cup	6.00
Olive, 7", leaf-shaped	5.00
Pickle, 8½", two hndl.	5.50
Pitcher, 39 oz.	495.00
Plate, 6"	2.50
Plate, 6", tab hndl.	3.00
Plate, 7¼", square, indent	9.00

	Crystal
Plate, 7¼", square, indent, 3-part	9.00
Plate, 8⅜", salad	6.00
Plate, 9⅜", dinner	10.00
Plate, 11½", sandwich	11.00
**Saucer	1.00
Sugar	4.50
Tumbler, 5 oz., 3½"	45.00
Tumbler, 9 oz., 4½"	40.00
Tumbler, 12 oz., 5½"	65.00

*Teal – $135.00
**Teal – $45.00

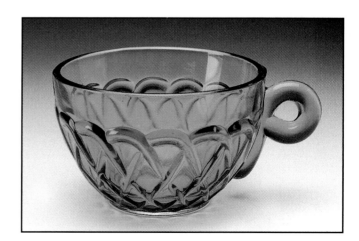

PYREX "BLUE WILLOW," CORNING GLASS WORKS, 1950s

Colors: Crystal with blue decoration

Corning's Pyrex was the main competition for Anchor Hocking's Fire-King Ovenware and "Blue Willow" was one of their patterns which collectors are beginning to gather. The major detraction is the blue design wore off with use. You can see the lack of blue on some of the pieces illustrated. Prices are for items with excellent blue design. There may be additional pieces than those in my listing; let me know what you find.

Bowl, 4½", dessert	12.00
Bowl, 6", cereal	15.00
Bowl, 10", soup	20.00
Casserole, w/cover, 1 pt.	18.00
Casserole, w/cover, 1 qt.	22.50
Casserole, w/cover, 2 qt.	30.00
Gravy boat	25.00
Gravy boat platter	12.50
Plate, 8"	12.00
Plate, 10"	20.00
Plate, 12"	25.00
Platter, 13"	42.50

PYREX TALLY HO, CORNING GLASS WORKS, 1960s

Colors: White w/decoration

Although labeled pieces of this pattern are Pyrex, there is an embossing of Made in England with a crown on the base of most pieces. Were it not for the Pyrex shapes and Pyrex labels on items being found, I would have ignored this pattern due to the embossing. With the Kentucky Horse Park seven miles from an antique mall where I had a booth, I started buying this pattern to sell there. It seems horse aficionados like horse decorated items too.

Bowl, 4½", dessert	10.00	Gravy boat platter	10.00
Bowl, 6", cereal	12.50	Mixing bowl, 7"	12.50
Bowl, 8", vegetable	20.00	Mixing bowl, 8"	15.00
Bowl, 9", soup	15.00	Mixing bowl, 9"	18.00
Casserole, w/cover, 1 pt.	18.00	Plate, 8"	9.00
Casserole, w/cover, 1 qt.	22.50	Plate, 10"	15.00
Casserole, w/cover, 2 qt.	30.00	Plate, 12"	20.00
Creamer	12.50	Platter, 13"	25.00
Cup	8.00	Saucer	3.00
Gravy boat	20.00	Sugar	12.50

RADIANCE #2700, FOSTORIA GLASS COMPANY, 1956 – 1957

Colors: crystal, aqua, peach, and white milk glass

Not many collectors have noticed Fostoria's Radiance which was only shown in catalogs for two years, making this one of the rarer Fostoria patterns from the 1950s. This heavier, linear design which was so "in" during the deco era wasn't very well accepted by the modernists of the fifties. So, right now, you can purchase designer Radiance almost cheaper than buying newly made glassware. We bought most of the pieces shown in one antique mall last year and have seen several sets sitting just waiting for a new owner.

By the way, this is a Sakier designed pattern which usually awakens some collector interest just by that magic name.

	Crystal		Crystal
Bowl, 5½", cereal	8.00	Relish, 12⅝", 3-part	22.50
Bowl, 11", oval, serving	22.50	Sauce bowl	18.00
Bowl, 12", salad	27.50	Sauce plate	6.00
Celery	16.00	Saucer	2.00
Creamer	9.00	Shaker, 2½", pr.	18.00
Cup	7.50	Sherbet, 3", 6 oz.	7.50
Plate, 7", salad	6.00	Sugar	9.00
Plate, 10", dinner	15.00	Tumbler, 4½", 5 oz., ftd. juice	10.00
Plate, 14", buffet	35.00	Tumbler, 5¾", 10 oz., ftd., beverage	12.50
Platter, 15"	35.00		

RAINBOW, ANCHOR HOCKING GLASS CORPORATION, 1938 – EARLY 1950s

Rainbow tableware was first shown in Anchor Hocking's 1939 catalog, but Tangerine (red) ball jugs were introduced the previous year. Along with Tangerine (2157) were Blue (2158), Green (2159), and Yellow (2160). For identification purposes, these are called Primary Rainbow colors and pictured on 209. The lighter colored Pastel Rainbow colors were designated Pink (159), Green (160), Yellow (161), and Blue (162).

I included Rainbow in the second edition of *Anchor Hocking's Fire-King and More* book to show what some collectors were beginning to buy. This fired-on ware became such a hot collectible that another company released a book on just Fire-King, and had only the non Fire-King Rainbow line on its cover which I found ironic. Many now think Rainbow is Fire-King. The "thousand words" that cover spoke was a tad misleading. None the less, it is a colorful and fun collectible glassware from the 1940s and was doubtless Anchor Hocking's answer to the colorful Fiesta color craze of the time.

Rainbow has always been around the fringes of collecting, but no name had been discovered for this ware so that collectors could identify it. A multitude of items surfaced in this decorated ware after exposing it in my book. Bidding wars were the norm on the Internet auctions and we sold a table full of it at the Fire-King Expo in Tulsa. Since then, prices have skyrocketed on the harder to find items, especially pitchers (except Tangerine), platters, and vegetable and cereal bowls.

We tried to have fun with this colorful pattern, and have included pieces below other than the dinnerware pictured on page 209 and 210 to show you how this pattern can be expanded to use vases, flower pots, bulb bowls, and even a lamp. The Pastel Rainbow below and on page 210 and the Primary colors on 209 are shown mixed for that rainbow effect that collectors are fond of now. This pattern adapts very well to that purpose, making Anchor Hocking either 60 years ahead of a collecting trend or it is just coming around again.

I have separated the pricing into Pastel and Primary headings; but to bring the prices listed, these pieces have to be mint (no missing paint spots). There are stems listed, which have a colored foot, but a crystal stem and bowl. These goblets were shown under Standard Glass Company listing in Anchor Hocking's 1940 catalog. They have cutting #112, called Criss-Cross & Punty, consisting of circular cuts and tic-tac-toe grids.

	*Pastel	Primary		*Pastel	Primary
Bowl, 5¼", utilty, deep		15.00	Plate, 9¼", dinner	15.00	18.00
Bowl, 6", fruit	25.00	22.00	Platter, 11"		65.00
Bowl, 9½", vegetable		65.00	Saucer	3.00	3.00
Creamer, ftd.	15.00	12.00	Shakers, pr.		25.00
Cup	7.00	7.00	Sherbet, ftd.	15.00	15.00
** Jug, 42 oz., ball	70.00	85.00	Stem, 10 oz., 7⅜"	15.00	25.00
Jug, 42 oz., Manhattan	65.00	55.00	Sugar, ftd.	15.00	12.00
Jug, 54 oz.		60.00	Tumbler, 5 oz., fruit juice		12.00
Jug, 64 oz.		65.00	Tumbler, 9 oz., bath, straight		12.00
*** Jug, 80 oz., ball	75.00	125.00	Tumbler, 9 oz., table	15.00	10.00
Jug, 80 oz., ball, Pillar Optic		80.00	Tumbler, 15 oz., ftd.		15.00
Plate, 6¼", sherbet	8.00	15.00	Tumbler, 12 oz., 4¾", straight		35.00
Plate, 7¼", salad	10.00	12.00			

* Add 25% for green   **Tangerine $30.00   ***Tangerine $20.00

ACCESSORY ITEMS

	*Pastel	Primary		*Pastel	Primary
Bulb bowl, 5½"	15.00	18.00	Lamp, 7", hurricane	35.00	
Cactus pot, 2¼", round		15.00	Vase, 3¾", 2 styles		10.00
Cactus pot, 2¼", square	20.00	20.00	Vase, 5¼", deco	15.00	12.00
Flower pot, 3¼"	18.00	15.00	Vase, 9", ruffled top	25.00	25.00
Flower pot, 4", 2 styles	18.00	15.00	Water bottle, 54 oz.	**40.00	30.00

* Add 25% for green   **Jade-ite

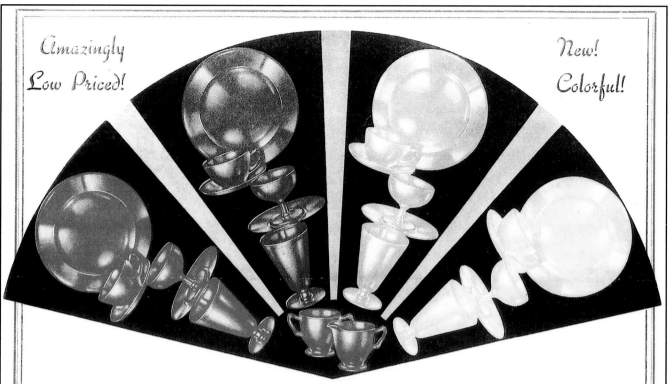

Amazingly Low Priced!

New! Colorful!

"RAINBOW" LUNCHEON SET

No. 1700/60

26 PIECES » » 26 PIECES

- . **SANITARY**
- . . . **EASY TO CLEAN**
- . . . . . **PERMANENT COLORS**

Composition of set:

Four Cups

Four Saucers

Four 9¼" Dinner Plates

Four 10 Oz. Footed Tumblers

Four Sherbets

Four Sherbet Plates

One Sugar

One Creamer

TANGERINE
BLUE
GREEN
YELLOW

Set can be had in assorted colors as illustrated above or will be packed only one color to a carton if desired.

ANCHOR HOCKING GLASS CORPORATION
HOCKING DIVISION
LANCASTER, OHIO, U. S. A.

RIPPLE, "CRINOLINE," "PETTICOAT," "PIE CRUST," "LASAGNA,"

HAZEL ATLAS GLASS COMPANY, EARLY 1950S

Colors: Platonite white and white w/blue or pink trim

This Hazel Atlas pattern had previously been known by all the names listed above in quote marks. A boxed set revealed the factory name and someone was thoughtful enough to share her find with us all. I am often asked how much an original box adds to the value of a set. It depends upon condition, desirability of pattern and whether the items enclosed are pictured in most cases. However, if the box is a discovery of a pattern name such as that of Ripple (or Gothic previously discussed under "Big Top"), it has enormous intrinsic value to me as a researcher and author, trying to get the names out there to the collecting public.

This pattern displays delightfully by mixing the colors. We deliberately varied the colors in the picture below to give you an idea of how it looks blended. Be aware that the cup, creamer, and sugar handles come both plain and beaded and that the small, shallow dessert bowl remains the most sought piece. I have had a number of collectors say they've never even seen one in either color. I see a lot of Ripple in central Florida, but have never encountered one of the shallow bowls for sale. Don't pass by these if you discover one. There is a collector waiting to take it off your hands.

Larger serving plates are not being found in any quantity and they seem to have been greatly used as they are rarely found without scratches and gouges. There was only one of these plates sold per set which makes them in much shorter supply than other pieces from the very beginning.

We know the tidbit set is found in both pink and white since we've encountered both of those. Has anyone found a blue one?

Collectors have discovered at least two different pitcher and tumbler designs that can be used with this set. Both of these sets were made by Anchor Hocking and are found with tumblers in four sizes. Hazel Atlas did make a fired-on blue or pink tumbler and mug that could accompany Ripple as accessory pieces. This ware displays attractively and is durable.

	All colors			All colors
Bowl, berry, shallow, 5"	12.50		Saucer, 5⅝"	1.00
Bowl, cereal, deep, 5⅝"	8.00		Sugar	7.50
Creamer	7.50		Tidbit, 3-tier	35.00
Cup	4.00		Tumbler, 5 oz., juice	7.00
Plate, 6⅞", salad	4.00		Tumbler, 6", 16 oz.	8.00
Plate, 8⅞", luncheon	5.00		Tumbler, 6¼", 20 oz.	10.00
Plate, 10½", sandwich	17.50			

ROMANCE, ETCHING #341, FOSTORIA GLASS COMPANY, 1942 – 1986

Color: crystal

Romance is occasionally confused with Fostoria's June because of the "bow" in the design. Compare the plain round shapes of Romance to those of June, which is found on the optic Fairfax blank. Also, there is a double line etch surrounding June which is not found on Romance. Thirty years into this business of buying and selling collectible glassware, I sometimes wonder if sellers look to see if a piece is priced higher in June than Romance, and if it is, price it as June.

Romance, found only in crystal, was distributed for over 40 years and still has charisma for collectors. I think some of the appeal is in the name itself, but some is apparently from the fantastic garland design; and putting it on the superb "Sceptre" stemware didn't harm it either.

There are a few pricing controversies for Romance. Some dealers have informed me my prices are too high and they can't sell this pattern at those prices; others consider my prices way too low on Romance and they can't keep enough of the pattern in stock to satisfy demand. I need to get these dealers together so they can trade stock. Pricing is something I work harder on than any other aspect of a book. It really is difficult to please everyone when it comes to pricing. I was recently informed by a customer at a show, that although they love my books, they are buying another more expensive guide because the prices are higher in it. I strongly believe I need to reflect actual selling prices in today's market and not "hoped for" prices. You can price an item for anything you wish, but if it won't sell for that, what good is that price? However, the prices herein are only a guide. You alone must ultimately decide what any item is worth to you; and that is your *real* price.

ROMANCE

Ashtray, 2⅝", indiv., #2364	20.00	Plate, 11", sandwich, #2364	37.50
Bowl, 6", baked apple, #2364	22.00	Plate, 11¼", cracker, #2364	27.50
Bowl, 8", soup, rimmed, #2364	100.00	Plate, 14", torte, #2364	60.00
Bowl, 9", salad, #2364	37.50	Plate, 16", torte, #2364	100.00
Bowl, 9¼", ftd., blown, #6023	175.00	Plate, crescent salad, #2364	55.00
Bowl, 10", 2 hndl., #2594	50.00	Relish, 8", pickle, #2364	22.50
Bowl, 10½", salad, #2364	45.00	Relish, 10", 3-pt., #2364	25.00
Bowl, 11", shallow, oblong, #2596	47.50	Relish, 11", celery, #2364	30.00
Bowl, 12", ftd., #2364	55.00	Salt & pepper, 2⅝", pr., #2364	60.00
Bowl, 12", lily pond, #2364	45.00	Saucer, #2350	5.00
Bowl, 13", fruit, #2364	50.00	Stem, 3⅞", ¾ oz., cordial, #6017	47.50
Bowl, 13½", hndl., oval, #2594	55.00	Stem, 4½", 6 oz., low sherbet, #6017	14.00
Candlestick, 4", #2324	20.00	Stem, 4⅞", 3½ oz., cocktail, #6017	20.00
Candlestick, 5", #2596	30.00	Stem, 5½", 3 oz., wine, #6017	35.00
Candlestick, 5½", #2594	32.00	Stem, 5½", 6 oz., champagne, #6017	16.00
Candlestick, 5½", 2-lite, #6023	40.00	Stem, 5⅞", 4 oz., claret, #6017	35.00
Candlestick, 8", 3-lite, #2594	67.50	Stem, 7⅜", 9 oz., goblet, #6017	25.00
Candy w/lid, rnd., blown, #2364	95.00	Sugar, 3⅛", ftd., #2350½	16.50
Cigarette holder, 2", blown, #2364	40.00	Tray, 11⅛", ctr. hndl., #2364	35.00
Comport, 3¼", cheese, #2364	25.00	Tumbler, 3⅝", 4 oz., ftd., oyster cocktail, #6017	16.00
Comport, 5", #6030	27.50	Tumbler, 4¾", 5 oz., ftd., #6017	18.00
Comport, 8", #2364	47.50	Tumbler, 5½", 9 oz., ftd., #6017	20.00
Creamer, 3¼", ftd., #2350½	17.50	Tumbler, 6", 12 oz., ftd., #6017	28.00
Cup, ftd., #2350½	18.00	Vase, 5", #4121	42.00
Ice tub, 4¾", #4132	125.00	Vase, 6", ftd. bud, #6021	42.00
Ladle, mayonnaise, #2364	6.00	Vase, 6", ftd., #4143	57.50
Mayonnaise, 5", #2364	25.00	Vase, 6", grnd. bottom, #2619½	60.00
Pitcher, 8⅞", 53 oz., ftd., #6011	335.00	Vase, 7½", ftd., #4143	67.50
Plate, 6", #2337	8.00	Vase, 7½", grnd. bottom, #2619½	75.00
Plate, 6¾", mayonnaise liner, #2364	15.00	Vase, 9½", grnd. bottom, #2619½	110.00
Plate, 7", #2337	10.00	Vase, 10", #2614	100.00
Plate, 8", #2337	15.00	Vase, 10", ftd., #2470	125.00
Plate, 9", #2337	47.50		

ROSE, ETCHING #1515 ON WAVERLY BLANK #1519, STEM BLANK # 5072, A.H. HEISEY & CO., 1949 – 1957

Colors: crystal

Heisey Rose pattern's oyster cocktails are rarely found except in Washington where evidently they actually ate oysters. Most Rose is found on the Waverly mould blank and stems are easily recognized with that rose incorporated into it. As with other Heisey patterns, stemware is showing up in abundance on the Internet. However, low sherbets are beating the trend by increasing in price. The very expensive, scarce 10½" dinner plate has a large center with a small border, while the 10½" service plate has a small center and large border. Six-inch epernettes are rare, as is the hurricane lamp.

Ashtray, 3"	37.50	Bowl, 10", crimped, floral, WAVERLY	75.00
Bell, dinner, #5072	150.00	Bowl, 11", 3-pt., relish, WAVERLY	77.50
Bottle, 8 oz., French dressing, blown, #5031	185.00	Bowl, 11", 3-ftd., floral, WAVERLY	165.00
Bowl, finger, #3309	100.00	Bowl, 11", floral, WAVERLY	70.00
Bowl, 5½", ftd., mint	37.50	Bowl, 11", oval, 4-ftd., WAVERLY	150.00
Bowl, 5¾", ftd., mint, CABOCHON	80.00	Bowl, 12", crimped, floral, WAVERLY	70.00
Bowl, 6", ftd., mint, QUEEN ANN	50.00	Bowl, 13", crimped, floral, WAVERLY	95.00
Bowl, 6", jelly, 2 hndl., ftd., QUEEN ANN	55.00	Bowl, 13", floral, WAVERLY	95.00
Bowl, 6", oval, lemon, w/cover, WAVERLY	695.00	Bowl, 13", gardenia, WAVERLY	80.00
Bowl, 6½", 2 pt., oval, dressing, WAVERLY	70.00	Butter, w/cover, 6", WAVERLY	175.00
Bowl, 6½", ftd., honey/cheese, WAVERLY	60.00	Butter, w/cover, ¼ lb., CABOCHON	325.00
Bowl, 6½", ftd., jelly, WAVERLY	45.00	Candlestick, 1-lite, #112	45.00
Bowl, 6½", lemon, w/cover, QUEEN ANN	250.00	Candlestick, 2-lite, FLAME	100.00
Bowl, 7", ftd., honey, WAVERLY	60.00	Candlestick, 3-lite, #142, CASCADE	85.00
Bowl, 7", ftd., jelly, WAVERLY	45.00	Candlestick, 3-lite, WAVERLY	100.00
Bowl, 7", lily, QUEEN ANN	125.00	Candlestick, 5", 2-lite, #134, TRIDENT	75.00
Bowl, 7", relish, 3-pt., round, WAVERLY	67.50	Candlestick, 6", epergnette, deep, WAVERLY	1,250.00
Bowl, 7", salad, WAVERLY	60.00	Candy, w/cover, 5", ftd., WAVERLY	195.00
Bowl, 7", salad dressings, QUEEN ANN	60.00	Candy, w/cover, 6", low, bowknot cover	175.00
Bowl, 9", ftd., fruit or salad, WAVERLY	195.00	Candy, w/cover, 6¼", #1951, CABOCHON	175.00
Bowl, 9", salad, WAVERLY	135.00	Celery tray, 12", WAVERLY	65.00
Bowl, 9", 4-pt., rnd, relish, WAVERLY	90.00	Celery tray, 13", WAVERLY	70.00
Bowl, 9½", crimped, floral, WAVERLY	75.00	Cheese compote, 4½" & cracker (11" plate),	
Bowl, 10", gardenia, WAVERLY	75.00	WAVERLY	145.00

ROSE

Cheese compote, 5½" & cracker (12" plate), QUEEN ANNE	145.00
Chocolate, w/cover, 5", WAVERLY	195.00
Cigarette holder, #4035	125.00
Cocktail icer, w/liner, #3304, UNIVERSAL	350.00
Cocktail shaker, #4225, COBEL	195.00
Comport, 6½", low ft., WAVERLY	65.00
Comport, 7", oval, ftd., WAVERLY	145.00
Creamer, ftd., WAVERLY	30.00
Creamer, indiv., WAVERLY	40.00
Cup, WAVERLY	55.00
Decanter, 1-pt., #4036½, #101 stopper	495.00
Hurricane lamp, w/12" globe, #5080	375.00
Hurricane lamp, w/12" globe, PLANTATION	495.00
Ice bucket, dolphin ft., QUEEN ANN	325.00
Ice tub, 2 hndl., WAVERLY	450.00
Mayonnaise, 5½", 2 hndl., WAVERLY	55.00
Mayonnaise, 5½", div., 1 hndl., WAVERLY	55.00
Mayonnaise, 5½", ftd., WAVERLY	60.00
Oil, 3 oz., ftd., WAVERLY	175.00
Pitcher, 73 oz., #4164	575.00
Plate, 7", salad, WAVERLY	20.00
Plate, 7", mayonnaise, WAVERLY	20.00
Plate, 8", salad, WAVERLY	30.00
Plate, 10½", dinner WAVERLY	175.00
Plate, 10½", service, WAVERLY	75.00
Plate, 11", sandwich, WAVERLY	60.00
Plate, 11", demi-torte, WAVERLY	70.00

Plate, 12", ftd., salver, WAVERLY	250.00
Plate, 15", ftd., cake, WAVERLY	295.00
Plate, 14", torte, WAVERLY	90.00
Plate, 14", sandwich, WAVERLY	110.00
Plate, 14", ctr. hndl., sandwich, WAVERLY	150.00
Salt & pepper, ftd., pr., WAVERLY	65.00
Saucer, WAVERLY	10.00
Stem, #5072, 1 oz., cordial	135.00
Stem, #5072, 3 oz., wine	95.00
Stem, #5072, 3½ oz., oyster cocktail, ftd.	60.00
Stem, #5072, 4 oz., claret	120.00
Stem, #5072, 4 oz., cocktail	38.00
Stem, #5072, 6 oz., sherbet	25.00
Stem, #5072, 6 oz., saucer champagne	27.00
Stem, #5072, 9 oz., water	36.00
Sugar, indiv., WAVERLY	40.00
Sugar, ftd., WAVERLY	30.00
Tumbler, #5072, 5 oz., ftd., juice	50.00
Tumbler, #5072, 12 oz., ftd., tea	58.00
Tray, indiv. creamer/sugar, QUEEN ANN	65.00
Vase, 3½", ftd., violet, WAVERLY	110.00
Vase, 4", ftd., violet, WAVERLY	120.00
Vase, 7", ftd., fan, WAVERLY	140.00
Vase, 8", #4198	175.00
Vase, 8", sq., ftd., urn	185.00
Vase, 10", #4198	245.00
Vase, 10", sq., ftd., urn	250.00
Vase, 12", sq., ftd., urn	295.00

ROYAL RUBY, ANCHOR HOCKING GLASS COMPANY, 1938 – 1960s; 1977

Color: Royal Ruby

    A Royal Ruby "High Point" #1201 nine-ounce glass was spotted for sale misidentified as ruby pattern glass with the name "Sword and Circle" — and priced as though it were rare. Though I am totally charmed by the name and amused that 1940s glassware has been so misrepresented, this tumbler really wasn't produced in the early 1900s.

    Royal Ruby is Anchor Hocking's patented name for their red color first produced in 1938. Many dealers and collectors incorrectly call all red glass Royal Ruby. Only true red glassware produced by Hocking or Anchor Hocking should be so called. That means that flashed red wares produced in recent years on patterns such as Wexford at Anchor Hocking cannot be labeled Royal Ruby either, which I have seen done by authorities who should know better.

    A Royal Ruby sticker was attached to each red piece, no matter the pattern. Red "Bubble" or Charm did not mean anything except Royal Ruby at the factory, so don't be shocked when you see a Royal Ruby sticker on Charm. In this book, Charm and "Bubble" Royal Ruby are covered under those pattern names. Priced below are only crystal stems with Royal Ruby tops (Berwick) as well as the stems that go with Royal Ruby "Bubble" (Early American Line). See a complete explanation of these stems in "Bubble" on page 15.

    Manufacturing of Royal Ruby was begun in the thirties after the merger of Anchor Hocking and Hocking glass companies, but what collectors typically identify as Royal Ruby was made after 1940. A Royal Ruby section in the sixteenth edition of *Collector's Encyclopedia of Depression Glass* covers the pieces made in patterns of the late 1930s. Royal Ruby will continue to be listed in both books since it can straightforwardly be divided into pre and post 1940 productions.

    An Anchor Hocking promotional ad shows the 6⅛" x 4" "card holder" cataloged as a cigarette box and sold with four Royal Ruby ashtrays. The lid is Royal Ruby on a divided crystal bottom. Using the Royal Ruby with crystal was a fairly common occurrence then.

    Either of two styles of quart water bottles used to be the hardest pieces to find in this pattern. Now you have to add a Royal Ruby globe for a hurricane lamp to that list. There are fired-on red ones, so don't be fooled. You can see one pictured in my *Anchor Hocking's Fire-King & More*. Those lids on the water bottles are identical. Bottles without a lid fetch about $100.00, but are hard to sell. The lids themselves will not fetch $135.00, but put them together and you can sell the completed bottle for $235.00. The mathematical rule about the sum of its parts does not always work with glassware or collectors. Oval vegetable bowls remain elusive in most parts of the country except the Midwest where they must have been a premium item for something everyone used regularly.

    The punch bowl base and the salad bowl with 13¾" underliner are rarely stumbled upon in today's market though they are not totally impossible to find. There are two styles of sherbets pictured in top row below. The stemmed one seems to be preferred by most collectors. Upright pitchers appear to have multiplied and I see less expensive prices on them now as compared to a few years ago.

    There were six sizes (7, 8, 12 [2 styles], 16, and 32 ounces) of beer bottles made in several shapes for Schlitz Beer Company in '49, '50, or '63. The date of manufacture is embossed on the bottom of each bottle. Thousands of these bottles were made, but labeled ones are not often found. Bottle collectors usually find these more charming than Royal Ruby collectors and prices are often higher at bottle shows than at glass shows. The quart size is the most commonly seen.

ROYAL RUBY

Ashtray, 4½", leaf	5.00	Punch bowl base	37.50
Beer bottle, 7 oz.	25.00	Punch cup, 5 oz.	3.00
Beer bottle, 12 oz.	75.00	Saucer, round	2.50
Beer bottle, 16 oz.	75.00	Sherbet, ftd.	8.00
Beer bottle, 32 oz.	45.00	Sherbet, stemmed, 6½ oz.	8.00
Bowl, 4¼", round, fruit	5.50	*Stem, 3½ oz., cocktail	10.00
Bowl, 5¼", popcorn	12.50	*Stem, 4 oz., juice	10.00
Bowl, 7½", round, soup	13.00	Stem, 4½ oz., cocktail	10.00
Bowl, 8", oval, vegetable	30.00	Stem, 5½ oz., juice	12.50
Bowl, 8½", round, large berry	17.50	Stem, 6 oz., sherbet	8.00
Bowl, 10", deep, popcorn (same as punch)	40.00	*Stem, 6 oz., sherbet	8.00
Bowl, 11½", salad	33.00	*Stem, 9 oz., goblet	14.00
Cigarette box/card holder, 6⅛" x 4"	60.00	Stem, 9½ oz., goblet	13.00
Creamer, flat	12.00	*Stem, 14 oz., iced tea	20.00
Creamer, ftd.	9.00	Sugar, flat	12.00
Cup, round	6.00	Sugar, ftd.	7.50
Goblet, ball stem	11.00	Sugar, lid	10.00
Ice bucket	35.00	Tumbler, 2½ oz., ftd., wine	14.00
Lamp	35.00	Tumbler, 3½ oz., cocktail	12.50
Pitcher, 3 qt., tilted, swirl	35.00	Tumbler, 5 oz., juice, ftd. or flat	7.50
Pitcher, 3 qt., upright	75.00	Tumbler, 9 oz., water	6.50
Pitcher, 42 oz., tilted or straight	40.00	Tumbler, 10 oz., 5", water, ftd.	6.50
Plate, 6¼", sherbet, round	4.00	Tumbler, 12 oz., 6" ftd., tea	15.00
Plate, 7", salad	5.00	Tumbler, 13 oz., iced tea	13.00
Plate, 7¾", salad, round	6.00	Vase, 4", ivy, ball-shaped	6.00
Plate, 9⅛", dinner, round	11.00	Vase, 6⅜", two styles	9.00
Plate, 13¾"	25.00	Vase, 9", two styles	17.50
Punch bowl	40.00	Water bottle (two styles)	235.00

SANDWICH COLORS, ANCHOR HOCKING GLASS COMPANY, 1939 – 1964

Colors: Desert Gold, 1961 – 1964; Forest Green, 1956 – 1960s; pink, 1939 – 1940; Royal Ruby, 1938 – 1939; White/Ivory (opaque), 1957 – 1960s

A Forest Green cookie with lid was reported to me me via e-mail and I got a bit excited. Unfortunately, a confirming picture showed a green cookie jar with a crystal lid on it. According to the collector, it was purchased that way years ago. Maybe it was, but, alas, it still was not a green cookie jar lid. It is not the first false alarm I've encountered regarding a green lid. About 30 years ago I drove 165 miles to check out a lid that had been seen at a flea market near Lexington the past weekend. When I finally found the dealer's shop, she explained she was looking for a lid and did not have one. Oh, the joys of chasing rainbows and the pot of gold at its end. I'd be willing to bet that every collector and dealer has some story like this one.

Forest Green Sandwich prices have slowed recently even though items (except for the five little pieces that were packed in Crystal Wedding Oats) remain hard to find. Thousands of those five pieces (4⁵⁄₁₆" bowl, custard cup, custard liner, and water and juice tumblers) are available today. Everyone had hot oats for breakfast; thus these pieces accumulated very fast. Prices for other Forest Green pieces have risen steadily over the years due to demand exceeding supply. All known pieces of Forest Green Sandwich are shown in the photograph. That rolled edge custard cup has never been accounted for in any quantity. It is more rarely seen than the pitchers.

Forest Green pitchers are in short supply. Everyone acquired the juice and water tumblers free in oats as explained above. Juice and water sets were offered for sale containing a pitcher and six tumblers. Most everyone already had enough tumblers, so they did not buy sets just to obtain a pitcher. Most of these pitcher sets were returned to Anchor Hocking for credit. Forest Green ads for Sandwich sugar and cookie lids have never surfaced. They probably do not exist; but I have learned in this business never to say never. The factories made sample runs sometimes that did not make regular production and therefore, no catalog listing.

Green Sandwich cups are seemingly more prevalent than saucers; as a result, the price of saucers is about to beat the price of cups.

I have priced Royal Ruby Sandwich here, but it is also found in *Collector's Encyclopedia of Depression Glass* in the Royal Ruby section of that book.

A very light pink pitcher was found a few years ago and pictured in the *Anchor Hocking's Fire-King and More* book. It is not a vibrant pink, but none of the pink is.

New collectors are starting to look at amber Sandwich. However, few are finding footed amber tumblers. That tumbler is cone shaped and like the one shown in crystal. The rest of the set can be completed with some work and luck. There are no pitchers to find in amber.

Ivory punch sets were first marketed in 1957, both plain and trimmed in 22K gold. There is little price difference today. That set edged in gold seems to be ignored because the gold has a tendency to wear away when used. In 1964 and 1965 Marathon gas stations in Ohio and Kentucky sold Ivory gold trimmed punch bowl sets for $2.89 with an oil change and lubrication. Many of these are still being found in their original boxes.

SANDWICH COLORS

	Desert Gold	Royal Ruby	Forest Green	Pink	Ivory/ White
Bowl, 4⁵⁄₁₆", smooth			6.00		
Bowl, 4⁷⁄₈", smooth	3.00	16.00		4.00	
Bowl, 5¼", scalloped	6.00	20.00		7.00	
Bowl, 5¼", smooth				7.00	
Bowl, 6½", smooth	6.00				
Bowl, 6½", scalloped		27.50	60.00		
Bowl, 6¾", cereal	12.00				
Bowl, 7⅝", salad			85.00		
Bowl, 8¼", scalloped		40.00	100.00	27.50	
Bowl, 9", salad	30.00				
Cookie jar and cover	37.50		*30.00		
Creamer			30.00		
Cup, tea or coffee	3.50		22.00		
Custard cup			3.00		
Custard cup, rolled edge			95.00		
Custard cup liner			2.50		
Pitcher, 6", juice			245.00	395.00	
Pitcher, ½ gal., ice lip			510.00		
Plate, 9", dinner	10.00		135.00		
Plate, 12", sandwich	15.00				
Punch bowl, 9¾"					15.00
Punch bowl stand					15.00
Punch cup					2.00
Saucer	3.00		20.00		
Sugar			*27.50		
Tumbler, 3⁹⁄₁₆", 5 oz., juice			4.00		
Tumbler, 9 oz., water			5.00		
Tumbler, 9 oz., footed	275.00				

* no cover

SANDWICH CRYSTAL, ANCHOR HOCKING GLASS COMPANY, 1939 – 1964; 1977

Color: crystal

Anchor Hocking's crystal Sandwich is popular with collectors due to its economical price and availability. I have separated the crystal from the colors to simplify the writing and price listings.

Four sizes of tumblers are available in crystal. The footed tumbler has never been easy to obtain, but the 3⅜" three-ounce (narrow) juice is missing from most collections. These juice tumblers were regularly found in the New England area. A dealer from Massachusetts tells me they have now disappeared in his area, too. When I met him in June 1973, I offered him six of my first books to sell, but he said people in New England didn't read books on glass and that is why he bought so well there. I ended up giving him six books and told him to mail me the money when they sold. Over a year later, he was at a show in Florida and handed me money for one and gave me five of the books back. He'd sold one to a friend and reiterated that people up there did not want to know about this glass. Boy, have times changed.

The rarely encountered, scalloped top, 6¾" cereal bowl has vaulted into a price range of $150.00. Not every collector wants these, which is good, since they are so scarce. Apparently, these scalloped edge pieces were a special order or a trial issue. It is interesting that heretofore unknown pieces continue to appear. Who knows what else will surface as more and more people enter the collecting world?

I was informed accurately by an avid collector that the 9" salad bowl and the punch bowl are not the same bowls. The true salad bowl will fit inside the punch bowl and the reason that there is a shortage of punch bowl bases is that there are too many salad bowls posing as punch bowls. The salad bowl was listed at 9" in the catalogs and the punch bowl 9¾"; so, if your punch bowl measures only 9" in diameter, you have a salad masquerading as a punch bowl.

Crystal pieces that are infrequently found are the regular cereal, 5" crimped dessert bowl, and perfect 12" plates. That 12" plate has disappeared from the market. A 5" crimped dessert listed by Anchor Hocking only measures 4⅞". Mould variation makes accurate size listings a major problem. Both this and the crimped sherbets are listed as occasional Sandwich pieces and only in the 1956 catalog. "Crimped" is their word used to describe these pieces. Listings in only one catalog normally mean pieces are in short supply today.

Prices continue to increase in this popular Hocking pattern. Surprisingly, Sandwich may be the most collected crystal pattern in this book except for Iris.

Remember that Anchor Hocking reintroduced a crystal cookie jar in the late 1970s that was larger than the old. For a comparison of these cookie jars, see measurements below. The newer one now sells in the $15.00 range.

Cups, saucers, and 8" plates were premiums for buying $3.00 (about ten gallons) of gas at Marathon stations in the mid-1960s. The promotion took a minimum of four weeks for cups, saucers, and plates. You could have gotten the crystal punch bowl set for only $2.89 with an oil change and lube. Ah, the good old days. Today, instead of giving you something for buying their product, we are slaves to whatever price they demand. Inventive minds need to find us acceptable alternatives.

COOKIE JARS	NEW	OLD
Height	10¼"	9¾"
Opening width	5½"	4⅞"
Circumference/largest part	22"	19"

Bowl, 4⁵⁄₁₆", smooth	5.00	Custard cup liner	21.00
Bowl, 4⅞", 5", crimped dessert	18.00	Pitcher, 6", juice	65.00
Bowl, 4⅞", smooth	6.00	Pitcher, ½ gal., ice lip	85.00
Bowl, 4⅞", scalloped	7.50	Plate, 7", dessert	12.00
Bowl, 6½", smooth	7.50	Plate, 8"	7.00
Bowl, 6½", scalloped, deep	8.50	Plate, 9", dinner	20.00
Bowl, 6¾", cereal	50.00	Plate, 9", indent for punch cup	5.00
Bowl, 7", salad	7.00	Plate, 12", sandwich	40.00
Bowl, 7⅝", scalloped	10.00	Punch bowl, 9¾"	20.00
Bowl, 8¼", scalloped	12.00	Punch bowl stand	30.00
Bowl, 8⅝", oval	8.00	Punch cup	2.25
Bowl, 9", salad	23.00	Saucer	1.50
Butter dish, low	45.00	Sherbet, footed	8.00
Butter dish bottom	25.00	Sugar	8.50
Butter dish top	20.00	Sugar cover	15.00
Cookie jar and cover	40.00	Tumbler, 3⅜", 3 oz., juice	20.00
Creamer	6.00	Tumbler, 3⁹⁄₁₆", 5 oz., juice	6.50
Cup, tea or coffee	2.50	Tumbler, 9 oz., water	8.00
Custard cup	3.50	Tumbler, 9 oz., footed	35.00
Custard cup, crimped, 5 oz.	14.00		

Colors: crystal late 1920s – 1980s; teal blue 1950s – 1980s; milk white, mid 1950s; amber, late 1920s – 1980s; Red, 1933/1970s; Smokey Blue, 1976 – 1977; Bi-Centennial Blue (vivid); Chantilly Green (light); Peach; Spruce Green (dark)

Indiana's Sandwich pattern is an appealing design with a historical basis and was re-made in various colors for Tiara Home Products from the 1970s to the 1990s. Many dealers and collectors have viewed it with cynicism for investment purposes due to the company's penchant for reissuing their glass patterns in older glass colors. This procedure has never allowed the older glassware to gain the status that other companies' older glassware has.

Pink and green Sandwich is priced in the *Collector's Encyclopedia of Depression Glass* since they were made in the 1930s; and although green (called Chantilly) has been made again, it is a different shade than the original. You can see examples of both greens in the Depression book. The older green Indiana Sandwich will glow under an ultraviolet (black) light while the newer will not. Do not use this as a blanket test for all old glass. Newer glass will glow, too, especially yellow or vaseline using the proper chemical formula; and that is a favorite trick of unprincipled dealers who portray their new glass as old. Speaking of vaseline, there is no such color as green vaseline, it is yellow. Old green glass glows because it was made with uranium oxide as was yellow. Just because glass glows under black light does not make it old.

Chantilly green was made in dinnerware sets whereas the original green was made only in occasional pieces. No dinner plates, cups, saucers, creamers, sugars, or water goblets were made in green until the 1980s. I actually don't care who told you how old these dinnerware items are; they were never made until the early 1980s. I say that because I received a letter from a lady who had taken her green Chantilly pieces to a popular television antiques show, and they explained to her they were from the 1930s; everybody, even the so called experts make some mistakes.

Tiara Exclusives took over Sandwich production by Indiana with an issue of red and amber in 1970, Smokey Blue in 1976, and crystal in 1978. Amber, Chantilly green, and crystal were made into the late 1980s.

Basically, the price list incorporates the original Sandwich line from the 1920s and the original Tiara listings from the early 1970s. Eventually, I may be forced to add all the Tiara listings throughout the 1970s and 1980s, but only if they become more collectible. So far, I've seen little evidence of this. You can probably stock up on Tiara sandwich pieces at a reasonable price if you have a friend who used to sponsor Tiara parties.

The mould for the old wine broke and a new one was designed. Older wines are 4½" tall and hold 3 ounces. The newer wines are shown in Tiara catalogs, but no measurements or capacities are given. Sorry, I didn't measure the one shown; but it appears to be about an eighth of an inch taller looking at the picture. I suspect it holds at least 4 ounces.

Teal blue and milk glass are colors distributed in the 1950s; but Tiara remade a teal Sandwich butter dish as an exclusive hostess gift that unconditionally destroyed the $200.00 price tag on the 1950s butter dish. This new Tiara one originally sold for approximately $15.00. "New" Sandwich has been heralded to prospective customers as glass that's going to be valuable based on its past; but the company eroded the collectibility of their older glassware by selling new glass copies in like colors. Of all the colors in the spectrum, you'd think they could have found some different shades — or dated the later wares. What a thought.

Amber and crystal prices are shown, but you must realize that most of the crystal and all the amber have been made since 1970. Prices reflect the small amounts of these colors that I see at flea markets and malls.

	Amber Crystal	Teal Blue	Red
Ashtrays (club, spade, heart, dmd. shapes, ea.)	3.50		
Basket, 10" high	30.00		
Bowl, 4¼", berry	3.50		
Bowl, 6"	4.00		
Bowl, 6", hexagonal	5.00	14.00	
Bowl, 8½"	11.00		
Bowl, 9", console	16.00		
Bowl, 11½", console	20.00		
Butter dish and cover, domed	22.50	*150.00	
Butter dish bottom	6.00	40.00	
Butter dish top	16.50	110.00	
Candlesticks, 3½", pr.	17.50		
Candlesticks, 7", pr.	25.00		
Creamer	9.00		45.00
Celery, 10½"	16.00		
Creamer and sugar on diamond-shaped tray	16.00	32.00	
Cruet, 6½ oz., and stopper	20.00	135.00	
Cup	3.50	8.00	30.00
Decanter and stopper	22.50		85.00

*Beware, recent vintage sells for $25.00

	Amber Crystal	Teal Blue	Red
Goblet, 9 oz.	13.00		45.00
Mayonnaise, ftd.	13.00		
Pitcher, 68 oz.	25.00		175.00
Plate, 6", sherbet	3.00	7.00	
Plate, 7", bread and butter	4.00		
Plate, 8", oval, indent for sherbet		6.00	12.00
Plate, 8⅜", luncheon	5.00		20.00
Plate, 10½", dinner	8.00		
Plate, 13", sandwich	13.00	25.00	35.00
Puff box	16.50		
Salt and pepper, pr.	16.50		
Sandwich server, center handle	18.00		47.50
Saucer	2.25	6.00	7.00
Sherbet, 3¼"	5.50	12.00	
Sugar, large	9.00		45.00
Sugar lid for large size	13.00		
Tumbler, 3 oz., footed cocktail	7.50		
Tumbler, 8 oz., footed water	9.00		
Tumbler, 12 oz., footed tea	10.00		
Wine, 3", 4 oz.	6.00		12.50

SEASCAPE, #2685 LINE, FOSTORIA GLASS COMPANY, 1954 – 1958

Color: Opalescent blue and pink

Seascape was added to this book, in part, because I got tired of seeing this 1950s pattern misidentified as Duncan and Miller glassware. Seascape was a short-lived pattern and collectors are often attracted to opalescent wares. Both of these reasons make Seascape a pattern to watch.

I don't believe I have ever seen a more divergent range of prices on any other pattern. Few pieces are advertised for sale; much is priced out of this world as Duncan and Miller. The more reasonably priced pieces of Seascape have been bought from dealers who knew what it was, who manufactured it, and when.

Seascape is found with Fostoria's Contour (#2666) shapes, but the company gave them different line numbers when they made the opalescent. Pictured with pink Seascape are three pink Contour stems. These are not opalescent, just pink. You can blend these with pink Seascape, but only crystal ones are likely with the opalescent blue.

By the way, the 12" footed salver is called a cake stand by many. You might even find one with an ivy-like design which came from a petite line of about 20 items that Fostoria called Vintage and made in 1955. So, this vine is obviously some designer's idea of a grape leaf. Half the items in this #347 Etch Vintage line were taken from the Seascape line and bring prices from 20% to 25% higher than the actual Seascape pieces; prices right now for Vintage items seem to depend more on size of the item than rarity. Since these were only made for a year, they all have to be pretty scarce; still, I see more collectors gathering the non-grape leaf items.

My wife likes this pattern, thinks it apropos for a time when people were thinking about space travel and going to the moon someday. She has stubbornly hunted it for this picture. Once I have enough pieces for a decent picture, I tend to get conservative in my buying, whereas she believes if we don't have it, we should. You have more pieces to view due to her efforts.

Bowl, 4½", pansy	35.00	Mint tray, 7½", ftd.	38.00
Bowl, 8", shallow	55.00	Plate, 14", buffet	80.00
Bowl, 8¾", ftd.	80.00	Preserve, 6½", handled	50.00
Bowl, 8¾", square, scalloped	70.00	Relish, 9" x 6", two-part	45.00
Bowl, 10", salad	70.00	Relish, 11¾" x 8½", three-part	60.00
Bowl, 11½", shallow	70.00	Salver, 12", ftd.	135.00
Candleholder, 2" high, 4½" diameter	25.00	Sugar, 2⅝"	25.00
Cream, 3⅜"	25.00	Sugar, individual	25.00
Creamer, individual	25.00	Tray, 7½", oval, ftd.	55.00
Mayonnaise, 3-pc. set	55.00	Tray, individual sug/cr	25.00

Color: opaque pink

    I have reduced Shell Pink from five to three pages. I will continue to show a variety of items, but not all in one book. I needed the space for new patterns. More were shown in previous editions should you wish to check there.

    Prices for Shell Pink have stabilized and there are new collectors buying it. All pieces that were seriously priced, still are. The Lazy Susan and heavy-bottomed National vase are continuing to outshine all commonly found pieces in price. This fashionable Jeannette pink milk color was made for only a brief time in the late 1950s. It included pieces from several standard Jeannette lines (Anniversary, Baltimore Pear, Floragold, Harp, Holiday, National, and Windsor). Like Anchor Hocking's colors, pattern was not the important idea, it was the color. Shell Pink was promoted as "a delicate coloring that blends perfectly with all kinds of flowers." That remains as true today as it was then.

    A couple of rarely seen Shell Pink pieces are pictured at the bottom of page 229, namely, the ashtray and the bird candle holder which was sold with the three-footed pheasant bowl. A solitary Anniversary cake plate was unearthed years ago. To my knowledge, no others have appeared. Anniversary pin-up vases are being found, though not by me to photograph. You can see a duck powder jar in *Very Rare Glassware of the Depression Years, Sixth Series.* I recently bought a Shell Pink "Genie" bottle that came from the same factory worker's relative who owned the rare duck powder jars. There was no stopper. I have photographed a collector's large Shell Pink plate with the same chevron striped pattern as the punch bowl pictured on the top of page 229. It may have been designed as a liner for the punch bowl, but the pattern was underneath where it didn't show. Speaking of the punch bowl reminds me that the original ladle was pink plastic and not crystal colored.

    Watch for the Butterfly cigarette box and ashtrays. They have become very popular with collectors. Be sure to check those butterfly wings. Pieces of those wings have a tendency to "fly off." The price below is for mint condition butterfly boxes. Out of the $17,000 worth of glassware destroyed when my van was totaled, there were only four pieces damaged but not broken into jigsaw puzzle pieces. I was amazed that one of these was this cigarette box which had a broken piece out of the bottom, but the lid was intact. The oval, four-footed Lombardi bowls turn up frequently, but those with an embossed design on the inside do not. The difference in price should be much greater; but some collectors feel one oval bowl is enough. The honey jar is easy to spot with its beehive shape, but it has begun to disappear from the market.

    That Harp tray is hard to find; but the greater demand for the Harp cake stand almost makes these two comparable in price. The five-part, two-handled oval tray, pictured with the punch bowl on page 229, is beginning to catch up with demand. For a while, it was on every collector's want list.

    Shell pink was used extensively by the floral industry and other pieces were made for "Napco Ceramics, Cleveland, Ohio." Each piece is marked thus with numbers (quoted in the price list) except for the piece with a sawtooth edge that only has "Napco, Cleveland." The National pattern candy bottom (with no lid) was promoted as a vase.

Ashtray, advertising, shell pink	325.00
Ashtray, butterfly shape	25.00
Base, for Lazy Susan, w/ball bearings	160.00
Bowl, 6½", wedding, w/cover	20.00
Bowl, 8", Pheasant, ftd.	37.50
Bowl, 8", wedding, w/cover	25.00
Bowl, 9", ftd., fruit stand, Floragold	32.00
Bowl, 10", Florentine, ftd.	30.00
Bowl, 10½", ftd., Holiday	45.00
Bowl, 10⅞", 4-ftd., Lombardi, designed center	40.00
Bowl, 10⅞", 4-ftd., Lombardi, plain center	27.00
Bowl, 17½", Gondola fruit	40.00
Cake plate, Anniversary	275.00
Cake stand, 10", Harp	45.00
Candle holder, 2-lite, pr.	45.00
Candle holder, Eagle, 3-ftd., pr.	80.00
Candy dish w/cover, 6½" high, square	30.00
Candy dish, 4-ftd., 5¼", Floragold	20.00
Candy jar, 5½", 4-ftd., w/cover, grapes	20.00
Celery and relish, 12½", 3-part	40.00
Cigarette box, butterfly finial	225.00
Compote, 6", Windsor	22.50
Cookie jar w/cover, 6½" high	125.00
Creamer, Baltimore Pear design	15.00
Honey jar, beehive shape, notched cover	50.00
"Napco" #2249, cross-hatch design pot	15.00
"Napco," #2250, ftd. bowl w/berries	15.00

"Napco," #2255, ftd. bowl w/sawtooth top	25.00
"Napco," #2256, square comport	12.50
"National," candy bottom	10.00
Pitcher, 24 oz., ftd., Thumbprint	25.00
Powder jar, 4¾", w/cover	45.00
Punch base, 3½", tall	30.00
Punch bowl, 7½ qt.	125.00
Punch cup, 5 oz. (also fits snack tray)	5.00
Punch ladle, pink plastic	25.00
Punch set, 15-pc. (bowl, base, 12 cups, ladle)	240.00
Relish, 12", 4-part, octagonal, Vineyard design	40.00
Stem, 5 oz., sherbet, Thumbprint	9.00
Stem, 8 oz., water goblet, Thumbprint	12.50
Sugar cover	17.50
Sugar, ftd., Baltimore Pear design	12.50
Tray, 7¾" x 10", snack w/cup indent	8.00
Tray, 12½" x 9¾", 2 hndl., Harp	60.00
Tray, 13½", Lazy Susan, 5-part	60.00
Tray, 15¾", 5-part, 2 hndl.	85.00
Tray, 16½", 6-part, Venetian	35.00
Tray, Lazy Susan complete w/base	225.00
Tumbler, 5 oz., juice, ftd., Thumbprint	8.00
Vase, 5", cornucopia	15.00
Vase, 7"	35.00
Vase, 9", heavy bottom, National	150.00
Vase, wall pin-up, Anniversary	295.00

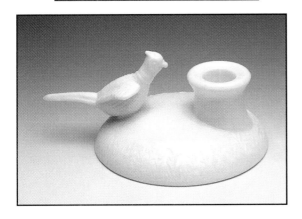

Color: white with crystal edge

Silver Crest is one of Fenton's patterns that started in the 1940s and is still in occasional production today. Every time Fenton has discontinued it, demand and/or financial matters persuade them into re-creating some pieces of it. There are a number of ways to date your pieces. Before 1958, the white was called opal and had an opalescence to it when held to the light. In 1958, a formula change to milk glass made the glass look very white without "fire" in the white. All pieces reinstated after 1973 will be signed Fenton. Fenton began marking carnival pieces in 1971, and in 1973 they continued this marking to all pieces. If you acquire items that have white edging encompassing crystal, this is called Crystal Crest and dates from 1942. Many of the very late silver crested items have violets, roses, or apple blossoms painted on the wares. There was also an embossed scrolled design added to pieces in 1968 called Spanish Lace Silver Crest. However, none of these latter decorations can be attained as actual dinnerware sets. Most of the newer decorations are occasional items, especially vases.

The pitcher, punch bowl set, and hurricane lamps are very hard to attain, but delightful in spite of the price tag. There's a floor lamp shade, which directs the light upward to the ceiling. Tumbler prices are edging upward; latch on to a few before they become too expensive. As with Fenton's Emerald Crest, you will encounter quite a few styles of tidbits using bowls and plates or both.

Some pieces of Silver Crest are assigned two different line numbers. Initially, this line was #36 and all pieces carried that classification. In July 1952, Fenton began issuing a ware number for individual pieces. That is why you see two distinct numbers for many of the items in the price listing.

See page 60 for prices of Emerald Crest. Aqua Crest has a blue edge around the white and prices for it tag along between those of Silver Crest and Emerald Crest. Remember that demand and a plentiful supply for Silver Crest is making it one of Fenton's most recognized line.

Basket, 5" hndl. (top hat), #1924	70.00	Bonbon, 5½", #36	12.00
Basket, 5", hndl., #680	40.00	Bowl, 5", finger or deep dessert, #680	22.50
Basket, 6½", hndl., #7336	40.00	Bowl, 5½", soup, #680	30.00
Basket, 7", #7237	40.00	Bowl, 7", #7227	20.00
Basket, 12", #7234	100.00	Bowl, 8½", #7338	32.50
Basket, 13", #7233	150.00	Bowl, 8½", flared, #680	32.50
Basket, hndl., #7339	65.00	Bowl, 9½", #682	40.00
Bonbon, 5½", #7225	10.00	Bowl, 10", #7224	50.00
Bonbon, 8", #7428	14.00	Bowl, 10", salad, #680	50.00

Bowl, 11", #5823	55.00
Bowl, 13", #7223	75.00
Bowl, 14", #7323	85.00
Bowl, banana, high ft., w/upturned sides, #7324	70.00
Bowl, banana, low ftd., #5824	50.00
Bowl, deep dessert, #7221	32.50
Bowl, dessert, shallow, #680	22.50
Bowl, finger or dessert, #202	20.00
Bowl, ftd. (like large, tall comport), #7427	75.00
Bowl, ftd., tall, square, #7330	75.00
Bowl, low dessert, #7222	22.50
Bowl, shallow, #7316	46.00
Cake plate, 13" high, ftd., #7213	45.00
Cake plate, low ftd., #5813	40.00
Candle holder, 6" tall w/crest on bottom, pr., #7474	65.00
Candle holder, bulbous base, pr., #1523	60.00
Candle holder, cornucopia, pr., #951	65.00
Candle holder, cornucopia (same as #951), pr., #7274	60.00
Candle holder, flat saucer base, pr., #680	55.00
Candle holder, low, ruffled, pr., #7271	55.00
Candle holder, ruffled comport style, pr., #7272	95.00
Candy box, #7280	65.00
Candy box, ftd., tall stem, #7274	110.00
Chip and dip (low bowl w/mayo in center), #7303	75.00
Comport, ftd., #7228	22.50
Comport, ftd., low, #7329	26.00
Creamer, reeded hndl., #680	26.00
Creamer, reeded hndl. (same as #680), #7201	26.00
Creamer, ruffled top	55.00
Creamer, straight side, #1924	32.50
Creamer, threaded hndl., #680	23.00
Cup, reeded hndl., #680	28.00
Cup, threaded look hndl., #7209	22.50
Epergne set, 2-pc. (vase in ftd. bowl), #7202	80.00
Epergne set, 3-pc., #7200	125.00
Epergne, 2-pc. set ,#7301	120.00
Epergne, 4-pc., bowl w/3 horn epergnes, #7308	150.00
Epergne, 5-pc., bowl w/4 horn epergnes, #7305	190.00
Lamp, hurricane, #7398	125.00
Mayonnaise bowl, #7203	14.00
Mayonnaise ladle, #7203	6.00
Mayonnaise liner, #7203	28.00
Mayonnaise set, 3-pc., #7203	60.00
Nut, ftd., #7229	20.00
Nut, ftd. (flattened sherbet), #680	20.00
Oil bottle, #680	85.00
Pitcher, 70 oz. jug, #7467	275.00
Plate, 5½", #680	7.00
Plate, 5½", finger bowl liner, #7218	7.00
Plate, 6½" #680, #7219	7.50
Plate, 8½" #680, #7217	15.00
Plate, 10", #680	40.00

Plate, 10½", #7210	55.00
Plate, 11½", #7212	45.00
Plate, 12", #680	47.50
Plate, 12", #682	45.00
Plate, 12½", #7211	40.00
Plate, 16", torte, #7216	60.00
Punch bowl, #7306	375.00
Punch bowl base, #7306	110.00
Punch cup, #7306	16.00
Punch ladle (clear), #7306	25.00
Punch set, 15-pc., #7306	700.00
Relish, divided, #7334	35.00
Relish, heart, hndl., #7333	24.00
Saucer, #680, #7209	5.00
Shaker, pr., #7206	110.00
Shaker, pr. (bowling pin shape)	175.00
Shaker, pr., #7406	225.00
Sherbet, #680	15.00
Sherbet, #7226	15.00
Sugar, reeded hndl., #680	26.00
Sugar, reeded hndl. (same as #680), #7201	26.00
Sugar, ruffled top	55.00
Sugar, sans hndls., #680	35.00
Tidbit, 2-tier (luncheon/dessert plates), #7296	50.00
Tidbit, 2-tier (luncheon/dinner plates), #7294	50.00
Tidbit, 2-tier plates, #680	50.00
Tidbit, 2-tier, ruffled bowl, #7394	75.00
Tidbit, 3-tier (luncheon/dinner/dessert plates), #7295	65.00
Tidbit, 3-tier plates, #680	50.00
Tidbit, 3-tier, ruffled bowl, #7397	85.00
Top hat, 5", #1924	125.00
Tray, sandwich, #7291	40.00
Tumbler, ftd., #7342	60.00
Vase, 4½", #203	15.00
Vase, 4½", #7254	15.00
Vase, 4½", double crimped, #36, #7354	20.00
Vase, 4½", fan, #36	20.00
Vase, 5" (top hat), #1924	125.00
Vase, 6", #7451	22.00
Vase, 6", doubled crimped, #7156	19.00
Vase, 6¼", double crimped, #36, #7356	20.00
Vase, 6¼", fan, #36	22.00
Vase, 7", #7455	35.00
Vase, 8", #7453	30.00
Vase, 8", bulbous base, #186	40.00
Vase, 8", doubled crimped, #7258	30.00
Vase, 8", wheat, #5859	45.00
Vase, 8½", #7458	70.00
Vase, 9", #7454	50.00
Vase, 9", #7459	50.00
Vase, 10", #7450	115.00
Vase, 12" (fan topped), #7262	135.00

Colors: crystal, some red and black

Cambridge Square was initially illustrated in the 1949 Cambridge catalog but was shown as "patent pending." Several of the unused Square pieces pictured still have "patent pending" as well as Cambridge labels. This is one of the few Cambridge patterns that completely falls into the time frame of this book.

The punch bowl set looks to be one of the more difficult pieces to find in crystal. I don't know if it didn't sell well or Cambridge avoided making large pieces of glassware since they were going into bankruptcy, or both. The icers with inserts are missing from many collections. These were used for shrimp and fruit with ice below, cooling the item in the insert. Square is reasonable for a Cambridge pattern; but there are not as many seeking Square as there are other Cambridge wares such as Rose Point or Gloria. Square was made during the financially troubled last years of Cambridge which may mean items are limited even more than we are aware. It will take a few years and more collectors buying it to resolve that.

Some Square was made in Carmen and Ebony; however, Ruby (Imperial's name) pieces were also made from Cambridge's Square moulds at Imperial in the late 1960s. Carmen pieces by Cambridge are rarely seen; Ruby can be found with some searching. I've been told that the "old timers" can tell the difference; personally, I can't.

In the totally unplanned department, I was walking down an aisle at a show and overheard a man tell his friends, "If only I could find one of those Cambridge Square punch bowls, I'd buy that in a heart beat." I said, "I've got one for sale in my booth." He looked a little shocked, or maybe, offended and said, "Really?" I pointed to my booth and he did meander by later; but his money wasn't where his mouth was that day. I think some people intentionally choose something they feel confident you won't possess to ask for at shows. That way they're safe from buying — but sound interested. Really, people, it's okay to just look and appreciate. We sold that bowl a few hours later, and I have never seen another.

	Crystal			Crystal
Ashtray, 3½", #3797/151	8.00		Bowl, punch	75.00
Ashtray, 6½", #3797/150	11.00		Buffet set, 4-pc. (plate, div. bowl, 2 ladles),	
Bonbon, 7", #3797/164	15.00		#3797/29	55.00
Bonbon, 8", #3797/47	24.00		Candle holder, 1¾", block, #3797/492, pr.	25.00
Bowl, 4½", dessert, #3797/16	12.00		Candle holder, 2¾", block, #3797/493, pr.	30.00
Bowl, 6½", individual salad, #3797/27	14.00		Candle holder, 3¾", block, #3797/495, pr.	30.00
Bowl, 9", salad, #3797/49	22.50		Candle holder, cupped, #3797/67, pr.	30.00
Bowl, 10", oval, #3797/48	25.00		Candy box and cover, #3797/165	33.00
Bowl, 10", shallow, #3797/81	30.00		Celery, 11", #3797/103	25.00
Bowl, 11", salad, #3797/57	40.00		Comport, 6", #3797/54	25.00
Bowl, 12", oval, #3797/65	32.00		Creamer, #3797/41	10.00
Bowl, 12", shallow, #3797/82	35.00			

	Crystal
Creamer, individual, #3797/40	10.00
Cup, coffee, open handle, #3797/17	10.00
Cup, tea, open handle, #3797/15	10.00
Decanter, 32 oz., #3797/85	95.00
Ice tub, 7½", #3797/34	37.50
Icer, cocktail w/liner, #3797/18	40.00
Lamp, hurricane, 2-pc., #3797/68	50.00
Mayonnaise set, 3-pc. (bowl, plate, ladle), #3797/129	30.00
Oil bottle, 4½ oz., #3797/100	25.00
Plate, 6", bread and butter, #3797/20	8.00
Plate, 7", dessert or salad, #3797/23	12.00
Plate, 7", salad, #3797/27	12.00
Plate, 9½", dinner or luncheon, #3797/25	30.00
Plate, 9½", tidbit, #3797/24	20.00
Plate, 11½", #3797/26	25.00
Plate, 13½", #3797/28	30.00
Relish, 6½", 2-part, #3797/120	20.00
Relish, 8", 3-part, #3797/125	25.00
Relish, 10", 3-part, #3797/126	27.50
Salt and pepper, pr., #3797/76	22.50
Saucer, coffee, #3797/17	5.00
Saucer, tea, #3797/15	5.00
Stem, #3798, 5 oz., juice	10.00
Stem, #3798, 12 oz., iced tea	12.00

	Crystal
Stem, #3798, cocktail	17.50
Stem, #3798, cordial	25.00
Stem, #3798, sherbet	11.00
Stem, #3798, water goblet	12.00
Stem, #3798, wine	20.00
Sugar, #3797/41	10.00
Sugar, individual, #3797/40	10.00
Tray, 8", oval, for individual sug/cr, #3797/37	17.50
Tumbler, #3797, 5 oz., juice	12.50
Tumbler, #3797, 14 oz., iced tea	18.00
Tumbler, #3797, low cocktail	12.00
Tumbler, #3797, low cordial	18.00
Tumbler, #3797, low sherbet	10.00
Tumbler, #3797, low wine	15.00
Tumbler, #3797, water goblet	14.00
Vase, 5", belled, #3797/92	22.50
Vase, 5½", belled, #3797/91	25.00
Vase, 6", #3797/90	22.50
Vase, 7½", ftd., #3797/77	24.00
Vase, 7½", rose bowl, #3797/35	35.00
Vase, 8", ftd., #3797/80	22.00
Vase, 9½", ftd., #3797/78	33.00
Vase, 9½", rose bowl, #3797/36	45.00
Vase, 11", ftd., #3797/79	42.00

Colors: yellow, crystal, and crystal w/gold trim

Cups in this pattern may have eluded your eye unless you find them in a set as I did. The Star cup is plan without a "star" on the bottom as on other Star pieces. This has caused collectors to unknowingly bypass these when out shopping because they were looking for the telltale star. You can view the cup and saucer, shown in yellow. I had to purchase a six-piece setting to get one cup and saucer; but having finally found a cup made it worth the cost. The saucers are like the 6³⁄₁₆" plate, but with an indented cup ring. Without a catalog listing for this pattern (except for the pitchers and tumblers), I have to discover pieces myself or from collector contributions. Please notice the 11" round platter standing in the back which was added to the listing in the last book.

Although there were only a few pieces made, you can put together a small set at a bargain price; and it is eye-catching. Notice the star-shaped design on each piece (except the cup and pitchers). Cathy remembers the pitchers being marketed with small colored soaps for the bath. Star pitchers were also sold as a set with Park Avenue tumblers.

You will find frosted, decorated juice pitchers with several designs and matching tumblers. Watch for a similar pitcher with painted flowers matching the red-trimmed Mountain Flowers Petalware. Both frosted and unfrosted pitchers are shown in the new *Collector's Encyclopedia of Depression Glass.*

That whisky tumbler is found with labels showing jelly was packaged in them as were those of Park Avenue.

	Yellow	Crystal
Bowl, 4⅝", dessert	7.00	4.00
Bowl, 5⅜", cereal		6.00
Bowl, 8⅜", vegetable	20.00	10.00
Butter dish, w/lid		95.00
Creamer	10.00	6.00
Cup	12.00	5.00
Pitcher, 5¾", 36 oz., juice		9.00
Pitcher, 7", 60 oz.		12.00
Pitcher, 9¼", 85 oz., ice lip		15.00
Plate, 6³⁄₁₆", salad	6.00	3.00

	Yellow	Crystal
Plate, 9⅜", dinner	10.00	5.00
Platter 11", round	18.00	12.00
Saucer (indented)	4.00	2.00
Sugar	8.00	5.00
Sugar lid	12.00	5.00
Tumbler, 2¼", 1½ oz., whisky		3.00
Tumbler, 3⅜", 4½ oz., juice	12.00	4.00
Tumbler, 3⅞", 9 oz., water	14.00	5.50
Tumbler, 5⅛", 12 oz., iced tea	18.00	8.00

STARS and STRIPES, ANCHOR HOCKING GLASS GLASS COMPANY, 1942

Color: crystal

Stars and Stripes is another Anchor Hocking pattern that is being mislabeled Fire-King.

At some stage of World War II, Anchor Hocking reworked their Queen Mary moulds and modified them to create this small, three-piece dessert service, which could double as a luncheon service. In their ad pictured below, they termed it an Early American Design. That eagle design, emblem of power and authority, has been used by several companies on their wares in the past, the most notable probably being the Dorflinger set cut for Abraham Lincoln in the 1860s. It was Hocking's patriotic acknowledgment of the country's struggle to survive during W.W.II. They were offering people a quick way to wave the flag.

Collectors have been totally charmed by this small pattern. Prices for tumblers are ever-increasing. Note that at least one plate has turned up with red backing over a golden eagle. It may be supposed that a glass and sherbet with like trim could be available. We would like there to have been more pieces; but three are sufficient to do the job for which they were intended; and that may be emblematic as well.

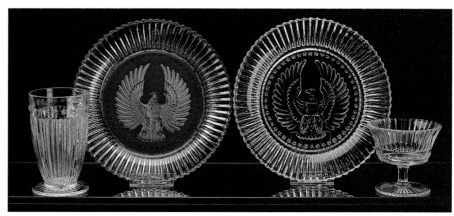

Plate, 8"	18.00
Sherbet	15.00
Tumbler, 5", 10 oz.	47.50

SWANKY SWIGS, 1930s – 1950s

Swanky Swigs were primarily sold as Kraft® cheese and bread spread containers. Exhibited here are the Swigs sold from the late 1930s into the 1950s with a collectible 1976 Bicentennial also displayed. Smaller size glasses (3¼") and the larger (4½") seem to have been circulated entirely in Canada. The limited distribution of these sizes in the States makes their prices increase more than those consistently found here. Tulip No. 2 was sold only on the west coast and prices are somewhat lower there. Earlier Swanky Swigs can be found in *Collector's Encyclopedia of Depression Glass* if you become enamored of collecting each design as many have. The two jars on row 2 of page 239 are store display Swankys (painted to look full of cheese). Some original lids from these Swigs are shown on page 241. Lids sell for $8.00 up, depending upon condition and the advertisement. Those with Kraft® caramels, Miracle Whip®, and TV show ads run $20.00 up in great condition. The most sought lid is pictured at the bottom center of page 241. Bing was a popular guy and his Swanky lid will fetch $25.00 to $30.00 depending upon condition.

Page 239:

Row 1: Tulip No. 1		
black, blue, red, green	3½"	3.00 – 4.00
black w/label	3½"	10.00 – 15.00
blue, red, green	4½"	15.00 – 20.00
green	3¼"	15.00 – 20.00
Row 2: Tulip No. 3		
lt. blue, yellow display jars	3¾"	30.00 – 35.00
lt. blue, red, yellow	3¾"	2.50 – 3.50
lt. blue, yellow	3¼"	15.00 – 20.00
red	4½"	15.00 – 20.00
Cornflower No. 1		
lt. blue	4½"	15.00 – 20.00
lt. blue	3½"	5.00 – 6.00
lt. blue	3¼"	15.00 – 20.00
Row 3: Tulip No. 2		
black, green, red	3½"	30.00 – 35.00
carnival blue, green, red, yellow	3½"	6.00 – 10.00
Tulip No. 3		
dk. blue	4½"	15.00 – 20.00
dk. blue	3¾"	2.50 – 3.50
dk. blue	3¼"	15.00 – 20.00
Row 4: Posy Jonquil		
yellow	4½"	20.00 – 25.00
yellow	3½"	7.00 – 8.00
yellow	3¼"	20.00 – 25.00
Posy: Tulip		
red	4½"	20.00 – 25.00
red	3½"	7.00 – 8.00
red	3¼"	20.00 – 25.00
Posy: Violet		
purple	4½"	20.00 – 25.00
purple	3½"	7.00 – 8.00
purple	3¼"	20.00 – 25.00
Row 5: Cornflower No. 2		
dk. blue, lt. blue, red, yellow	3½"	2.50 – 3.50
dk. blue, lt. blue, yellow	3¼"	15.00 – 20.00
Forget-Me-Not		
dk. blue,	3½"	2.50 – 3.50
dk. blue or yellow w/label		
(yel p 220)	3½"	10.00 – 12.50
dk. blue	3¼"	15.00 – 20.00

Page 240:

Row 1: Forget-Me-Not		
lt. blue, red, yellow	3½"	2.50 – 3.50
lt. blue, red, yellow	3¼"	15.00 – 20.00
Daisy		
red & white	3¾"	25.00 – 30.00
red & white	3¼"	35.00 – 40.00
Rows 2 – 5: Daisy		
red, white & green	4½"	15.00 – 20.00
red, white & green	3¾"	2.00 – 3.00
red, white & green	3¼"	15.00 – 20.00
Bustling Betsy		
all colors	3¼"	15.00 – 20.00
all colors	3¾"	4.00 – 5.00
Antique Pattern		
all designs	3¼"	15.00 – 20.00
all designs	3¾"	4.00 – 5.00
clock & coal scuttle brown		
lamp & kettle blue		
coffee grinder & plate green		
spinning wheel & bellows red		
coffee pot & trivet black		
churn & cradle orange		
Kiddie Cup:		
all designs	4½"	20.00 – 25.00
	3¾"	4.00 – 5.00
	3¼"	20.00 – 25.00
bird & elephant, red		
bear & pig, blue		
squirrel & deer, brown		
duck & horse, black		
dog & rooster, orange		
cat and rabbit, green		
bird & elephant w/label	3¾"	10.00 – 15.00
dog & rooster w/cheese	3¾"	25.00 – 30.00
Bicentennial issued in 1975;		
yellow, red, green	3¾"	4.00 – 5.00

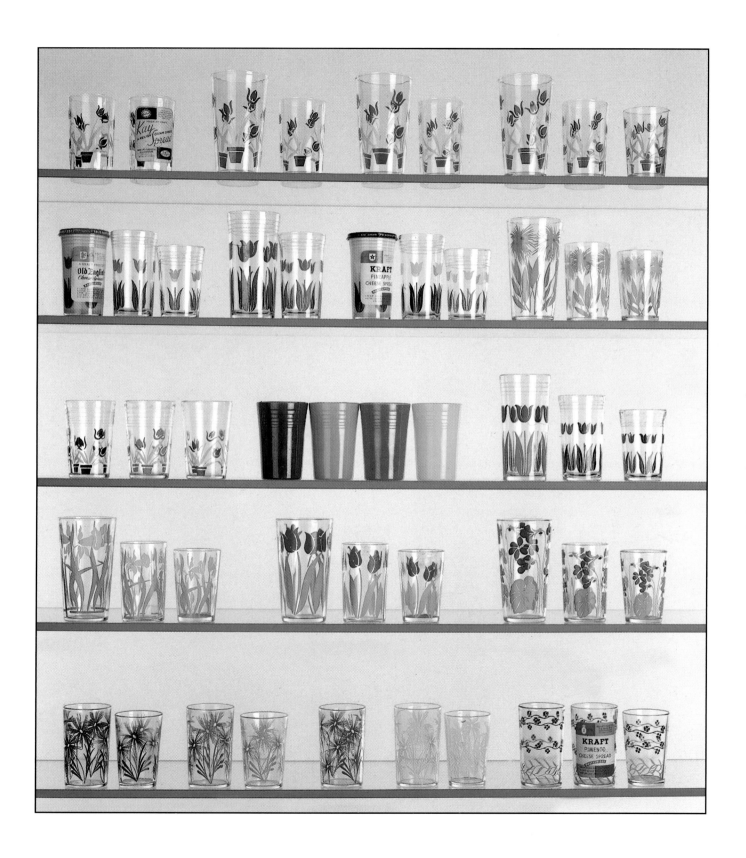

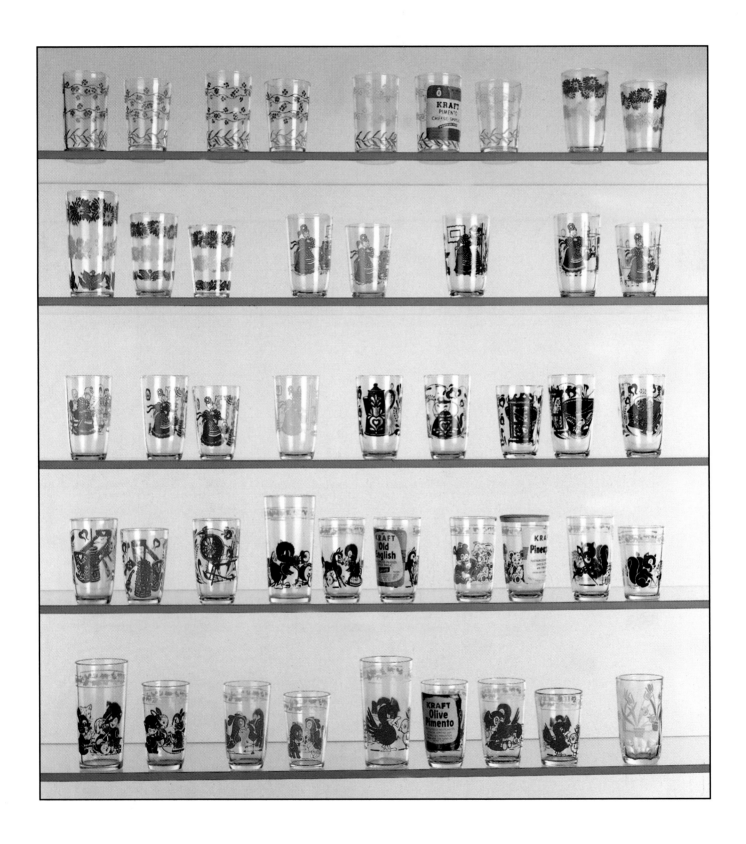

TEARDROP, LINE NO. 1011 INDIANA GLASS COMPANY, 1950 – 1980s

Colors: crystal, crystal decorated, white and white decorated

Teardrop is a recognizable pattern due to its abundance of pieces being seen in the marketplace today. Those comports seem to be everywhere in a multitude of sprayed on colors as well as white. After I bought one to photograph, I swore to myself that I would not buy another white item. However, when I spotted the banana stand, I had to relent and dig in my pocket. As with all newly listed patterns, you may find additional pieces.

The decorated white creamer and sugar in the top row are well done. The translucent effect shows off the decoration. The opaque white shown on the banana stand is not as collected as the crystal or decorated crystal.

	Crystal
Banana stand (white)	35.00
Bowl, 9", 2-handled	20.00
Bowl, 10", deep, ftd.	25.00
Bowl, 13", ftd.	25.00
Bowl, 5"	8.00
Cake stand	22.50
Candlestick	17.50
Candy dish w/lid	25.00
Comport	12.00

	Crystal
Creamer	7.50
Plate, 11", 2-handled	20.00
Plate, 15", punch liner	20.00
Punch bowl	30.00
Punch cup	2.00
Server, center handled	15.00
Sugar	7.50
Tray, for creamer/sugar	7.50

*decorated add 50%

THISTLE, LA FLO GLASS COMPANY, C. 1960

Color: crystal

Former Cambridge Glass Company employees were hired by this company when Cambridge closed in 1957. This glass was cut with a very-like-Cambridge Thistle pattern from various companies' blanks. We have been able to find a few more La Flo cut items in the last two years. I'm very certain there are other pieces to be found. We'd appreciate knowing what you find to add to our listing.

This cutting is almost identical to #1066 Cambridge Thistle. The mould shapes of items differ from those of Cambridge and the Cambridge wares had plain centers whereas these are cut with a starred center. You will note the pieces pictured are not close to any known Cambridge shapes. Cambridge Thistle pieces also had an ovoid shape on the stem cut with bars, which forms a kind of webbing on one part of their stem. To further confuse this issue, Cambridge also had a similar cutting to their Thistle called Silver Maple which had two round, fuzzy balls cut at the base of that three petal flower before the stem.

Bowl, 6", crimped	22.00
Bowl, salad, deep, belled	35.00
Ice tub	75.00
Pitcher, martini	45.00
Pitcher, milk	40.00
Plate, 13", torte plate	32.50
Shot glass	20.00
Stem, cocktail	17.50

Colors: crystal, satinized green

Thousand Line is the line number listed for this pattern in Anchor Hocking's catalogs. I have heard this line called "Stars and Bars" as well as "Rainbow Stars." Both of these collector names have a certain appeal, but we will stick to its original designation for now. This minor Hocking line is beginning to be noticed by collectors of Fire-King and Early American Prescut. All Early American Prescut pieces have line numbers in the 700s.

Many collectors buy the Thousand Line large salad bowl and tray to use for salads. A glass fork and spoon may be found with these. You can find these more reasonably priced than buying newly made glassware items. I was in a shop in Sanford, Florida, a week before the Depression glass show when the owner asked me to identify this pattern for a customer. I showed him the pattern in the copy of my book the shop owner had. He got excited about a piece he found in the shop just like his Mom had.

The luncheon plate may be the most difficult item to find in this pattern; bowls seem to be everywhere in the markets; and sugar and creamer sets are just as plentiful. We've found one large bowl with a ground bottom which might indicate an early production prototype.

You may find some satinized pieces in Thousand Line, and many of these will be color decorated.

	Crystal			Crystal
Bowl, 6", handled	10.00		Plate, 8", lunch	11.00
Bowl, 7½" deep	10.00		Relish, 12", six-part	15.00
Bowl, 8", vegetable	12.00		Relish, three-part, round	8.00
Bowl, 10½", salad, flat base, 7" ctr.	25.00		Relish, 10", two-handled, oval	6.00
Bowl, 10⅞", vegetable, rim base, 5½" ctr.	15.00		Spoon	7.50
Candle, 4"	4.00		Sugar, 2½"	4.00
Candy w/lid	20.00		Tray, 12½", sandwich	12.50
Creamer, 2½"	4.00		Vase, bud	12.50
Fork	7.50			

WILD ROSE WITH LEAVES & BERRIES, INDIANA GLASS COMPANY, EARLY 1950S – 1980S

Colors: crystal, crystal satinized, iridescent, milk glass, multicolored blue, green, pink, and yellow; satinized green, pink, and yellow; sprayed green, lavender, and pink

    Wild Rose with Leaves and Berries is a small serving ware pattern that collectors in increasing numbers are noticing. I only wish I could find more of the multicolored ware which flies off the table at shows. Even non-collectors have grabbed pieces because it is so "pretty" or "neat" or "cool." A rather wide range of colors is available in Wild Rose including some iridescent and satinized items.

    I have encountered a multitude of prices, some exorbitant on the multicolored pieces. I admit they are nicely colored, but it is not Victorian pattern glass as I once saw it marked. There is a pretty blue seven-piece berry set in a shop near here for $150.00 and they have no idea what it is or who made it. We have enjoyed our multicolored sherbet dishes at many family meals. Those we hand wash for fear that the color will fade in the dishwasher. Using crystal presents no such problem. One collector told me she was using the two-handled tray as a plate so she could set a table with her ware. Collectors are becoming quite innovative.

	Crystal Milk Glass Crystal Satinized	Sprayed & Satinized Colors Iridescent	Multicolored
Bowl, handled sauce	4.00	7.00	12.50
Bowl, large vegetable	10.00	15.00	50.00
Candle	5.00	9.00	22.00
Plate, sherbet	2.00	3.00	10.00
Relish, handled	7.00	12.00	27.50
Relish, two-part, handled	7.00	12.00	30.00
Sherbet	4.00	6.00	15.00
Tray, two-handled	15.00	22.00	45.00

WAKEFIELD, LINE #1932, WESTMORELAND GLASS COMPANY, C. 1932; WATERFORD, 1950s – 1960s; WAKEFIELD W/RED TRIM, C. 1970s AND BEYOND

Colors: crystal, crystal with red

Wakefield, the birth home of George Washington, was so named according to Charles West in his book on Westmoreland, because it made its appearance in the 200th year following Washington's birth. We know there was quite a bit of hoopla surrounding that bicentennial occasion because of glasses honoring the event which survive today. That was also the birth year of our Washington quarter.

Wakefield was initially made in crystal of quality materials and it cost twice as much as West-moreland's normal wares. Westmoreland was hoping to put good crystal (on par with the enormously expensive Waterford wares) within reach of the public at large. Indeed, the ware was re-introduced to the market in the 1950s and once again in the 1960s (in ruby stain) under the Waterford name. In the 1970s and 1980s, before the company's demise, Wakefield was made with the red trim staining that is so very popular with collectors today. I have a 1963 catalog, which lists the pattern as Waterford with ruby stain instead of Wakefield; I am not exactly sure when the change of name occurred. The applied stain wears and will not hold up to washing in the dishwasher. You have to treat this as the fine crystal it was intended to be and hand wash pieces. It's funny that the latest issues are the ones sought by collectors today, rather than great-grandma's crystal Wakefield without the stain.

Amazingly, in the many catalog references I checked, there were no creamer and sugar sets listed with ruby stain. In that 1963 price manual accompanying the catalog, the ruby stained wares cost twice what the same piece in crystal cost. If a piece were $5.00 in crystal, it was $10.00 in ruby stain.

Thanks for all the compliments on the layout for this pattern. I did pass those comments along to the editorial staff at Collector Books who were responsible for the great art work.

	Crystal w/red stain		Crystal w/red stain
Basket, 6"	70.00	Compote, 7", hi ft.	50.00
Bonbon, 6", crimped, metal hndl.	35.00	Compote, 7", hi ft., crimped	55.00
Bowl, 5", heart, w/hndl	30.00	Compote, 12", low ft. fruit	85.00
Bowl, 5", nappy, round, w/hndl	25.00	*Creamer, ftd.	25.00
Bowl, 6", cupped	22.50	Fairy lamp, 2-pcs	60.00
Bowl, 6", heart, w/hndl	45.00	Plate, 6"	12.50
Bowl, 8", heart, w/hndl	75.00	Plate, 8½", luncheon	22.50
Bowl, 10½", bell, ftd.	75.00	Plate, 10", dinner	65.00
Bowl, 11", flat, lipped	65.00	Plate, 14", torte	75.00
Bowl, 12", flat, crimped	85.00	Stem, 1 oz., cordial	50.00
Bowl, 12", ftd., straight edge	65.00	Stem, 2 oz., wine	30.00
Bowl, 12", ftd., crimped	85.00	Stem, 6 oz., sherbet	25.00
Bowl, 13", shallow server	70.00	Stem, 10 oz., water	25.00
Cake stand, 12", low ft.	85.00	*Sugar	25.00
Candlestick, 6"	60.00	Sweetmeat, crimped top	35.00
Compote, 5", low ft.	30.00	Tidbit tray, ruffled, metal handle	35.00
Compote, 5", low ft., crimped	35.00	Tumbler, 12 oz., ftd. tea	25.00
Compote, 5½", hi ft., mint	35.00	Vase, crimped top	65.00

*crystal

WILLOW, ETCHING NO. 335, FOSTORIA GLASS COMPANY, 1939 – 1945

Colors: crystal with etch

Fostoria's Willow is etched predominantly on blank #2574 (Raleigh) and on stemware blank #6023 (Colfax). Willow patterns have always been popular whether they are on china or glass. Everyone has heard of Blue Willow china if they have been into collecting at all, and this design is based upon similar scenes. There are three pattern shots (bridge, house, and willows) so you can see each of the scenes etched.

What I noticed as I looked for the pattern was a lack of knowledge about who made it, but it was recognized as excellent made ware since the prices were never economical enough to buy more than a piece or two at a time.

Bonbon, 5", hdld.	32.00		Plate, 8"	18.00
Bowl, finger	22.00		Plate, 9"	38.00
Bowl, 8½", hdld.	38.00		Plate, 10", cake, 2 hdld.	48.00
Bowl, 9", ftd.	75.00		Plate, 14" torte	67.50
Bowl, 9½", hdld.	48.00		Relish, 10", 3-part	45.00
Bowl, 12", flared	45.00		Shaker, pr.	75.00
Bowl, 13", fruit	50.00		Saucer	5.00
Celery, 10½"	38.00		Stem, 3⅜", 1 oz., cordial	35.00
Comport, 5"	45.00		Stem, 3⅝", 4 oz. oyster cocktail	17.50
Cream, ftd.	25.00		Stem, 4⅛", low sherbet	15.00
Cream, individual	25.00		Stem, 4¾", 4 oz. claret-wine	22.50
Cup	25.00		Stem, 4⅜", 3¾ oz., cocktail	17.50
Ice Tub	75.00		Stem, 4⅞", 6 oz., saucer champagne	17.50
Lemon dish, 6½", hdld.	20.00		Stem, 6⅜", 9 oz. water	25.00
Mayonnaise	33.00		Sugar, ftd.	25.00
Mayonnaise plate	12.00		Sugar, individual	25.00
Oil bottle, 4¼ oz.	110.00		Sweetmeat, 5¼", hdld.	33.00
Olive, 6"	20.00		Tray, 8", muffin, hdld.	45.00
Pickle, 8"	25.00		Tumbler, 4½", ftd., 5 oz., juice	15.00
Pitcher, 53 oz., ftd.	250.00		Tumbler, 5⅛", ftd., 9 oz., water	18.00
Plate, 6"	9.00		Tumbler, 5¾", ftd., 12 oz., tea	22.50
Plate, 7"	12.00		Whip cream, 5", hdld.	33.00

WILLOWMERE, ETCHING NO. 333, FOSTORIA GLASS COMPANY, 1938 – 1968

Colors: crystal with etching

Willowmere was made by Fostoria for a little over 30 years, so many brides received this as their wedding crystal. I am seeing more and more of this for sale in my travels. Thanks to a generous collector from St. Louis, I was able to show you a variety of pieces. Most Willowmere is etched on blank #2560 (Coronet); in addition, the stems are etched on blank #6024 (Cellini).

Bonbon, 5¾", hdld.	30.00
Bonbon, 7¼", 3-toed	30.00
Bowl, finger	22.00
Bowl, 5⅞", 3-toed nut	33.00
Bowl, 6", cereal	24.00
Bowl, 8½", hdld.	40.00
Bowl, 10½", 2-part, salad	85.00
Bowl, 10", salad	60.00
Bowl, 11½", crimped	60.00
Bowl, 11", hdld.	62.50
Bowl, 12", flared	60.00
Bowl, 13", fruit	65.00
Candlestick, 4½",	32.50
Candlestick, 4",	30.00
Candlestick, 5⅛", duo	45.00
Celery, 11"	33.00
Cheese comport, 3¼"	35.00
Comport, 6"	60.00
Creamer	25.00
Creamer, individual	25.00
Cup	18.00
Ice bucket, 4⅞", ftd.	110.00
Lemon dish, 6¼", hdld.	18.00
Mayonnaise	35.00
Mayonnaise, 2-part	40.00
Mayonnaise plate	14.00
Oil bottle, 3 oz.	100.00
Olive, 6¾"	22.00
Pickle, 8¾"	28.00
Pitcher, 32 oz.	250.00
Pitcher, ftd.	350.00
Plate, 6"	7.00
Plate, 7"	14.00
Plate, 8"	16.00
Plate, 9"	40.00

Plate, 11", cracker	45.00
Plate, 11½", cake, hdld.	57.50
Plate, 14", torte	65.00
Relish, 6½", 2-part, hdld.	30.00
Relish, 10", 3-part, hdld.	45.00
Relish, 10", 4-part	55.00
Relish, 13¼", 5-part	80.00
Sani-cut server	350.00
Saucer	4.00
Shaker, pr.	100.00
Stem, 3½", 4 oz., oyster cocktail	18.00
Stem, 3¾", 1 oz., cordial	40.00
Stem, 4½", 6 oz., sherbet	16.00
Stem, 4¾", 3½ oz., cocktail	18.00
Stem, 5⅜", 6 oz., saucer champagne	18.00
Stem, 5⅜", 3½ oz., wine	35.00
Stem, 5¾", 4 oz., claret	40.00
Stem, 7⅜", 10 oz., water	24.00
Sugar	25.00
Sugar, individual	25.00
Sweetmeat, 5½", hdld.	22.00
Tid bit, 3-toed	32.00
Tray, 7½", sugar/creamer	22.00
Tray, 8¼", hdld., muffin	68.00
Tray, 11", center hdld,. Lunch	50.00
Tumbler, 4⅝", ftd., 5 oz., juice	16.00
Tumbler, 5¼", ftd., 9 oz., water	20.00
Tumbler, 5¾", ftd., 12 oz., tea	25.00
Vase, 6", hdld. (2560)	125.00
Vase, 7½" (2567)	125.00
Vase, 9" (2568)	125.00
Vase, 10" (2470)	175.00
Vase, 10" (5100)	175.00
Whip cream, 5", hdld.	22.00

WINDSOR, FEDERAL GLASS COMPANY, c. 1974

Colors: crystal, Aegean blue, Sun Gold, pink

   This pattern was shown in Federal's 1974 catalog but was not in that of 1979. This gives us fairly accurate dates for Federal's "jewel-like" Windsor. Pink was not listed as a color and I suspect Indiana is responsible for this color, having bought the molds after Federal's ensuing demise.

   I am not sure who made the lamp, but if you collect this pattern, it would be an important piece to own.

	Crystal	Colors		Crystal	Colors
Ashtray, 6"	2.50	4.00	Marmalade, w/notched lid	4.00	8.00
Bowl, 5½"	3.00	5.00	Plate, 6½"	1.50	2.00
Bowl, 6½"	3.50	6.00	Plate, 9¼", snack	2.00	3.00
Bowl, 10½"	6.00	10.00	Plate, 11"	7.50	11.00
Butter w/cover, ¼ lb.	7.50	12.00	Relish, 8½, divided	3.50	6.00
Cake stand	12.50	22.50	Shaker, pr.	5.00	8.00
Candy dish w/cover	8.00	12.50	Sugar w/cover	4.00	8.00
Cigarette box	6.00	11.00	Sundae, ftd.	3.00	5.00
Coaster/ashtray	3.00	4.50	Tumbler, ftd., water	3.00	5.00
Creamer	3.00	5.00	Tumbler, ftd., tea	3.50	5.50
Cup, 6 oz., snack	2.00	3.00	Tray, rectangular	4.00	6.00
Lamp		35.00			

Color: crystal; white, aqua and peach milk

We recently found a few more pieces of Wistar pattern, unfortunately not soon enough to photograph for this book. A Wistar is a twining vine with showy clusters of flowers, according to Mr. Webster. Wisteria was named for a C. Wistar, an anatomist who was born in 1760. I got curious about the term when I ran into Duncan and Miller stemware with the same name. Up until this revelation, I had thought that Fostoria was doing its part for the country at war by creating a pattern with stars and stripes, on the order of the Stars and Stripes pattern by Hocking.

In 1958, Fostoria revived this pattern in their milk and colored (pink and blue) milk wares. This revival was named the Betsy Ross pattern, still a patriotic principle of sorts, whether they originally intended that or not. The stemware and tumblers for Betsy Ross were the Wistar design exactly. However, the other items in Betsy Ross did not have the stars, just the ribbing and vine.

	Crystal	White		Crystal	White
Bowl, 4", sq., hndl.	11.00		Celery, 9½"	20.00	
Bowl, 4¼", ftd., round, hndl.	10.00		Creamer, 4", ftd.	10.00	12.50
Bowl, 4½", triangular, hndl.	13.00		Mayonnaise, 2⅞", ftd., w/ladle	30.00	
Bowl, 5", ftd., hndl.	12.50		Plate, 7"	7.50	10.00
Bowl, 5½", 3-toe, nut	12.50		Plate, 14", torte	30.00	
Bowl, 6⅝", 3-toe, bonbon	17.00		Stem, 6 oz., high sherbet	8.00	12.00
Bowl, 6¾", 3-toe, tri-corner	17.00		Stem, 9 oz., water	12.50	17.00
Bowl, 10", salad	25.00		Sugar, 3½", ftd.	10.00	12.50
Bowl, 12", lily pond	25.00		Tumbler, 5 oz.	8.00	12.00
Bowl, 13", fruit		27.50	Tumbler, 12 oz.	12.50	17.00
Candlestick, 4"	17.50				

YORKTOWN, FEDERAL GLASS COMPANY, MID 1950s

Colors: yellow, crystal, white, iridized, and smoke

I added this pattern to the book to try to eradicate some of the letters I receive every year announcing that some rare Heisey's Provincial has been discovered in yellow (Sahara) and wondering how much it's worth. Provincial was not made in yellow; therefore, readers assume that they have found a really rare piece of Heisey. Rare pieces and colors do show up sporadically in various other patterns; but Heisey's colors are well documented and discoveries there are usually Imperial-made wares from Heisey's moulds. This Federal pattern is very like Heisey's Provincial and another ware named Pilgrim.

Crystal Yorktown can be collected within a brief period if you search for it. The punch set is easy on the pocket. There is enough yellow around to collect a set, also, but it will take a bit longer to piece together. I am pricing both colors the same for now, based strictly upon what I have paid or seen priced. I have not paid any more for yellow than crystal. Time will tell us if a difference will evolve. I see only a few pieces of the iridized, mostly the punch bowl set and mugs.

	Crystal/Yellow		Crystal/Yellow
Bowl, 5½", berry, #2905	4.00	Plate, 11½", #2904	8.50
Bowl, 9½", large berry, #2906	11.00	Punch set, 7 qt., base, 12 cups	42.50
Bowl, 10", ftd., fruit, #2902	18.00	Saucer, #2911	.50
Celery tray, 10", #2907	9.00	Sherbet, 2½", 7 oz., #1744	3.00
Creamer, #2908	4.00	Sugar w/lid, #2909	7.50
Cup, #2910	3.00	Tumbler, 3⅞", 6 oz., juice, #1741	4.00
Cup, snack/punch, 6 oz.	2.00	Tumbler, 4¾", 10 oz., water, #1742	5.50
Mug, 5¹⁄₁₆"	17.50	Tumbler, 5¼", 13 oz., iced tea, #1743	9.00
Plate, 8¼", #2903	4.00	Vase, 8"	16.00
Plate, 10½" x 6¾", snack w/indent	3.00		

OTHER BOOKS BY GENE FLORENCE

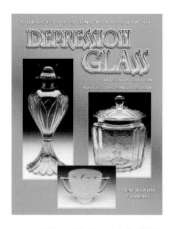

Collector's Encyclopedia of DEPRESSION GLASS, 16th Edition *Gene Florence*

Since the first edition of *Collector's Encyclopedia of Depression Glass* was released in 1972, it has been America's #1 bestselling glass book. Gene Florence now presents this completely revised 16th edition, with the previous 133 patterns and 15 additional patterns, to make this the most complete reference to date. With the assistance of several nationally known dealers, this book illustrates, as well as realistically prices, items in demand. Dealing primarily with the glass made from the 1920s through the end of the 1930s, this beautiful reference book contains stunning color photographs, vintage catalog pages, updated values, and a special section on reissues and fakes. This dependable information comes from years of research, experience, fellow dealers and collectors, and millions of miles of travel by full-time glass dealer Gene Florence, America's leading glassware authority.

Item #6327 • ISBN: 1-57432-353-9 • 8½ x 11 • 256 Pgs. • HB • $19.95

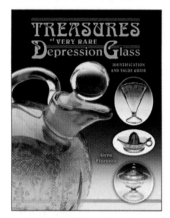

Treasures of VERY RARE DEPRESSION GLASS *Gene Florence*

Our *Very Rare Glassware of the Depression Years* books have been bestsellers for many years, helping collectors spot those rare and valuable pieces of Depression glass that may come around once in a lifetime. Rarity can be determined by an unusual color or pattern; many pieces here are one of a kind or can be found only in limited quantities. Gene Florence is America's leading glassware authority, and his books are considered required reading. This new book features over 1,000 rare examples of Depression items, as well as elegant and kitchen items. It features many famous glass companies, including Duncan & Miller, Federal, Fostoria, Fenton, A.H. Heisey, Hocking, Imperial, Jeannette, Paden City, Tiffin, and more. Values are given for these rare items. The essential information and experience that Florence provides in his books will help you know what to look for in your glass searches and teach you to be an informed collector. This book is a must for your glassware library. 2003 values.

Item #6241 • ISBN: 1-57432-336-9 • 8½ x 11 • 368 Pgs. • HB • $39.95

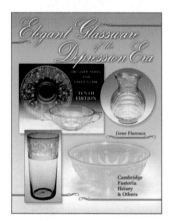

ELEGANT GLASSWARE of the Depression Era, 10th Edition *Gene Florence*

This new edition holds hundreds of new photographs, listings, and updated values. This book features the handmade and acid-etched glassware that was sold in department and jewelry stores from the Depression era through the 1950s, not the dimestore and give-away glass known as Depression glass. As always, glassware authority Gene Florence has added many new discoveries, 10 additional patterns, and re-photographed many items from the previous books. Large group settings are included for each of the more than 100 patterns, as well as close-ups to show pattern details. The famous glassmakers presented include Fenton, Cambridge, Heisey, Tiffin, Imperial, Duncan & Miller, U.S. Glass, and Paden City. Florence provides a list of all known pieces, with colors and measurements, along with 2003 values.

Item #6125 • ISBN: 1-57432-298-2 • 8½ x 11 • 240 Pgs. • HB • $24.95

KITCHEN GLASSWARE of the Depression Years, 6th Edition *Gene Florence*

This exciting new edition of our bestselling *Kitchen Glassware of the Depression Years* is undeniably the definitive reference on the subject. More than 5,000 items are showcased in beautiful professional color photographs with descriptions and values. Many new finds and exceptionally rare pieces have been added. The highly collectible glass from the Depression era through the 1960s fills its pages, in addition to the ever-popular Fire-King and Pyrex glassware. This comprehensive encyclopedia provides an easy-to-use format, showing items by color, shape, or pattern. The collector will enjoy the pages of glass, from colorful juice reamers, shakers, rare and unusual glass knives, to the mixing bowls and baking dishes we still find in our kitchen cupboards. 2003 values.

Item #5827 • ISBN: 1-57432-220-6 • 8½ x 11 • 272 Pgs. • HB • $24.95

Anchor Hocking's FIRE-KING & More, 2nd Edition
Gene Florence

From the 1940s to the 1970s Anchor Hocking Glass Corp. of Lancaster, Ohio, produced an extensive line of glassware called Fire-King. Their lines included not only dinnerware but also a plethora of glass kitchen items — reamers, measuring cups, mixing bowls, mugs, and more. This is the essential collectors' reference to this massive line of glassware. Loaded with hundreds of new full-color photos, vintage catalog pages, company materials, facts, information, and values, this book has everything collectors expect from Gene Florence. 2002 values.

Item #5602 • ISBN: 1-57432-164-1 • 8½ x 11 • 224 Pgs. • HB • $24.95

Glass CANDLESTICKS of the Depression Era
Gene Florence

Florence has compiled this book to help identify the candlestick patterns made during the Depression era. More than 500 different candlesticks are shown in full-color photographs. The book is arranged according to color: amber, black, blue, crystal, green, iridescent, multicolor, pink, purple, red, smoke, white, and yellow. Many famous glassmakers are represented, such as Heisey, Cambridge, Fostoria, and Tiffin. The descriptive text for each candleholder includes pattern, maker, color, height, and current collector value. A helpful index and bibliography are also provided. 2000 values.

Item #5354 • ISBN: 1-57432-136-6 • 8½ x 11 • 176 Pgs. • HB • $24.95

Florence's Glassware
PATTERN IDENTIFICATION Guide
Gene Florence

Florence's Glassware Pattern Identification Guides are great companions for his other glassware books. Volume I includes every pattern featured in his *Collector's Encyclopedia of Depression Glass, Collectible Glassware from the 40s, 50s, and 60s,* and *Collector's Encyclopedia of Elegant Glassware,* as well as many more — nearly 400 patterns in all. Volume II holds nearly 500 patterns, with no repeats from Volume I. Volume III also showcases nearly 500 patterns with no repeats from the previous volumes. Carefully planned close-up photographs of representative pieces for every pattern show great detail to make identification easy. With every pattern, Florence provides the names, the companies which made the glass, dates of production, and even colors available. These guides are ideal references for novice and seasoned glass collectors and dealers, and great resources for years to come. No values.

Vol. I • Item #5042 • ISBN: 1-57432-045-9 • 8½ x 11 • 176 Pgs. • PB • $18.95
Vol. II • Item #5615 • ISBN: 1-57432-177-3 • 8½ x 11 • 208 Pgs. • PB • $19.95
Vol. III • Item #6142 • ISBN: 1-57432-315-6 • 8½ x 11 • 272 Pgs. • PB • $19.95

Pocket Guide to
DEPRESSION GLASS & More, 13th Edition
Gene Florence

Gene Florence has completely revised his *Pocket Guide to Depression Glass* with over 4,000 values updated to reflect the ever-changing market. Many of the photographs have been reshot to improve the quality and add new finds. There are a total of 119 new photos for this edition, including 29 additional patterns that have not appeared in previous editions. These gorgeous photographs show great detail, and the listings of the patterns and their available pieces make identification simple. There is even a section on re-issues and the numerous fakes flooding the market. This is the perfect book to take with you on your searches through shops and flea markets and is the ideal companion to Florence's comprehensive *Collector's Encyclopedia of Depression Glass.* 2003 values.

Item #6136 • ISBN: 1-57432-309-1 • 5½ x 8½ • 224 Pgs. • PB • $12.95